VALOUR
A History of the Gurkhas

VALOUR

A History of the Gurkhas

Text by E. D. SMITH

Photographic material co-ordinated
by M. H. Broadway

THE OVERLOOK PRESS
WOODSTOCK & NEW YORK

First published in the United States 1998 by
The Overlook Press, Peter Mayer Publishers, Inc.
Lewis Hollow Road
Woodstock, New York 12498

Library of Congress Cataloging-in-Publication Data

Smith, E.D.
Valour: a history of the Gurkhas / E. D. Smith.
p. cm.
Bibliography: Includes index.
I. Gurkha soldiers-History. 2. Great Britain. Army. Brigade of Gurkhas-History.
I. Title.
UA853.N35565 1998 355.3'5-dc21 97-23833

First published in 1997 by
Spellmount Publishers
The Old Rectory
Staplehurst
Kent TN12 0AZ
United Kingdom

Printed in Great Britain

ISBN 0-87951-817-0

3 5 7 9 8 6 4 2

CONTENTS

LIST OF MAPS

Introduction and Acknowledgements

UNLIKE a more conventional regimental history, this book covers a truly wide canvas, beginning in 1815 and ending in 1995. For much of that time and certainly up to 1947 – when the Gurkha Brigade was split between the armies of independent India and Great Britain – there were ten regiments. During the period prior to 1914, many campaigns were fought which included the Indian Mutiny of 1857, the Afghan Wars and numerous forays against rebellious tribesmen on the North-West and North-East Frontiers of India. In all these campaigns, one or more battalions of the Gurkha Brigade took part: some of their stories can only be given in outline as, inevitably, I have had to be selective. For that, I alone take the responsibility, while apologising to those who feel that their regiment or battalion should have had a prior claim to the limited space available.

During both World Wars, the British-Indian Army Gurkha Brigade was expanded from twenty regular battalions to thirty-three (First World War) and forty-five (Second World War). Every man that came down from the hills of Nepal to enlist was a volunteer, coming from a small kingdom that was not part of the British Empire; truly a magnificent response to this country's cry for help. It would be a monumental task, and would require an inordinately lengthy book, to cover the exploits of so many battalions in so many campaigns – in Europe, the Middle East and in South-East Asia. Despite that, I have tried to give some background to each of the campaigns, since otherwise the narrative would be unduly 'bald'. For such a reason, the bibliography is fairly lengthy as, perforce, I have had to consult a great many sources during my research. After 1948, the narrative covers Britain's Brigade of Gurkhas only, as to have included the six regiments that now serve in the Indian Army Gurkha Brigade would not have been possible without unduly increasing the size of the book.

'Qui s'excuse, s'accuse': enough of apologies! I could not have written this book or obtained the vast majority of the photographs without the unstinted help given by the Gurkha Museum, first under the curatorship of Major John Lamond, and now, Brigadier Christopher Bullock. As one of the Museum 'volunteers', Lieutenant-Colonel Mike Broadway has played a dual role in the production of this book. It has been he who has searched for and produced most of the photographs as well as acting as a proof-reader of the first rough draft. I must also pay tribute to the painstaking editorial efforts of Toby Buchan, whose copious notes helped me considerably – as well as giving my wife, Jill, the task of amending the final draft! I thank her, too. For the ready help they have afforded me, my heartfelt thanks are due to the Secretaries of the ten Gurkha Regimental Associations and the three Gurkha Corps.

To Mrs Gloria Tanner, my profound gratitude for typing and retyping drafts, as well as deciphering my intricate corrections, which must have tried her patience more than somewhat on numerous occasions.

To you all, 'Dhanyabad' (thank you).

E.D.S. 1997

1 NEPAL – THEN AND NOW

NEPAL lies between the great alluvial plains of India and the cold, wind-seared tablelands of Tibet. On a map of the world, the small country is sandwiched between giant neighbours, India and China, something that the Nepalese have learnt to live with over the years. It is a land of great beauty, of high mountains and mighty rivers, a land that is crisscrossed by mountain tracks where generations of hillmen have moved over centuries past as traders, farmers or to tend flocks on high pastures. Truly the home of the Gurkha warriors is a mountain kingdom.

With thousands of tourists now pouring into Nepal by land and air each year, it is difficult to imagine what the country was like in years gone by. Ever since the East India Company came into contact with the mountain kingdom 200 years ago, and until the late 1940s, when India was given her independence, the Nepalese Government saw to it that except for the tiny handful who were invited, from time to time, by the Court, foreigners were excluded from the country. The movements of those favoured few were confined to the Valley of Nepal and only on very special occasions was permission given them to travel elsewhere in the country. Nepal was a forbidden country as far as foreigners were concerned, even more inaccessible than its neighbour, Tibet, was at the time. The exclusion of Europeans was not only insisted upon by the Gurkha state but also by the British Government of India, in deference to Nepalese feelings and in order that the country should not suffer prematurely from contact with 'modern civilisation'. Backward and primitive though the country was up to the end of the Second World War, most of the inhabitants living in the mountains were content with their simple circumstances and respected their rulers, the Maharajah and his Rana relatives, and knowing no other existence outside their country, there was no great desire for change.

There were no roads, no airports, while frontier posts existed to deter intruders rather than to welcome tourists into the country. But in 1947, with events moving

A typical bridge over a mountain torrent, East Nepal

An aerial view of Kathmandu, taken in the 1960s

with such speed in India as it gained its independence, inevitably there were bound to be repercussions in the little country of Nepal. The Indian-based Nepalese National Congress sponsored armed insurgents across the frontier from India and there were political strikes in the Terai, particularly at the mills of Biratnagar. Under pressure the Maharajah (who was also Prime Minister) in Kathmandu promised to introduce a measure of democracy but on all important matters decisions were still to be left in his hands. Moreover, the rights of the ruling Rana family to succession in the premiership were declared to be unalterable and inalienable for all time. In addition, although there was to be a National Chamber of sixty to seventy members, twenty-eight of these were to be nominated by the Maharajah who still retained power to veto any question or proposal made in the legislature which, in his opinion, was not in the public interest. Shortly afterwards, there were more riots and open unrest but it is fair to say that the hillmen in East Nepal, the Rais and Limbus, and the Magars and Gurungs in West Nepal, still continued their normal lives, untouched by the simmering political climate that was coming to the boil in Kathmandu and in the Terai Plain which runs along the border with India.

The main tribes of the hillmen tended to live in their own areas in the mountains of Nepal: there was little mixing and intermarrying between tribes was rare. To reach villages meant walking along winding tracks, up ridges and down to steep valleys, over frighteningly slender bridges swaying

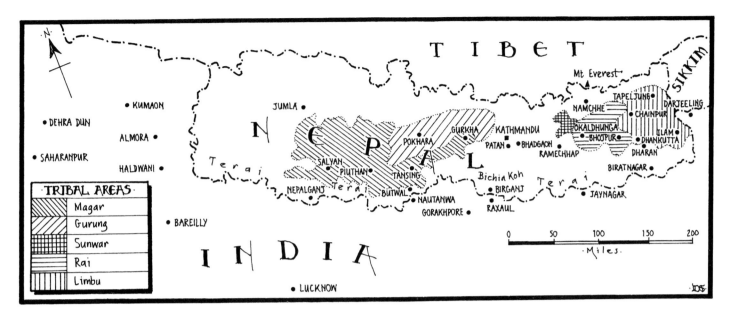

above ice-cold roaring rivers: these tracks were the hill folk's lifeline and many were the songs sung about them as porters toiled up the hillside or as relaxation when the day's walking was over. Without roads, everyone and everything had to go up and down these tracks.

The hill people have bodies that could endure the backbreaking loads that had to be carried by all, including women and children as well as young boys and old men. Nature made the Gurkha villagers short and stocky, with thigh and leg muscles exaggerated in size and shape. Added to their physique there was a simple and strong sense of humour, deep pride in race, village and family; a people that asked little but the right to cultivate their little plot of land, build their own house and, when the work was done, to enjoy the occasional village party. Such a hardy and independent people remained masters in their own villages and sent thousands of first-class soldiers to the many parts of the world visited by the British and Indian Armies. Advisedly the past tense has been used but much of that description of life in the hills remains true today, albeit with certain modifications.

Although Nepal remained in virtual isolation from world forces until the end of the 1940s, the country's rulers had seen portents of the future and began taking belated steps to liberalise their regime. In 1948 the Constitution Act was promulgated by the Maharajah which envisaged a form of government such as India had earlier in the century, with a Legislature and Council of Ministers, consisting of a mixture of nominated and elected members. The latter were to be returned by a system of indirect election, based primarily upon village and town 'panchayats' (councils of elders). The Maharajah, Padma Shamsher, in the eyes of his fellow Ranas was moving too fast; they pointed out that out in the hills life went on as usual, as in some respects it does to this day. At that time the majority of the simple hillmen were not persuaded by the blessings of self-government and shared little enthusiasm for exercising their franchise, still less for standing for election. But Padma was not strong enough to cope with affairs and in April 1948 he retired voluntarily. Political agitation in Kathmandu contrived to keep the Valley in turmoil, with the police being used on several occasions to break up gatherings, while decrees were issued banning the pro-Congress Party as well as imposing a stringent censorship on the press. From years past there had always been a struggle between the King and his Maharajah, and now this was exploited by ambitious politicians. The Indian press played a big part and actively supported any movement opposed to the Rana regime. Towards the end of 1950 the Nepal border was crossed at nine points by the forces of the Indian-inspired Nepal Congress Party, and a few days later, India's Prime Minister, Pandit Nehru, admitted that his government wanted progressive democracy in Nepal, adding that he officially recognised King Tribhuvana as the supreme authority in that land.

For a time there was no large or significant uprising in the Valley of Nepal, while the hillmen in West Nepal remained unruffled

Her Majesty Queen Elizabeth II
with His Majesty King
Mahendra on a state drive
through Kathmandu during her
visit to Nepal in March 1961

and quiet. However, in the east – where the quicker-tempered Limbus and Rais live – there were widespread outbreaks of violence and within a few weeks many of the main centres in East Nepal had been taken over by rebel forces. King Tribhuvana took matters into his own hands in February 1950 by proclaiming the termination of the hereditary premiership and transferring most of the Maharajah's powers to himself. In December 1951 the last Maharajah retired to live in south India: his departure marked the end of Gurkha political supremacy in Nepal and heralded the final twilight of the Ranas.

Tribhuvana's son, King Mahendra Bir Bikram Sah was crowned in May 1956 and until his death in 1972 he attempted to keep the panchayat system in being as he felt it was ideal for a backward country like Nepal. At least that method of government had the advantage of stopping the quarrelling among the politicians, but it allowed virtually no political expression as only people who actively supported the system were allowed to stand for election. In several places, it was corrupt, with local panchayats working the system to their own advantage. When Mahendra's son, Birendra Bir Sah Dev, took over in 1972, like his father the new King affirmed his belief in the panchayat system

but beneath the surface there were strong undercurrents which could not be suppressed for ever. In 1979 these came to the fore when serious riots erupted in Kathmandu involving clashes between students and the police; eventually the police lost control of the situation and order had to be restored by the Nepalese Army.

That was enough to spark the King into action and he announced that there would be a nationwide referendum to determine whether the citizens of Nepal wished to continue the existing system of government – under which party politics were forbidden – or to replace it with a multi-party system. The referendum showed that the panchayat system had won, with most of the rural areas clearly in favour while the towns, in general, voted for a party-political system. However, this referendum gained a short respite only and eventually in 1982 elections were held on political lines, with the King losing much of his power, although he was still regarded by many as a reincarnation of the Hindu god Vishnu. This factor alone ensures a measure of support for him, particularly in the mountain villages. The present political set-up is involved and is constantly changing; suffice it to say that multi-party democracy has made an understandably faltering start in a country that, inevitably, is still backward.

Nepal is now open to the world, and tourism brings some £30 million annually into the kingdom. However, it must be remembered that a large portion of that sum is spent on importing luxury goods, foods and other items required to support an international tourist industry. Commendable strides have been made in education and in communications, the two major factors which in the past had helped to keep the country in the dark ages under the Rana regime. Foreign aid has poured in from donor countries and international organisations and is by far the greatest source of foreign currency. Nepal is a staunch member of the non-aligned group in the United Nations and is at pains to be friendly with all states but, inevitably, her greatest preoccupation must be with her big neighbours, India and China. Her policy is to be on good terms with both, although on several occasions since the Second World War relations with India have not been smooth, chiefly because there has been a tendency on the Government of India's part to play the big brother and wield a heavy stick. Nepal's landlocked position means that the bulk of her imports and exports have to pass overland through India; her giant neighbour is always in the position to strangle her economically, a hard fact of life which does not help to establish a cordial relationship between the two countries.

Outside the world of politics there are other major problems to resolve. Nepal's population since 1958 has grown from just under 8.5 million to somewhere in the region of 19 million. With the improved communications, there has been a mass exodus from the hills down to the Kathmandu Valley, to the Plain of Pokhara in the west, and to the Terai in the south. In 1954, 71 per cent of the population were living in the hill regions, now it is only about 40 per cent. Many of the shanty towns in the Terai are dirty, dilapidated and unhygienic so that, at first, it is difficult to understand why so many people have abandoned the tidy hill villages and the cool, clean air of the mountains. However, life in the hills is burdensome with no modern facilities on the spot. Precious loads of water have to be carried in pitchers and buckets from springs up to the houses, just one of the many tiresome chores that women have to perform throughout the year. Cooking is done on firewood and the houses have to be heated in the same way during the winter months. This means a daily trek to the nearest copses and lone trees around the villages which inevitably, has led to serious deforestation in many parts of the hills. In the monsoon the deluge causes landslides and turns rivers into raging torrents. Life in the hills is no fun for the old, the infirm, or the badly disabled, although these unfortunates are given as much help as possible by relatives and neighbours.

It is not altogether surprising that many hill people turn their backs on their old homes to seek easier conditions down in the Terai or in Kathmandu itself. Instead of backbreaking climbs for the women carrying heavy loads of water and firewood, piped water of a sort is usually available in the shanty towns along the Terai. The children can go to school by bus instead of meandering over mountain tracks, often walking for up to two hours each way. The surroundings may be more sordid but life is generally less stressful, especially for the women. Moreover, there are a handful of hospitals that can be reached by bus or taxi, instead of a sick person being carried by a porter in a huge basket on his back, over hill tracks during the rains, journeys that can be both dangerous and frightening. The exodus from the hills increases every year and the extensive roads which have been constructed by foreign countries – India, China, the USA and the UK – undoubtedly have sped up the process rather than inducing the hill tribes to stay put. The Nepal of today, with its thousands of tourists, its expanding roads and shanty towns and, most alarming of all, its ever-increasing population, has changed dramatically since the British and the Nepalese fought their war, way back in 1815.

When Nepal was a country forbidden to foreigners, British officers never saw the fields or mountains, the villages or their inhabitants, so that recruiting had to be carried out in a special way. Once permission had been given for Gurkhas to serve the East India Company and, eventually, the Indian Army under British rule, up to the time of the Great Mutiny of 1857 no recruiting party was allowed to enter Nepal. As a consequence, recruiters had to haunt the border villages in the hope of enticing young men who, as porters, had carried loads down to India's plains, into enlisting. A favourite time and place was a country fair, where drink and other unaccustomed luxuries persuaded the hill youths to seek fame and fortune with 'John Company'. Recruiters roamed far and wide in their search for likely lads, going to places where Gurkha families had resided after Nepal had spread beyond its borders in the eighteenth century. However, the aftermath of the Indian Mutiny led to much friendlier relations between those in authority in Kathmandu and the British Government of India, so that in the 1860s the military cantonment of Gorakahpore, conveniently near the Nepalese border, became the official centre for would-be recruits. From there, appointed recruiters, all of whom were ex-Gurkha soldiers, were allowed to return to their own villages and surrounding districts and shepherd volunteers down to Gorakhpore, journeys that could take several days, and on occasions, even weeks to accomplish. This system continued until the Rana regime collapsed after the Second World War, thus heralding the end of Nepal's isolation when the doors were opened to tourists. Thereafter in 1957 Great Britain was allowed to establish recruiting depots on Nepalese soil, 140 years after the first Gurkha soldiers began serving the British Crown.

2 HOW IT ALL BEGAN

THE CONCEPT OF NEPAL as a nation is a comparatively recent one: the state which developed until today came into being under the vigorous leadership of Prithwi Narain of Gorkha, founder of the Gorkha nation. Before he died in 1774 Prithwi Narian had laid the foundations of the present nation. His successors continued his policy and a period of rapid expansion followed but, as has happened to other countries in modern times, the Nepalese overreached themselves. Using the highly efficient war machine created by Prithwi Narain, they conquered Sikkim, including Darjeeling, and parts of Tibet to the east as well as Garhwal and Kumaon in the west. Further incursions were made into the Dogra country around the fertile Kangra Valley. It was not long before the intruders began to come into conflict with the British Honourable East India Company; moreover, the boundary between the territories of Nepal and those of the Company was ill-defined, which tempted the Nepalese into exploiting the situation by seizing villages, as well as committing other crimes. Meanwhile, in Kathmandu, there was divided counsel about what to do with the East India Company, now on Nepal's borders. Prime Minister and Maharajah Bhim Sen Thapa was a fire-eating advocate of expansion who failed to understand the power of the British. Addressing his young Rajah (King) in Kathmandu, he declared:

How will the British be able to penetrate into our hills? The small fort of Bhurtpore was the work of man, yet the English, being worsted before it, desisted from the attempt to conquer it. Our hills and fastnesses are formed by the hand of God and are impregnable.

To this end Bhim Sen instigated a deliberate policy of infiltration throughout the Terai, the narrow strip of plain adjoining India. Village after village was taken either in areas under dispute or within British territory itself. These incursions went on for seven years until open conflict became inevitable.

Not everybody in the capital, Kathmandu, was in agreement with Bhim Sen's aggressive policy including one of his more distinguished generals, Amarsing Thapa, who warned the Prime Minister not to stir up the British to the point at which they would resort to arms to settle their differences with Nepal. He wrote:

We have hitherto but hunted deer: if we engage in this war, we must be prepared to fight tigers... The advocate of war [Bhim Sen] who proposes to fight and conquer the English has been brought up in court and is a stranger to the toil and hardships of a military life.

Not for the first time in history did the soldier advocate peace while his political master banged the drum, seeking glory in a war in which he would not have to face death or disablement. Bhim Sen continued to seek possession of the disputed villages along the frontier and as the revenue from those villages was passing into the hands of the Prime Minister's family, Amarsing's warning went unheeded. In May 1814 Gurkha soldiers, without warning, raided three frontier police posts in the Butwal district, killing eighteen policemen and putting the headman to death with singular brutality. In India the Governor-General of Bengal, Lord Moira (later first Marquess of Hastings), sent an ultimatum to Bhim Sen, whose response was, 'If the English want war against the Gurkha conquerors, they can have it.'

Lord Moira set his army in motion to assemble at Dinapore, Benares, Meerut and Ludhiana, planning to split the force into four columns. From the Dinapore area General Marley, with the main force of 8,000 men, was to march on Kathmandu; from Benares,

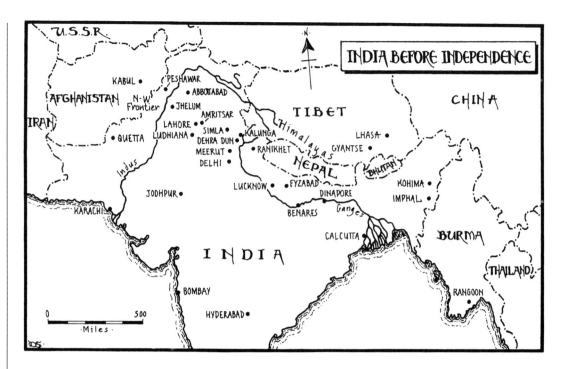

General Wood with 4,000 men was to move towards the frontier district of Butwal and thence into Palpa; from the Saharanpore area, Major-General Rollo Gillespie, also with 4,000 men, was to invade the valley of the Doon, thence to strike towards the capital of Garhwal, Srinagar; finally, Major-General David Ochterlony, in command of 6,000 men and supported by 12 guns, was to move up the left bank of the River Sutlej and engage Amarsing's main forces at Malaun.

This was the first mountain campaign in which the East India Company's British-Indian army had been engaged, and the country in which they fought favoured the defenders. The Company's army, including its allies and detachments, amounted to some 30,000 men with 60 guns, while Bhim Sen had only some 12,000 men with which to engage this formidable expedition. Under Amarsing's nephew, Balbahadur, the nation's crack troops, 600 men of the Purana Gorakh Regiment, were to defend the small fort of Kalunga, which stood on a wooded hill, guarding the track to Garhwal, some 500 feet above the surrounding country. The Company's army had a vast superiority in numbers and, moreover, their communications were far more efficient, so that the four main columns could be supplied and reinforced from the plains behind them. On the other hand, Amarsing had lines of communication stretching back to Kathmandu which were truly horrific,

including a two-month walk over narrow winding mountain tracks.

The British strategy was to cut the Nepalese supply route, and to bring this about Gillespie was told to occupy the Doon Valley, thus forcing the Gurkha commander to retreat to the east, where he could be attacked and destroyed by the columns led by Ochterlony and himself. In the east, meanwhile, the other columns under Marley and Wood were to move towards Kathmandu and Palpa, taking full advantage of Gurkha preoccupation in the far west. Undoubtedly the country favoured the defenders, but fortunately for the British, Ochterlony was a born master of operational tactics, a highly efficient commander and one who was bold in spirit. He devised a stockaded post to protect his main body and was interested to discover, after the first brush with the Gurkhas, that his enemies conducted their defence in a similar manner. Not surprisingly, it was Ochterlony's army that met with success; the other three columns forgot to fortify their outposts and were punished with unwelcome reverses.

The Gurkha soldiers who opposed the British were described as follows by Captain Hearsey, who knew the Nepalese well:

Their muskets are infamous and their gunpowder the same. They have little or no clothing and are very ill-paid. They are armed with a musket with or without a bayonet, a sword, and stuck in their girdles is a crooked

*instrument called a Kookuree...
They are hardy, endure privations
and are very obedient... Under our
Government they would make
excellent soldiers.*

They were an ill-equipped force, although a highly mobile one, while another disadvantage which the Nepalese suffered was that the countries they had recently conquered were quick to turn on them: it did not take very much persuasion or bribery by the British for those who had been subjugated by Nepal to take up arms against their recent conquerors.

From Lucknow on 1 November 1814, the Governor-General of India issued the formal declaration of war with Nepal. It was a conflict that was to change the relationship between the two nations from direct enmity into a warm friendship which has lasted until this very day. The four English columns advanced from their points of forward concentration in the late autumn of 1814, only to meet with severe checks along the line. The aged General Wood bumped into a stockade near Butwal and his force suffered casualties. To the disgust of his soldiers, he ordered them to withdraw just as the Gurkhas had begun to fall back after having attacked a force that was twice the size of their own. Seizing the chance the Gurkhas turned round and followed up the British, harassing them unmercifully. Marley's column was no more successful, with its commander being so dumbfounded by the aggressive spirit shown by the Gurkha hillmen that he too ordered his men to move back. Before long, however, he found the responsibility of this operation too much for him, so, without telling a soul or arranging for anyone to act for him, quietly he rode away by night into a self-imposed retirement. Not surprisingly, the Governor-General placed this over-reluctant commander on the invalid list, an appropriate punishment for his irresponsible behaviour. He was not the only officer in this campaign to be sent on pension – on the Nepalese side, a commander called Bhagatsing had refused to attack Marley's force on the grounds that he was opposed by an army that was ten times the size of his own. Bhim Sen ordered him back to Kathmandu where he had to face a court martial and attend an open 'Durbar',* dressed in petticoats.

In the west there was a different story to tell where the gallant, though ageing, Gillespie, still as brave as a lion, seized Dehra Dun, thus further isolating Amarsing Thapa from his supporting forces. Indeed, Amarsing was 400 miles from Kathmandu and forced to defend a wide front in recently subjugated territory, in country whose inhabitants were hostile to the Nepalese. Although the overall British strategy may have had its faults, in the long term it was a sensible one. But the most dramatic battle was fought in and around the stockade of Kalunga, where some 600 defenders under Balbahadur manned the walls, watching Gillespie's formidable column, with its 4,000 men and its guns, as it moved towards them.

That night, 29 October 1814, a message offering terms came from the British commander. Balbahadur, remarking that he did not accept letters at that late hour, tore it up. Before daylight on the 30th, the British guns opened up on the stockade while the leading troops assembled for the assault. Gillespie, an impatient commander, gave the signal for the attack some hours before the time at which, previously, he had notified that it should be given, and as a result, the British and Indian regiments attacked piecemeal and were thrown back. Once more Gillespie tried, leading the assault in person but, again, this was defeated with severe loss.

At the height of the bombardment a Gurkha suddenly appeared, advancing through the shells and smoke, waving his hands. The firing ceased, whereupon he was welcomed into the British camp. His lower jaw had been shattered by a shot and he had come for treatment by the British surgeon. When discharged from hospital, he asked permission to return to his own army in order to fight the British again!

The courageous Gillespie put himself at the head of his own regiment, the Royal Irish Dragoons, to lead a third assault on the fort. With him by his side was one Lieutenant Frederick Young of the 13th Native Infantry, now commanding a company. Dashing towards the gate, Rollo Gillespie was shot down thirty yards from the palisade and mortally wounded: he died in the arms of Lieutenant Young.

Again the attack failed, after which the British force waited for over a month until its

---

* Durbar – a meeting or court.

The Kalunga Memorial, Dehra Dun. The Memorial consists of two obelisks: one of these commemorates the British casualties, the other carries an inscription that pays tribute to Balbahadur, the Gurkha commander, and 'his brave Gurkhas'

siege train arrived from Delhi. Once more they assaulted, but with no more success than before. Every time a breach was made, the Gurkhas, with their women helping them, drove the assailants back using an assortment of missiles, including bullets, arrows, rocks and stones. Food and water were running out in the beleaguered, battered post, and the ranks of the defenders were thinning fast under the bombardment. Balbahadur was now in a desperate plight.

'To capture the fort was a thing forbidden but now I leave of my own accord.' Accompanied by his last seventy hale men, Balbahadur slipped away in the night of 1 December through the besiegers' lines, and they saw him no more. When the British entered the place they found it empty save for the dead and the grievously wounded, among them women and children. They rescued the living, then razed Kalunga to the ground. Balbahadur had lost 520 men, his enemy 31 officers and 750 men. On the hillside at Kalunga, now known as Nalapini, are two small white obelisks, the one commemorating Gillespie and those who fell with him, the other 'the gallant adversary'. 'They fought in fair conflict like men, and in the intervals of actual combat showed us a liberal courtesy…' wrote a British historian.

The one British commander who understood how these brave mountain folk could be defeated was David Ochterlony. He was opposed by the experienced Nepalese commander in the west, General Amarsing Thapa, who had no more than 3,000 troops under his command. Amarsing, in his turn, could appreciate good generalship and in his despatches to Kathmandu he paid tribute to Ochterlony, saying that he could never fight at the time and place of his own choosing against the wily British general. Ochterlony conducted a careful series of operations; step by step he brought his artillery forward to bear on Amarsing's defences at Ramgarh. The gallant Gurkha commander found that his position was neatly turned so he had no option but to evacuate it and retreat to Malaun.

In spite of the occasional dashing counter-attacks by the Gurkha warriors, Ochterlony's force pursued a policy of attrition, probing forward to seize the advantages they needed. Indeed, the battle fought at Malaun was won before the actual fighting began, for Ochterlony found that two of the peaks, in the very centre of the Nepalese position, were not fortified, a gamble that Amarsing might have taken against any other British general but not when opposed by this one. After a night's march, both points fell before daylight on 15 April 1815, and the Gurkha position was neatly bisected. In fury, Amarsing launched all he had, 2,000 men, against the key peak of Deothal.

*The Gurkhas came on with furious intrepidity, so much so that several were bayoneted or cut to pieces within our works. Amarsing stood all the while just within musket range with the Gurkha colours planted beside him, while his nephew Bhagte was everywhere inciting the men to further efforts.**

Gallant, but fruitless and disastrous; at the end of the day over 500 Gurkhas lay dead on the field of battle. Amarsing withdrew his remaining men into the fort of Malaun where he hoped to make a last stand but, realising the Ochterlony now surrounded his small garrison, he was forced to ask for terms. 'In consideration of the bravery, skill and fidelity with which he defended the country entrusted to his charge,' Ochterlony agreed that Amarsing should march out with his arms, colours and all his personal property. Courtesy after the battle was one thing, but in other matters the British general was definite and severe. Nepal was to cede to the British the Plain of the Terai and to hand back the districts which are today called Kumaon, Garhwal and Simla, to evacuate parts of Sikkim and, the bitterest pill of all, to accept a British Resident at the Court of Kathmandu. This last provision was the nearest Nepal ever came to accepting a modicum of control from the British but, as it turned out, it was a tenuous one. Moreover, they gave the British a site in a highly malarial part of Kathmandu so that life expectancy, in the early years, was often governed by the mosquito. The tombstones bear witness to the many young men who died in the nineteenth century as a result of malaria.

Back in Kathmandu, Bhim Sen faltered and evaded. Why should he surrender the Terai, the buffer region that afforded Nepal a high measure of security? Why should they be

Major-General Sir David Ochterlony

* Henry Thoby Prinsep, *Political and Military Transactions in India*, 1825

forced to have a British Resident? Inevitably negotiations broke down and the Prime Minister refused the terms. Once again a British force assembled, this time at Dinapore, and again under the inspiring leadership of Sir David Ochterlony. In January 1816, 14,000 regular soldiers, supported by irregulars and 83 guns, set off to capture Kathmandu. Once again the Gurkhas were outmanoeuvred and outwitted, being forced to pull back until their small force, under its leader, Ranjursing, stood at Makwanpore. The fighting was intense and bitter: a British subaltern wrote: 'The havoc was dreadful for they still scorned to fly. On going round the hill afterwards, the dead bodies there astonished me.' At the end of the day there were 500 dead Gurkhas around the British positions; the British and Indian losses were about half that number. It was the beginning of the end. Sensibly, Bhim Sen was determined that the British would not set foot in the Valley of Kathmandu so, in March 1816, he signed a treaty with Sir David Ochterlony. The latter said: 'You take either a Resident or War,' words which for years were resented in Nepal and made the Resident's task no easier. The Treaty of Segouli was signed on 4 March, to end the hardest-fought campaign of all those that the East India Company had engaged upon since the first arrival of English merchants in India in the seventeenth century.

The short bloody war was to have a happy outcome as it was to precede a long and lasting friendship between the two countries. That war taught the British to respect the Nepalese highlanders, to such an extent that no attempt was ever made to colonise Nepal or coerce that country into becoming part of the Indian Empire. The respect and affection were not one-sided. Some years later, when Gurkha soldiers were being praised for their gallantry by British comrades, they returned the flattering partiality of the latter with the following characteristic remark: 'The English are as brave as lions; they are splendid sepoys and very nearly equal to us!'

At the height of the campaign Ochterlony had recommended the enlistment of Gurkhas into the Company's army, a novel idea at such a time in the middle of a war. Shortly afterwards Lieutenant Frederick Young was selected to raise and command an irregular force of 2,000 men for operations on Ochterlony's inner flank. This band of irregulars met the Gurkhas who at once attacked them. Young and his handful of officers stood aghast while the irregulars fled, leaving them alone on the battlefield. The Gurkhas gathered round and asked why he did not run off with his men.

'I have not come so far in order to run away,' replied Young. 'I came to stop,' and he sat down.

'We could serve under men like you,' observed their leader, a prophetic saying as events were to transpire. Young was held as an honoured prisoner and treated well, so that he made friends with his captors who taught him their language. When he was released, he went to the prisoner-of-war camps in India to select an initial batch of recruits. When he sought permission to ask for volunteers to form a Corps of Gurkha soldiers, it was readily granted and, as he said afterwards: 'I went there one man and I came out 3,000.' From these volunteers he raised the Sirmoor Battalion which eventually became the 2nd King Edward VII's Own Gurkha Rifles. Frederick Young was then thirty years old: he had been commissioned in 1800 after appearing before a board in London, where he was asked his age and whether he was prepared to die for King and Country. He confirmed that he was fifteen years old and gave an affirmative reply to the second question. Young was granted a commission and remained Commandant of the Sirmoor Battalion for twenty-eight years, truly the father figure of that famous regiment.

Two more battalions, called the Nasiri, or Friendly, battalions were raised at Subathu, near Simla, which subsequently became one unit, and in the twentieth century were granted the title of the 1st King George V's Own Gurkha Rifles. Meanwhile the Kumaon Battalion had been raised in 1815 at Almora in Kumaon: its personnel were not all Gurkhas but men from Nepal's feudatory districts such as Kumaon and Garhwal. The battalion was to police the Nepalese border for forty years before the outbreak of the Indian Mutiny in 1857 summoned it to Delhi. It eventually became the 3rd Queen Alexandra's Own Gurkha Rifles. There were no further Gurkha units raised for another forty years but during that interval the existing battalions more than justified themselves in a number of operations. (As the titles of all the Gurkha

A Gurkha officer
and sepoys of the Sabathu
Battalion in 1834.
This was probably the
Nusseree (Nasiri) Battalion
based in Sabathu; it later
became the 1st Gurkha Rifles

regiments changed several times during the nineteenth century, details are shown in Appendix 1, pages 161-5.)

But what were these Gurkhas like, the men who enlisted under the British flag after 1816? Ensign John Shipp, himself renowned as being an extremely brave soldier, wrote in his memoirs:

I never saw more steadiness or bravery exhibited in my life. Run they would not, and of death they seemed to have no fear, though their comrades were falling thick around them, for we were so near that every shot told.

Brian Hodgson, who spent several years in Nepal, ending up as Resident in Kathmandu, wrote:

In my humble opinion they are, by far, the best soldiers in India; and if they were made participators of our renown in arms, I conceive that their gallant spirit, emphatic contempt of madhesias [people residing on the plains] and unadulterated military habit might be relied on for fidelity.

A few years later, Doctor Oldfield in his book (1860) paid tribute to the Gurkha soldiers:

Their fighting qualities, whether for sturdy unflinching courage or enduring elan are, 'nulli secundus' amongst the troops we enrol in our ranks from the varied classes of our Indian Empire and no greater compliment can be paid to their bravery than by quoting one of their sayings: 'Kafar hone bhanda morne ramro' (It is better to die than be a coward).

Following 1816 the reputation of these newly raised Gurkha corps was to be enhanced by actions carried out in the years, prior to the Indian Mutiny, which broke out in 1857. The first major action occurred in 1826 when men of the Nasiri and Sirmoor Battalions took part in the siege operations that preceded the storming of the great fort of Bhurtpore, where their behaviour under fire earned the warm commendation of the Commander-in-Chief, Lord Combermere.

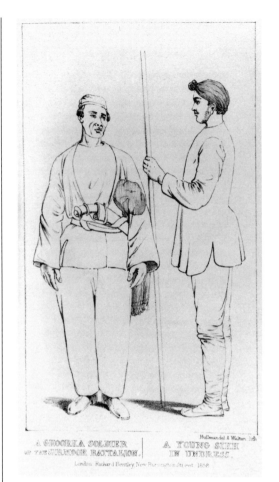

A GOORKHA SOLDIER OF THE SIRMOOR BATTALION. | A YOUNG SIKH IN UNDRESS.

London: Richard Bentley, New Burlington Street 1858.

'A Goorkha soldier of the Sirmoor Battalion.' This battalion later became the 2nd Gurkha Rifles; the soldier on the right is a young Sikh

Other despatches after the battle paid generous tribute to these Gurkha soldiers. General Sir Harry Smith wrote: 'The intrepid little Goorkas of the Naseree and Sirmoor Battalions in bravery and obedience can be excelled by none.'

Such praise was to be echoed twenty years later when both battalions took part in the great battles against the Sikhs at Aliwal and Sobraon during the first Sikh War of 1845-6. Here, too, written reports after the battle were generous in their praise, with the Commander-in-Chief, General Sir Hugh Gough, writing in his despatches of

the determined hardihood and bravery with which our two battalions of Goorkas, the Sirmoor and Naseree, met the Sikh whenever they were opposed to them. Soldiers of small stature and indomitable spirit, they vied in ardent courage in the charge with the Grenadiers of our own nation and, armed with the short weapon of their mountains [the kukri], were a terror to the Sikhs throughout the great combat.

While these battalions of the original

Corps were laying the foundations for the future, events both in Nepal and in India were to accelerate that process. From 1846 Nepal had a strong man at the helm, Jangbahadur Rana, whose rise to the dual post of Prime Minister and Commander-in-Chief had been mercurial as well as blood-stained. Jangbahadur, virtual dictator of Nepal until his death in 1877, was a great anglophile and the year he spent in the United Kingdom in 1850 induced him to take some long overdue steps towards modernising Nepal. His admiration for Queen Victoria and her country heralded a dramatic change in Anglo-Nepalese relations which was to come to the fore when the Indian Mutiny broke out.

In 1857 the flames of insurrection threatened to engulf the tenuous British hold over India.

With the passing of the years misconceptions about the Mutiny have grown, especially in the minds of modern Indian historians, supported by a few academics who seek to denigrate the British role in India. The temptation to present it as part of the struggle against the British beginning in 1857 and ending in 1947, has proved difficult to resist. Nevertheless, definitive and authentic accounts written during and immediately after the Mutiny show that it was in fact a rising by parts of the Native Army as opposed to a national movement. (E. D. Smith, *Johnny Gurkha*, 1986.)

Apart from the province of Oudh – where there was an appearance of a national rising because affairs had been brought to a head by tactless handling of much-needed land reform by the British officials concerned – elsewhere it remained a military mutiny by discontented sepoys: although, for a variety of reasons, other Indians supported the disaffected soldiers in order to spread anarchy and destruction. The majority of Indian princes believed that the English could never win India back, but Jangbahadur was one of a handful who still felt that, in the end, the power of the British was bound to prevail. Having been to England, he realised that the few thousand British soldiers and administrators in India were but the tip of the iceberg. It is also worth remembering that he had pledged his faith to Queen Victoria during an audience at Buckingham Palace, which as a Gurkha he had not given lightly. Consequently, Jangbahadur threw the whole power of Nepal into the struggle on the British side, and among other things committed the East India Company to raising more Gurkha regiments, as a reward for his loyalty and help during the Mutiny.

The first of these to be raised was to become, in time, the 4th Prince of Wales's Own Gurkha Rifles, but was known initially as the Extra Gurkha Regiment. Its first operational task was to hold the Kumaon Hills after the outbreak of the Mutiny, putting much reliance on a draft of experienced soldiers from the 1st Nasiri Battalion (later the 1/1st Gurkha Rifles).

Meanwhile Jangbahadur's initial offer of 6,000 soldiers from his own army was turned down by the Governor-General, Lord Canning, albeit in the politest of terms. It was but a temporary refusal, however, because the situation at Lucknow, which had been besieged by the mutineers since July 1857, deteriorated, thus influencing Canning into gratefully accepting Jangbahadur's offer of help. Three thousand Nepalese soldiers, under General Dhir Shamshur Rana, moved down into India where they drove out the mutineers from two or three towns: then on 19th September 1857 the fortified position at Manduri was taken, with the defenders fleeing from the kukris wielded with such ferocity by the highland warriors.

Manduri was but the prelude to a much fiercer battle, when, a few weeks later, the small force under Dhir Shamshur attacked an army some four or five times their number at Chanda. The fighting was savage and the

The Maharajah Jangbahadur Rana, the Ruler of Nepal, 1845-1877

outcome was in doubt, with the Nepalese contingent suffering grievous losses before forcing their way into the defences to win a hard-earned victory. The rebels left some 300 dead on the battlefield. Lieutenant

Lucknow soon after the Indian Mutiny. The buildings show the scars of the siege

Gambirsing was singled out for mention because although covered in wounds, he 'took a gun, cutting down five artillery men and wounding and driving away the others'.

At such a moment did Lord Canning ask Jangbahadur Rana to move down into India at the head of 9,000 men, reinforcements that Nepal's ruler had held ready for such a purpose for four months. Jangbahadur did not hesitate – especially when there was the prospect of a fight. In later years he affirmed that the campaign that followed was the most important work of his whole life: certainly it was a highly significant moment in the long friendship between Britain and Nepal when the short, stocky soldiers from the mountains went into battle against the enemies of their friends, the British. Moving down to besieged Lucknow, they joined General Sir Colin Campbell's forces and played an important role in a series of attacks which led to the relief of that city in March 1858, after a siege that had lasted some eight months.

Lord Canning was quick to reward such loyalty, returning the much disputed strip of plain, the Terai, to Nepal. Jangbahadur's soldiers were not slow to enrich themselves and returned to their hills loaded with plunder, followed by a baggage train of several thousand bullock carts, heavily laden with loot collected during their year's campaigning.

In those days, battalions of infantry in the East India Company's army consisted of eight companies, each of about one hundred and twenty men. The battalion commander, called the Commandant, initially had a British adjutant – although as the years passed, other British officers were added to the establishment. It was with such an establishment that two Gurkha battalions, the Kumaon and the Sirmoor, played such a significant part in the struggle for possession of India's most important city, Delhi.*

That we know so much about the Sirmoor Battalion's exploits is due to the fact that the Commandant, Major Charles Reid, wrote and retained letters throughout the march to Delhi and, thereafter, during the siege that lasted for over four months; from him we learn how the conflict went until the final victory in mid-September 1957. On 14 May a tired camel sowar (trooper) arrived in Dehra Dun with instructions that the Sirmoor Battalion was to move with the greatest possible urgency to Meerut where the Europeans were in dire straits already. Four hours later they left, and by dint of forced marches, Reid and his men covered distances of thirty miles a day in the heat of the mid-May Indian summer, with the soldiers wearing what today would be considered thick, unhealthy clothing. The first brush with the mutineers came on the fifth day near the Ganges Canal, where some of the rebels were captured. They were tried by a drumhead court-martial and thirteen were convicted. Reid ordered them to be shot, a punishment that was carried out immediately: these executions were a test of his own Gurkhas because five of the prisoners were brahmins and there were many brahmins serving under his command.

Shortly afterwards, the Commandant learned that Major-General Archdale Wilson, who was marching towards Delhi, was in danger of being attacked,. By dint of a considerable feat of stamina, the Gurkhas marched through a night of terrific heat, covering twenty-seven miles before dawn broke on the following day. After a short rest, the men continued until they reached General Wilson's camp, dead beat and footsore, on 1 June. When they did meet up with the 60th Rifles (now part of the Royal Green Jackets), the British battalion thought they were the enemy and fired on them, though fortunately, no blood was shed. Reid found that the British soldiers were, in his words, 'Knocked down by the sun and completely exhausted'. Nevertheless, the 60th Rifles turned out and cheered the Gurkhas into camp. As Reid wrote later; 'My poor little fellows were so dead beat that they could not return the hearty cheers with which they were welcomed.' In such a way was to begin a most long-lasting regimental friendship, one that has endured to this day. Events over the next few weeks were soon to dispel that initial British mistrust of the Gurkhas, loyalty and the highest degree of mutual admiration was attained.

Space does not allow a detailed description of the lengthy struggle for the city of Delhi. As far as the Sirmoor Battalion was concerned, the key position was Hindu Rao's House which owed its name to a former owner, a Mahratta nobleman. This strongly built mansion, together with a

---

* Calcutta was the capital of India from 1773 until 1912, when Delhi was made the administrative capital.

Gurkhas of the Sirmoor Rifle Regiment in front of Hindu Rao's House, Delhi

neighbouring observatory, provided accommodation and cover from fire for a substantial garrison and was to be the pivot of the British defences on the right flank of the Delhi Ridge. In Reid's words:

Hindu Rao's House was the key of the position... which the enemy were not long in discovering; they tried their utmost to drive me out of it on the first day and it became ever after the object of almost every attack, often by as many as 8,000 rebels at a time.

But Charles Reid knew his men and, being no believer in static defence himself, realised that their morale would remain high if they were given the chance to close with the mutineers and wield their kukris in hand-to-hand conflict. On 15 June he wrote in his diary:

I gave the word forward; our little fellows were up like a shot and advanced in beautiful order to the top of the hill. By way of bringing the enemy on, I sounded the retreat having previously warned my men what we were going to do. It had the desired effect; on came the mutineers, we met just as I got over the brow of the hill. I gave them one well-directed volley and then ordered my guns to open. This sent them to a round-about and about 50 were killed and a great number wounded.

Nevertheless, the Sirmoor Battalion's casualties were mounting steadily, because although the mutineers tended to adopt the same tactics day by day, under leadership that was poor, they fought with extraordinary tenacity. By the end of July,

Reid was becoming extremely concerned at the number of his 'little fellows' who had been killed or wounded and only the timely arrival, at the end of July, of a draft of recruits and men returning from furlough saved the situation. It is worth recording that Charles Reid's admiration for his men was no greater than the opinions he expressed about the 60th Rifles under his command.

The feeling that existed between the 60th Rifles and my own men was admirable: they call one another brothers, share their grog with each other... My men used to speak of them of 'Our Rifles' and the men of the 60th as 'Them Gurkhees of ours'.

This close fellowship and admirable discipline was never to waver until the end of the siege, which came after a total of three months and eight days' continuous struggle. As it neared its end, the King of Delhi promised ten rupees for every Gurkha's head, the same price being offered for that of an English soldier, as an incentive to his wavering army. They were due to fight in front of the ladies of the city, seated in specially erected chairs with the princes in attendance, dressed in green velvet suits covered with gold.

Reid was ready for them:

I shall be very happy to see him and hope he will come out of the Moree Gate on the largest elephant he has got. A 24-pound shot would double up his Majesty, elephant, gold Howdah* and all!

The promised spectacle was the hope that his rebels would raise the green standard over Hindu Rao's House. To this end, the

---

* A seat for an elephant's back, usually quite an elaborate affair with a canopy over it.

The Truncheon. Presented by Queen Victoria in 1863 to the 2nd Gurkha Rifles to commemorate its service in the Mutiny, the Truncheon replaced the colours no longer carried when the unit became a rifle regiment

King with a large retinue and a number of his wives, arrived at their vantage point; alas for them, the end was not as good as the beginning, for the assault proved very costly and the royal spectators were forced to withdraw hurriedly into the city.

During the first week of August the long-awaited British reinforcements arrived under the command of the legendary Brigadier-General John Nicholson. Among these reinforcements was the Kumaon Battalion and despite a series of forced marches at the height of the hot weather, that battalion's stamina and resilience were unimpaired. On 12 August the newly arrived unit participated in a silent attack which was launched against the rebels and their guns at Ludlow Castle. This proved to be a great success and a number of the rebels were killed during the fierce assault.

Away from Delhi the mutiny still ebbed and flowed in various parts of India. Up in the Kumaon hills, the 66th Gurkhas (eventually to become the 1st Gurkhas) were part of a British force holding the town of Haldwani. Opposing them were two rebel contingents, each of about 4,000 men with supporting guns, reported to be converging from their different directions to make a combined attack on the town. The commanding officer of the 66th decided to defeat them in detail before they joined forces. Some 500 men from the 66th Gurkhas, supported by two guns and a contingent of the Nepalese Army, marched all night through the forest and took the rebel army by surprise at the village of Charpura. Although the little force was heavily outnumbered they did not hesitate, with the Gurkhas firing rapidly as they advanced towards the rebels. Nothing could check that discipline under fire and the rebels fled. That was but the first of their efforts: they set off back to Haldwani and, after forced marching thirty-four miles, arrived there after midday – all within the space of thirteen hours. In the event Haldwani was not attacked and when the remnants of the rebel force trickled back to the town of Bareilly, their leader castigated them with the scathing denunciation: 'You worthless cowards! You took ten days to march from Bareilly to Charpura, only to come back in a matter of hours after seeing the British troops.' In this context no doubt he meant the British-led Gurkhas and their fellow countrymen of the Nepalese Army.

'The Nusseree Battalion,
c. 1857' (later the 1st Gurkha
Rifles)

In the action at Charpura the 66th Gurkhas lost a promising young officer, Lieutenant Gepp. After the officer's death, his parents gave the regiment some of the letters he had written from 1855 until his death in 1858. While serving as an ensign he had frequently praised his regiment: 'I am sure there is not a more celebrated corps in the world … I fear you will be quite tired of hearing their praises sung but you must forgive my regimental esprit de corps.'

The CO's letter of condolence to Lieutenant Gepp's grieving father may strike an odd note in today's society: 'You have, my dear sir, much to be thankful for that your poor son died a soldier's death and was not brutally murdered as many of our countrymen, women and children have been.' The Mutiny witnessed much brutality and before it was suppressed, both sides had been guilty of many atrocities.

Back at Delhi, 14 September 1857 was the date selected for the grand assault which the forces under Nicholson hoped would bring the siege to an end. Living up to his title of 'Lion of the Punjab' and waving his sword, Nicholson led the party which took possession of the ramparts but tragically he was mortally wounded at the moment of his triumph.

Behind him the main body of the Kumaon Regiment drove the rebels from the Korwali and from Delhi's famous street, the Chandni Chauk, until it came up against the great mosque, the Jamna Masjid. Here the battalion waited for the artillery before it occupied itself in clearing the rebels out of

'A British Officer of the 66th
or Goorkha Regiment, c. 1855.'
Taken from a portrait of
Lieutenant T. S. Gepp, who died
of wounds received at the Battle
of Charpura in February 1858

Veterans of the Mutiny at the Coronation Durbar, Delhi, in 1911

the narrow alleyways of the great city, a task that took some days to complete.

Meanwhile, Reid's column, which consisted of about 2,500 men from various units – in addition to his own battalion – suffered some setbacks, particularly when the Commandant himself was wounded. In the violent battle the defending mutineers fought stubbornly as the struggle ebbed and flowed. Nevertheless, the attackers slowly fought their way forward until organised rebel resistance ceased, although bitter fighting was to continue in parts of the city until 20 September. Regrettably, unbridled vengeance was taken against the innocent as well as the guilty by the less disciplined members of the attacking army. On this point Reid compliments the soldiers under his command for being forbearing in the heat of battle and at the moment of victory, a trait which they have invariably shown during the aftermath of many battles in subsequent campaigns. Lieutenant-General Sir Francis Tuker, one of the most distinguished of Gurkha officers, was to write in his book *Gorkha*: 'As a result of these achievements the reputation of the Gurkha as a fighting man was hailed in the British and Indian Armies: these battalions had established Nepal in India.'

3 THE BRIGADE EARNS ITS SPURS

So far, no mention has been made of the regiments which had their original, non-Gurkha, roots in Assam (6th and 8th Gurkha Rifles), Bengal (9th Gurkha Rifles), and Burma (7th and 10th Gurkha Rifles). The omission is deliberate because although the first three were in existence well before the Mutiny, they did not become all-Gurkha units until late in the nineteenth century. (See Appendix I) This is not to decry their earlier exploits, when they were composed of Indian as opposed to Gurkha soldiers – but those deeds do not form part of the Gurkhas' history.

The 5th Gurkha Rifles did not evolve via the Bengal Army but was raised at Abbottabad to hold the Hazara frontier with Afghanistan. Abbottabad was to remain the regimental home for almost ninety years. In 1861 their title became the 5th Gurkha Rifles or Hazara Gurkha Battalion. After the turn of the century, by agreement with Nepal there were to be ten Gurkha regiments, each consisting of two battalions, with each regiment having its 'home' station in North India where, in theory, one of its battalions was stationed, while the other battalion was on 'active' service on the North-West Frontier or elsewhere. Every Gurkha battalion trained its own recruits, with an extra major being authorised, that officer having command of the training company.

The period after the Indian Mutiny up to the beginning of the First World War was by no means devoid of active operations for the Indian Army. There were wars in Afghanistan, and tribal uprisings on the Frontier posed problems which the British never resolved despite numerous punitive expeditions mounted against rebel tribesmen, in addition to waging two of the Afghan Wars between 1878 and 1920, in both of which battalions from the Gurkha Brigade fought.

During the latter half of the nineteenth century British statesmen were highly

General Sir Frederick Roberts,
VC, GCB, CIE, (*standing*)
with General Sir Donald
Stewart (*left*) and General the
Hon. A. E. Harding

sensitive about Russia's blatantly displayed ambitions in Afghanistan, which came to a head in 1878 when a Russian Mission was established in the Afghan capital, Kabul. This act was like a red rag to a bull so General Sir Neville Chamberlain, C-in-C of the Madras Army, was instructed to establish an equivalent British Mission at Kabul. He left Peshawar for the Afghan border, only to be turned back by a show of superior force. In Kabul, the Amir, Sher Ali, refused to make an apology so that the British prepared for what was to become known as the Second Afghan War.*

The part played by the 5th Gurkha Rifles during this war was to be a notable one. The regiment formed part of the Kurram Field Force, whose commander was Major-General Frederick Roberts, VC, later Field Marshal Lord Roberts of Kandahar. When campaigning in a hostile land with a small force, Roberts was not the sort of commander to be deterred by problems and believed in the spirit of aggression whenever possible. Four out of his six Indian regiments contained a large proportion of Muslims who, for obvious reasons, were not so enthusiastic about fighting tribesmen who shared their faith. For such a reason, the 5th Gurkhas were asked by Roberts to play a leading role and in every respect they lived up to his trust. It was their dash and courage that won the day when Roberts's force attacked the Spingawi Kotal, with the 72nd Highlanders (later the 1st Seaforth Highlanders) in support. It was during this battle and its aftermath that Captain John Cook of the 5th Gurkhas won the Victoria Cross for gallantry in charging the enemy and saving a fellow officer's life. In addition, five Gurkhas from the same regiment were awarded the Indian Order of Merit. During these operations the 5th Gurkhas formed an enduring friendship with the 72nd Highlanders with whom they were brigaded throughout the campaign. Their dual role

* First Afghan War, 1838–42; Second, 1878–80; Third, 1919.

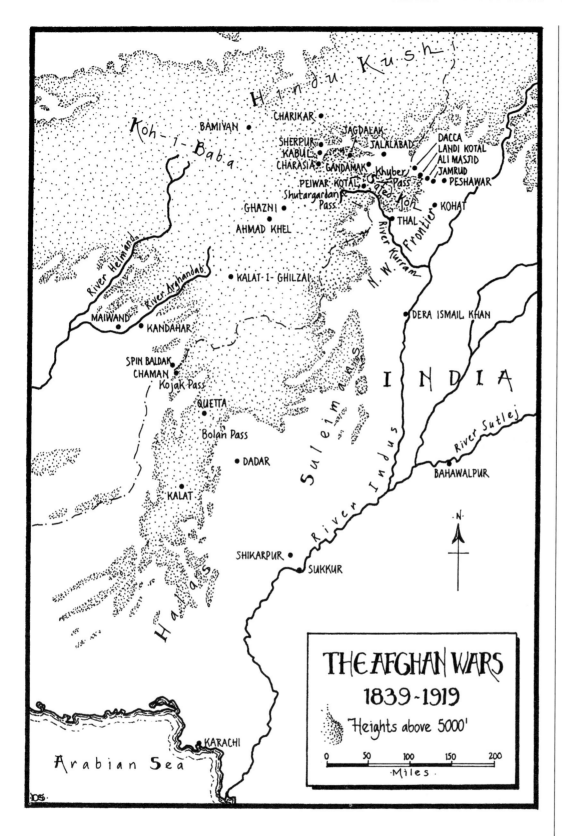

THE AFGHAN WARS
1839-1919
Heights above 5000'

0   50   100   150   200
· Miles ·

was recognised when, in 1892, General Roberts was raised to the peerage, because he chose, as supporters for his arms, a representation of a 72nd Highlander on one side and a rifleman of the 5th Gurkhas on the other.

In addition to the 5th Gurkhas, the 1st, 2nd, 3rd and 4th Gurkhas all participated in the campaign, taking their full share in the actions which eventually led to the relief of Kabul and Kandahar, where British garrisons and civilians were besieged.

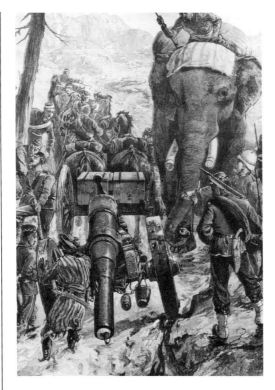

'On the road to Ali Masjid.'
An artist's impression of an incident in the Second Afghan War, depicting men of the 2nd Gurkha Rifles on the advance against the Afghan fortress of Ali Masjid at the head of the Khyber Pass

When in December 1878 the 3rd Gurkhas entered Afghanistan via Quetta, the terrain over which they had to march was so difficult that the bullocks of the gun teams broke down, whereupon the Gurkha soldiers were ordered to manhandle the guns on their march to Kandahar. As part of the Kandahar Field Force – which also included the 1st Gurkhas – their advance was not contested and Kandahar was reached on 8 January 1879. A year later, when marching from Kandahar to Kabul, as part of a column commanded by Lieutenant-General Sir Donald Stewart, the 3rd Gurkhas were attacked by a fanatical force of Afghan tribesmen: it was only when the commanding officer, Colonel Lyster, VC, ordered his men to form a square that the attack was thwarted: The unique battle honour 'Ahmed Khel' was awarded to the regiment in recognition of this action.

The 2nd Gurkhas, who had returned to India from Cyprus, arrived too late to participate in the capture of Kabul by General Roberts on 24 December 1811. One hundred and twenty-nine men from the unit, however, had been present at the defence of Charasiah in October the same year, where they had launched a counter-attack which, in the end, threatened to outflank the tribesmen who then fled. The campaign continued into the 1880s during which negotiations between the Afghan leaders and the Viceroy's representatives were carried out against a background of intrigue and violence. This continued until there was a dramatic reversal when, on 27 July 1880, a brigade of the Kandahar Field Force was defeated by a contender to the throne of Afghanistan, Ayub Khan; this setback meant that Kandahar was directly threatened.

A relief force was raised with speed and, once more, command was given to the best general in the campaign, Roberts. The choice of commander dictated the choice of troops because Roberts had strong prejudices in

Men of the 4th Goorkha Regiment at Kabul in 1880. They are dressed in khaki drill (hot-weather uniform)

favour of Highlanders, Sikhs and Gurkhas, which, in turn, meant that the 72nd Highlanders and 5th Gurkhas, who had served under him since the start of the war and had been present in all his major actions, found themselves, once more, marching towards Kandahar. So, too, were the 92nd Highlanders and 2nd Gurkhas, already comrades in a previous battle, which was to herald a long and lasting friendship that was to be tested, once again, seventeen years later in the Battle of the Heights of Dargai on the Frontier, 20 October 1897.

General Roberts's epic march to Kandahar from Kabul in August 1880 was commemorated by the award of a special ribbon and bronze star to all units which took part in it. The award was fully earned because in 23 days they covered 305 miles, an average of nearly 15 miles a day over the most difficult country imaginable. This rapid advance was not to be in vain nor were the soldiers to be denied a stirring battle as a reward for these feats of endurance. During the march only nine soldiers and eleven followers* were listed as killed or missing but the daily sick list averaged some 550 soldiers and up to 200 followers – mainly as a result of diarrhoea from the poor food, blistered feet, heat stroke and exhaustion. Great feat though it was, the march to Kandahar was by

no means the smooth efficient operation it has been made to appear in some accounts or regimental histories.

Nevertheless, the drama of the force's sudden appearance on 31 August at the besieged Kandahar, after a virtual absence of news for three weeks, plus the crowning victory over the Afghans outside the city within twenty-four hours of its arrival, accentuated by the charisma of Roberts himself, all combined to catch the British public's imagination and to make the march an episode known to all, from Queen Victoria down to the humblest of her subjects.

After his arrival outside Kandahar, Roberts assumed overall command and was determined to seize the initiative as soon as possible. On 1 September 1880 the battle for Kandahar was joined near a village called Sahibad. By 10.30 in the morning the village had been taken but the 92nd Highlanders and 2nd Gurkhas then found themselves confronted by some thousands of the enemy, occupying a position around two guns. Volleys of fire poured into the massed tribesmen causing them to waver but not to retire. Major White of the 92nd Highlanders rode along the front line and ordered the charge to be sounded. Cheering highlanders from the mountains of Scotland and Nepal

The Battle of Kandahar, 1 September 1880

* Non-combatants – sweepers, water carriers and syces (grooms).

sprang forward and went for the guns, which they captured; an incident that has been painted by Colonel Hobday, RA, shows a rifleman of the 2nd Gurkhas thrusting his cap down the muzzle of the Afghan guns in order to claim ownership. Legend has it hat he shouted in Hindustani: 'This gun belongs to my Regiment – 2nd Gurkhas! Prince of Wales!' One of the guns was subsequently presented to the regiment and before the 2nd Gurkhas amalgamated as a result of the recent cuts in the army under 'Options for Change', it always stood outside the Officers' Mess, wherever the unit was serving.

The enemy were routed and the fighting was over, with the 92nd Highlanders suffering the heaviest casualties. Thereafter the contingent was broken up and for the 4th and 5th Gurkhas that battle marked the end of two years' active service: they were the last battalions of the original Kabul Field Force engaged in active operations beyond the Frontier. As a result of the second Afghan War, Lord Roberts, as C-in-C India, decided to expand considerably the Gurkha units of the Indian Army by raising second battalions for each of the five all-Gurkha regiments then in being. It was not to be long before three of these newly formed second battalions – those of the 2nd, 3rd and 5th Gurkhas – were in action when participating in the expedition to raise the siege of Chitral in 1895. Prior to that, however, active operations were being conducted on India's eastern frontier and these will now be considered.

From 1860 until the outbreak of the First World War, peace there was a rare commodity. Throughout this time one or other of the battalions which were later to form part of the Indian Army Gurkha Brigade was on active service either in Assam or in north-eastern Bengal. The hilly province of Assam was the main eastern boundary of the British Indian Empire until 1865 and during this period Britain's interest in the area grew as the tea industry developed. Encroachments were made into tribal areas in the name of trade so it is easy to understand why the tribesmen viewed it all with more than a little suspicion. As time went by the local tribes found it wise to make promises to obey the orders of the Government even if they had no intention of keeping their word.

The 1st Assam Light Infantry (later to become the 6th Gurkhas) carried out a series of operations against the unruly tribesmen, the major one being an armed sortie against the Abors which was successful - although the battalion suffered forty-five casualties before the rebel villages were captured. At that time the regiment contained only two companies of Gurkhas but after 1864 an Army Order stated that it would be 'chiefly Gurkhas and hillmen [Assamese] with a proportion of not exceeding one fourth of strength of Hindustanis'. The title of the regiment – which changed with monotonous regularity every few years – did not reflect the increased Gurkha contingent until 1886, when it became the 42nd Regiment Gurkha Light Infantry. As it transpired, this was the final step in the process of becoming a completely Gurkha unit, the ultimate transition from its Indian origin to the modern 6th Gurkha Rifles. It is of interest, however, that there was a great controversy about the future class composition of the regiment, with most officers advocating that the Indian and Sikh other ranks should be posted elsewhere. However, Colonel Sheriff (who commanded for over eleven years) wanted to replace all the Gurkhas with Sikhs. The regimental history commends two junior officers who 'appear to have been able to exert their influence, and saved the Regiment from this fate'.

As the 42nd Regiment, the battalion carried out actions against several tribes including the Nagas and the Lushai. Both the Nagas and the Lushai were warlike people and in the early 1870s, carried out a series of raids against neighbouring tea gardens, particularly in the Char district, where they massacred many local coolies and some Europeans. In a sense, such a situation had been brought about by the British, who did the worst thing possible by alternating between an aggressive 'forward' policy, and vacillating prior to withdrawing.

However, the raids that the Lushai carried out finally stirred the Government into action and, on 3 January 1872, a considerable battle resulted at Lal Gnoora's village. The 2nd Gurkhas had entered the south Lushai hills, marching with a column commanded by Brigadier-General Brownlow, with the 42nd Regiment accompanying a second column, of which a certain Colonel F. S. Roberts, VC, (later of Kandahar fame) was the senior staff officer. The Lushai hills proved difficult country for the troops operating in them.

There were several skirmishes before the main battle occurred at Lal Gnoora's village which was attacked by the 2nd Gurkhas – the unit's first real action since their last tour of duty on the North-West Frontier. The Government troops had found each village difficult to assault particularly as the houses were surrounded by lines of bamboo spikes, *panjis*, which at times were about eight or nine feet in height. At Lal Gnoora's village the Lushais opened fire at the same time as some of their number began burning the village, prior to evacuation. The Gurkha casualties in the centre of the assault could well have been heavy had it not been for Major Donald McIntyre, the left flank commander, who scrambled over the stockade and disappeared into the smoke to attack the Lushais from an unexpected quarter. This gallant act was recognised by an award of the Victoria Cross.

One campaign was over although other minor ones continued throughout the 1870s and 1880s. Casualties in these actions were never high but sickness, added to the tough nature of the country, meant that 'the history of the expedition has been sheer hard work,' as General Bouchier was to write about the Lushai operations.

Before the end of the nineteenth century there occurred an episode in the small state of Manipur which afforded little credit to the British reputation in India. Manipur was a protected state in south-eastern Assam, and somewhat larger than Wales. In 1890 a revolution there led by the Senapati, the Chief Minister, ousted the Maharajah who was replaced by his younger brother. This coup d'état was not recognised by the Indian Government and Mr J.W. Quinton, Chief Commissioner of Assam, marched with a force to investigate and, if necessary, deal with the rebels. The troops that accompanied him were 400 men of the 42nd Gurkha Rifle Light Infantry and 44th Gurkha Regiment but from the start there was complacency: for example, the mountain guns, then in the possession of the 42nd

Chin Field Force, Burma, 1888. Seated on the right is Subedar-Major Bhole Bajur, 42nd Gurkha Light Infantry (later 6th Gurkha Rifles)

Naga/Lushai Campaign, Burma, 1890. 42nd Gurkha Light Infantry with two guns

Regiment, were not taken with the escort, which included several young recruits, while each man was armed with only forty rounds and no reserves of ammunition. Quite why there was such complacency is difficult to understand, because a private warning was said to have been given to Mr Quinton which stated that 'A big tiger was to be killed in Manipur.' The tiger was to be Quinton himself.

The Gurkha contingent was commanded by Lieutenant-Colonel C. Skene who, on reaching Imphal, the Manipur capital, launched an abortive attack on the Senapati's palace on 24 March 1891. Thereafter the story of the blunders that ensued makes sorry reading: bluster, vacillation and half-measures only served to embolden the Manipuri rebels. The tragic outcome was that Quinton, his Assistant Secretary, Skene, and two other officers, accepted a cease-fire, followed by an invitation to attend a durbar in the palace grounds where they went without any escort whatever. By the time they reached the main gate a large crowd of Manipuri soldiers and civilians had gathered and the five were surrounded by an excited jeering mob. One of the officers was speared, which was the signal for the soldiers to seize the other four Englishmen who were dragged and buffeted into the citadel: a few hours later they were brought out and beheaded by the public executioner.

The troops withdrew to the British Residency which, shortly afterwards, was attacked by the Manipuris. The two senior British officers remaining escaped with a handful of men and headed for the safety of Cachar, 100 miles to the west while, shamefully, over 200 Gurkha soldiers were left behind, seemingly without any orders. Besieged in the Residency by several thousand Manipuris, they fought on until their ammunition gave out. By now the house was ablaze, and in the firelight they fought with kukris and bayonets until they were overpowered by sheer weight of numbers. About 50 survived as prisoners in the hands of the Manipuri rebels. Later the two officers who fled, Major L. Boileau and Captain G. Butcher, were court-martialled and cashiered for gross neglect of duty in the face of the enemy.

News of the disaster quickly caused the Government to send forces to seek retribution even if it was too late to retrieve reputations. Three columns set out from Manipur which included the rest of the 42nd Regiment and the 1st Battalion of the 2nd Gurkhas, the original Sirmoor battalion. There was to be little fighting and the rebel leaders were soon seized, to be tried and executed in due course. What was to remain in the men's memories were the marches across forest-clad hills in the great heat, with each man carrying a greatcoat, waterproof sheets and 170 rounds of ammunition – plus all his other kit. Cholera struck and the 2nd

Gurkhas were to lose 32 men out of 58 cases that occurred; later the 42nd Regiment also suffered from the same disease, losing 58 officers and men out of 105 victims. Throughout this campaign many more men died from cholera and malaria than were killed on the field of battle.

In the years that preceded the First World War, there were no more dramatic or large-scale operations on the North-East Frontier. In 1899 the 42nd Regiment moved away from Assam to Abbottabad after a tour of duty in the east which had lasted for seventy-seven years: it was to be the final severing of its connection with the old Cuttack Legion, raised in 1817. Four years later the title of 6th Gurkha Rifles was adopted,* one that was only to disappear in 1994 when amalgamation, under 'Options for Change', witnessed the birth of the Royal Gurkha Rifles.

Events which brought Burma into the old British Empire also gave birth to the future 10th Gurkha Rifles. Following the Third Burma War of 1885 – which only lasted nine days – the aftermath witnessed anarchy and confusion with dacoits swarming over the countryside, spreading terror and destruction. When the situation improved, most of the regular troops from upper Burma were withdrawn, and in their place a semi-military force was raised to maintain law and order which became known as the Burma Military Police.

One of its original units was designated the Kubo Valley Military Police Battalion, and was well led and trained from the outset. It was soon to make a name for itself on operations against the dacoits. The majority of its men had been recruited from the little known Kiranti (Limbu and Rai) tribes of Eastern Nepal, until then rarely recruited in any of the other Gurkha units. In 1890, the old 10th Madras Native Infantry was converted into a Gurkha regiment,† with the officers and men of the Kubo Valley Battalion forming the nucleus of the new unit which was stationed near Maymyo in Burma. During this period a close association was formed with the Royal Scots who trained and equipped the new battalion's pipers, and this became a recognised affiliation, with the Gurkha pipers – until 'Options for Change' – wearing the Hunting Stewart tartan. During

the last few years of the nineteenth century, the battalion's title underwent several changes until finally, in 1901, it became the 10th Gurkha Rifles. Like the other regiments in the Indian Army Gurkha Brigade, thereafter most active soldiering, both prior to and between the two World Wars, was carried out on the North-West Frontier of India.

The number of times that titles changed in the Gurkha Brigade between 1890 and the beginning of the twentieth century can be confusing to the historian, let alone the general reader: hence it is not surprising that Appendix 1 is somewhat lengthy and complex. In 1903, the 8th Gurkhas came into existence and formed part of a military expedition into Tibet led by Colonel Francis Younghusband: six companies of the 8th Gurkhas went along, and for the first time in their lives, the Gurkhas were given pack ponies and mules on operations. Prior to setting out, riding practice was carried out and in May 1903 the column started its advance towards Gyantse. The expedition had been mounted because the government in Lhasa had been dallying with Russia, a flirtation which was anathema to the Government of India at that time; Russian arms and ammunition had begun to appear in Tibetan hands and there had been encroachments into Indian territory.

The expedition encountered a bitterly cold winter in the Himalayan uplands, blizzards struck a supply column and there were seventy cases of snow blindness among the Gurkhas, who also suffered from lack of food. However, Gyantse was occupied and its fort stormed in July 1904: it was here that Lieutenant John Grant of the 8th Gurkhas was to win a Victoria Cross and Havildar Karbir Pun the Indian Order of Merit – Gurkha soldiers not being eligible for the award of the Victoria Cross until 1911. Both Grant and Karbir Pun showed great courage as they stormed the fort at Gyantse and inspired by their leadership the rest of the force was encouraged to follow them and capture the building. The treaty that resulted after this campaign agreed that a company of Indian infantry should be stationed in Gyantse for the next fifty years, nominally as escort to the British and, later, Indian Trade Agents.

* Not without yet another name-change – to 42nd Gurkha Rifles – in 1901. See Appendix 1.
† See Appendix 1.

Men of the 1st Battalion, Gordon Highlanders bring Gurkha wounded down after the battle for the ridge at Dargai, during the Tirah Campaign of 1897-8

Before the First World War began, there was one more major campaign yet to be fought on the North-West Frontier, in 1897. Discontent had been spreading from tribe to tribe until the two main ones, the Waziris and Afridis, resorted to open aggression. At first the Indian Government was patient before deciding to burn some of the tribesmen's villages and destroy their crops. In the past such action had been effective but on this occasion the initial raids were met with resolute opposition and a large-scale campaign resulted which was to prove expensive, both in money and in lives.

The 1st Battalion of the 2nd Gurkhas went on this, the Tirah Campaign of 1897-8 and, because of the short notice, the equivalent of one company from the 2/2nd was drafted in to make the unit up to full operational strength. The Gurkhas found themselves in 1 Brigade where they renewed their old friendship with the Gordon Highlanders, an association that, once more, was to be fully tested on the ridge at Dargai. On 18 October 1897, the brigade was told to move to and secure the heights above Dargai village. These were known to be held by a large number of Afridis, stout-hearted tribesmen who had fought hard to stem the advance. At first, the steep craggy hill was secured by the British above the village, but as evening approached the Afridis reoccupied the hills

above Dargai when the British withdrew to concentrate their force for the night. It was to be an expensive error because the Afridis prepared and fortified 'sangars'* throughout the 19th while their opponents awaited the arrival of their guns.

On 20 October, at 10 am, the Gurkhas led the way up the ridge with the Dorsetshire Regiment in support and the Gordon Highlanders and the 95th (Rifle Brigade) in reserve. Scarcely a shot was fired as they worked their way up the hill against a total and unearthly silence until they reached a position barely 300 yards from the Afridis. The tribesmen knew that these last 300 yards from their position led across an open saddle, a fact that had not been discovered by Brigade Headquarters when the plan was made. The 2nd Gurkhas were to pay for this lack of reconnaissance because their attack was shot to ribbons. An eyewitness stated that:

When all was ready, Colonel Eaton Travers commanding the 2nd Goorkhas, stepped out in front, and drew his sword and called on his men to follow him. With a smothered shout the men scrambled up the few yards of shale and coarse grass which separated them from the glacis in front and pouring over the top came into view with the loopholes above.

* Sangars – stone breastworks, much used in operations on the Frontier.

Instantly the whole line of sangars burst into smoke and flame and a torrent of bullets from the front, right, and left, tore through the ranks; men literally fell in heaps on the stony slope that was strewn with dead and wounded.

Over sixty men fell; wounded lay in the open, often receiving further wounds as the Afridis' rifles pumped bullets into the strip of ground, the size of two tennis courts. Meanwhile, on their left, the Dorsets had suffered a similar reverse, with their survivors joining Colonel Travers's small party, hiding in dead ground under the final steep cliff before their objective. The first attack at Dargai had failed, at great cost to the two units concerned.

A further attack was arranged with the Gordons in the centre, supported by the 3rd Sikhs and in the final rush, by Colonel Travers's remaining Gurkhas. The assault went in and, in the face of such numbers, the Afridis melted away. The Dargai Heights were in British hands but if there was a victory it belonged to the Afridis, whose casualties throughout the battle were comparatively few. The Gordons held the heights and helped to carry down the wounded men from the Gurkhas and Dorsets, a touching show of comradeship that has been commemorated in a painting (see opposite). This rebuff in the opening action of the Tirah Campaign had been a grievous one as far as the 2nd Gurkhas was concerned.

Other Gurkha regiments took part in the Tirah Campaign, among them the newly raised 2nd Battalion of the 1st Gurkha Rifles; both battalions of the 3rd Gurkha Rifles, which gained three significant battle honours; the 2/4th and the 1/5th Gurkha Rifles. During the Tirah Campaign, the regimental scouts of the 1/5th Gurkhas combined with those of the 2nd and the 1/3rd to form the Gurkha Scouts, a body of three British officers and some one hundred and twenty riflemen intended to exploit the well-known performance of Gurkhas in hill operations. Indeed, one thread appears in all the historical accounts of Gurkha units which served on the North-West Frontier: the agility and incredible speed shown by the Gurkhas when faced with the steepest of cliffs or confronted by the most dangerous of ravines. At the same time, they knew it was never a one-sided encounter and all ranks learnt much from their tribesmen enemies:

The Tirah Campaign. A rifleman of the 9th Gurkha Rifles, and a Sikh

they came to appreciate the value of unwinking, unsleeping alertness. The Pathans and Afridis taught them how to use ground tactically, and rarely, if ever, showed mercy, constantly reminding them that the penalty of carelessness was death. The Gurkha soldiers came to respect the tribesmen, even if they never grew to like them.

By the year 1908 there were ten regiments in the Gurkha Brigade, two of which have not been mentioned so far. The 9th Gurkhas was a senior regiment in the sense that it had served the British since 1817: however, it did not become an all-Gurkha unit until 1893. Then the decision was taken that the regiment should be composed principally of Khas Gurkhas, who were more strictly Hindu than the other Gurkha clans enlisted in the rest of the Brigade. Their performance in the first Tirah Campaign of 1897-8 left no doubt about their ability, and in 1901 the regiment finally became the 9th Gurkha Rifles.

The evolution of the 7th Gurkhas was somewhat complex and details are shown in Appendix 1. Suffice it to say that when the Nepal Durbar agreed in April 1907 to the number of Gurkha units in the Indian Army being increased, it was decided that two of the regiments should be composed entirely of men enlisted from the Kiranti tribes of Eastern Nepal, the Rais and Limbus. A new battalion was raised, whereupon the 2nd Battalion 10th Gurkha Rifles was split into two, with the Right Wing becoming the 1st Battalion 7th Gurkha Rifles while the Left Wing became the 2nd Battalion. The 1907 Durbar also agreed to allow recruitment in Nepal to maintain the minimum strength of twenty regular Gurkha battalions in the Indian Army during peacetime.

After the turn of the century, no more major wars were fought on the North-West Frontier until the First World War broke out, so that the years immediately preceding that terrible conflict allowed the Gurkha Brigade to concentrate on peacetime activities such as shooting competitions, field manoeuvres, attendance at durbars and large-scale ceremonial parades, as well as on routine training. With each regiment having two battalions, the Indian Army Gurkha Brigade became an efficient and well-trained body of men, the majority of whom were still awaiting their first taste of active service. Sadly, they did not have long to wait before they were to participate in many battles in several theatres of war – so that, for the first time, the world at large, and especially the British public, came to hear about the mountain warriors from Nepal.

4 THE FIRST WORLD WAR

THE FRIENDSHIP between Britain and Nepal was given great impetus when the Prime Minister, Maharajah Chandra Shamsher Rana, visited England in 1908 where he was given an enthusiastic and warm reception. At the end of his visit the Maharajah wrote an effusive letter of thanks to the British people:

Wherever we have gone we have found everyone anxious to make us feel that we were friends. I want to and do thank the British people for all their kindness. Yours is a great country. But to me the greatness of your country is best seen in the good that is done for our great neighbour, India, in the peace, security of life and property, justice and numerous other benefits that it has given to that country.

Those words should be remembered today by those who denigrate the British and the way they governed their Indian Empire.

Three years later, in 1911, the newly-crowned King George V visited India and accompanied Chandra Shamsher on one of the biggest shooting expeditions ever organised in Nepal. The British King, one of the best shots of his day, was reputed to have accounted for twenty-one tigers, ten rhinoceros and two bears – a bag that would make conservationists today shudder in horror! There was a genuine rapport between the British King and the Maharajah and after his visit the King sent the message: 'Dear Maharajah, I can always count upon you and your people as my truest friends.'

Three years later, in 1914, such words were translated into action with an alacrity that surprised friend and foe alike. The

Tigers, bears and the heads of rhinoceroses shot on a *shikar* (hunt) organised by the Maharajah of Nepal for King George V during his visit to Nepal in 1911

Maharajah wrote to the British Resident in Kathmandu in these words: 'I have come to request you to inform His Excellency the Viceroy and through him the King-Emperor that the whole military resources of Nepal are at His Majesty's disposal.' The little nation, which at that time boasted a population of less than 5 million people, was to send nearly 200,000 of its manhood down from the mountains to fight for a King-Emperor they had never seen, one who lived across the *kalo pani*, the 'black water'.* Prior to 1914, the training of all battalions had been geared to the tactics required for fighting the tribesmen of the North-West Frontier: they had not been trained to fight a long war of attrition in trenches nor were they mentally prepared for the terrible artillery bombardments and the deadly machine-gun fire they were soon to experience. But that also applied to the British, French and German soldiers, too, as the world was to witness a modern war, with all its horrors and horrendous casualties.

The Maharajah's immediate response to the British cry for help included the despatch of four Nepalese Army regiments to the North-West Frontier of India, as well as sending other regiments to the United Provinces, until over 16,000 men of Nepal's own army were serving within the garrison of India. These Nepalese units helped to keep the peace on the important and touchy Frontier, thus relieving British, Indian and Gurkha battalions to join in the struggle overseas. Indeed, when the war ended, the help the Nepalese army continued to give the Indian Government was invaluable, especially when, in 1919, the Wazir and Mahsud tribesmen rose against the British at a time when much of the army in India was demobilising.

By that time, all the Gurkha units contained many young, raw recruits, while eight out of the ten regiments had raised a third battalion which, in most cases, did not disband until 1921. That those third battalions served for about three years after the First World War was very much due to Maharajah Chandra Shamsher of Nepal, who advised the British to delay disbandment of the wartime battalions of the Indian Army because he suspected that there would be strife on the Frontier in 1919. As a consequence, the dangerous Mahsud rising

was put down because the Indian Army, at a most critical time, was able to deploy several experienced Gurkha battalions to crush the widespread threat posed by the tribesmen.

The only Gurkha regiments that did not raise a third battalion during the First World War were the 4th and 10th. The fact that the former did not do so was due to a clerical error at GHQ New Delhi; instead of the newly raised unit being called the 3/4th Gurkha Rifles – as it should have been – it was designated the 4/3rd Gurkha Rifles with complete companies from the 2nd, 3rd, 5th and 6th Gurkha Rifles being transferred on posting to form the 4/3rd Battalion.

Between 1914 and 1918 soldiers of the Gurkha Brigade fought and died in France and Flanders, Mesopotamia, Egypt, Gallipoli, Salonika and Palestine. During those years they were to gain a worldwide reputation as first-class soldiers; by 1918 the warriors from Nepal had stepped on to the world's stage.

In France, the efficient German Army expected a repetition of the Franco-Prussian War of 1870-1 when a series of brilliantly executed moves defeated their French enemy in a remarkably short campaign. In the minds of senior generals on both sides, such tactics seemed inevitable and would be repeated unless defeated by aggressive Allied counter-moves, on both of Germany's frontiers, with Russia and her huge armies posing a threat in the east. Unfortunately, only the first few weeks in late August and September 1914 were to witness the type of fighting expected by the generals and, by the end of September, the power of the artillery and the accuracy of the machine-guns had caused soldiers on both sides to dig and dig for protection. Trenches were prepared, dugouts constructed, and strong fortifications appeared along the whole of the front. Trench warfare had begun.

The British Expeditionary Force in France, outnumbered and ill-equipped, fought magnificently but was soon reduced to hanging on grimly. Back in the United Kingdom the large Territorial Force was still under training; fresh troops had to be found from somewhere in a hurry and it was not surprising that eyes were turned towards India, where there were many British, Indian and Gurkha regiments with a fine history of soldiering behind them. On 15 October 1914, two Indian divisions arrived at

* *Kalo pani* - the black water which Hindus were forbidden to cross without a special dispensation.

A group of British and Gurkha officers and men of the 1st Gurkha Rifles in France in 1914

Marseilles where they were designated the Indian Corps. Travelling from India by sea had been for the Gurkhas an experience they had never had before: always poor sailors, most of the men were dreadfully seasick. As mountain people from a landlocked kingdom it was the first time in their lives that they had seen salt water or the large ships that sailed on it. Moreover, as Hindus, they were forbidden to cross the sea on pain of loss of caste unless given special dispensation, so that the Maharajah had to use his influence to persuade the Raj Guru, Nepal's supreme religious authority, to give his approval for the troops to cross the 'black water'. Before the Great War ended six Gurkha battalions had sailed to and fought in France, four had landed and fought at Gallipoli: ten had seen active service in the Middle East and, in particular, in Palestine; and finally, between 1916 and 1918 twelve battalions fought in Mesopotamia. Every Gurkha soldier was a volunteer, fighting for a country he had never seen.

The decision to send the Indian Corps to France is one that has been queried by several military historians. The reasons for their despatch have already been examined; what can be questioned, however, is the state of the troops introduced, as they were,

to trench warfare with so little preparation. Their equipment was poor, they had no machine-guns nor men trained to fire them, and their clothing was pitifully inadequate for soldiers unused to the damp cold of Northern Europe.

The two divisions of the Indian Corps were the 17th (Meerut) Division and the 3rd (Lahore) Division and each contained three Gurkha battalions. On 29 October 1914, the first Gurkha battalion, the 2/8th Gurkha Rifles, arrived on the Western Front and went into the front line near Festubert, south of the Ypres Salient, for a grim introduction to life and death in the trenches. Like the other Gurkha battalions that followed, they found that the trenches were far too deep for the short, stocky soldiers which meant higher firesteps had to be constructed in a hurry to enable them to see and be able to shoot at the Germans. Not long after the 2/8th Gurkhas had arrived, the Germans began a heavy artillery programme before attacking. The enemy were beaten back but only with the greatest difficulty and within twenty-four hours six out of the battalion's ten British officers had been killed, with three more wounded. This heavy loss of their leaders can be explained, to some extent, by the necessity for the British officers to

A havildar (sergeant) of the 1st Gurkha Rifles in France, 1915

Gurkhas assaulting a trench during training in France

expose themselves and take risks while their Gurkha soldiers learnt to adjust themselves to the hell of trench warfare.

Shortly afterwards, in early November

1914, the 2/2nd Gurkhas was to lose all its British officers and it was very much to the credit of the battalion that it still stuck it out and inflicted heavy losses on the Germans. The surrounding country and the heavy autumn rain did little to help the morale of the troops, with the low-lying nature of the ground producing areas of severe flooding, while incessant artillery fire denuded the trees of foliage and digging 'hit' water almost at once. During the early weeks it was to be a severe test of the British officers' leadership, always at a heavy cost in lives, and it was their example which played a big part in the successes eventually achieved by the units. Soon all the Gurkha battalions were to be heavily engaged – the 1st Battalions of the 1st, 4th and 9th and, as already mentioned, the 2nd Battalions of the 2nd and 8th as well as the 2/3rd. All suffered grievous losses: for example, the 1/4th Gurkhas, after setting sail from India with a strength of 736 officers and men, went into the trenches in Givenchy 650 strong on 17 November 1914 – one week later only 423 fighting soldiers remained in action. To add to the discomfort of the combatants, the 1914/1915 winter was intensely cold so that frostbite was a major problem among the troops of all nations.

By the middle of December 1914, the Indian Corps – although now very short of men – was called on to make a series of diversionary attacks in order to assist the big offensive, launched at Messines by General Sir Horace Smith-Dorrien, GOC Second Army. As before, these attacks led to such heavy losses that, at the end of December, the Indian Corps had to be withdrawn from the front line for a much-needed rest. After two months of constant combat its casualty figures were: killed 1,397, wounded 5,860 and missing 2,322 – which represented nearly half of its total strength. During the short respite, equipment was replaced while badly needed reinforcements arrived from India and essential training exercises were carried out. When the men first came out of the trenches, their feet were almost green from being constantly immersed in mud and water so that the march back to their billets in the rear was a nightmare for many of them. During the rest period, their feet grew hard again as a result of route marches until, on 15 January 1915, they started moving back once more into the front line, once again to face appalling wintry conditions of heavy rain,

snow and bitter winds. The first two months of 1915 were comparatively uneventful although full of cold discomfort and the never-ending process of repairing and strengthening trenches, constantly extending them by day and night. During this period, fortunately, casualties were light so that the newly arrived drafts were given ample opportunities to learn how to patrol and accustom themselves to the routine of life in the front-line trenches, without too much pressure being put upon them. This period of acclimatisation was to help the Gurkha units when the battle of Neuve Chapelle began in the spring of 1915, a long and bloody struggle which was to end without victory; although each of the six Gurkha battalions that participated in the fighting more than earned the battle honour 'Neuve Chapelle'.

The overall aim of the assault at Neuve Chapelle was to seize the Aubers Ridge near Lille. On this occasion it was a well-planned attack and in terms of relative strength within the area the British were much better off than the Germans. The administrative arrangements had been meticulously prepared and the logistic support for such a big offensive had entailed weeks of preparation. Neuve Chapelle was to be the first of the major trench battles to be fought after the armies on the Western Front had settled down into conditions of stalemate. So much was experimental: the vast scale of the operations; the difficulty of observation over the low ground; the passage of information along archaic communication systems; all these still had to be satisfactorily resolved. The artillery relied on reasonable observation posts but these were hard to find in the low-lying plain. Great efforts were made to maintain secrecy but inevitably the unusual movement forward in the British lines did not pass unnoticed by their adversaries. That an attack was imminent the Germans knew well; only the timing was shrouded in mystery, and it was not until the last moment that they were certain as to from where it would be launched.

Initially, on the morning of 10 March, there was success especially when Nos. 1 and 2 Companies of the 2/2nd Gurkhas, ordered to advance on the Bois du Biez during the hours of darkness, reached and patrolled the north-west corner of the wood, to find few signs of any enemy. A great opportunity appeared to exist but orders

His Highness Maharajah Sir Chandra Shamsher Rana, GCB, GCSI, GCMG, GCVO, 1863-1929

from above told the companies to dig in and consolidate. Even more tragic, a little while later fresh orders were received ordering a withdrawal of some 500 yards – a fleeting chance to inflict a heavy defeat on the Germans and break out of the trench war

Gurkhas training in France – learning the technique of bombing

Inspection by a general

Out of the line – pipers of the 3rd Gurkha Rifles in France

Men of the 9th Gurkha Rifles in France, 1914

deadlock was lost for ever. Why this happened was undoubtedly due to the inordinate delay taken for orders to be passed up and down the long chain of command, usually by word of mouth or written messages, so that sufficient time was never allowed for this process. After an order had been issued by a general in his headquarters, several hours often elapsed before the troops concerned actually moved; likewise, accurate reports of progress made by units took an excessively long time to filter back to the commanders in the rear. That excellent opportunity having been lost, fighting then intensified so that the Indian Corps alone suffered 4,000 casualties in 10 days.

The left centre attack was made by the 2/3rd Gurkhas who also reached the German first-line trenches without too much trouble, but when crossing the road into Neuve Chapelle, they came under heavy machine-gun fire from the ruined houses near the village brewery. It was at this moment of severe crisis that Havildar* Bahadur Thapa led his men into one house, stormed the barricade and killed sixteen Germans as well as capturing two machine-guns. Rifleman Gane Gurung, a man of small stature but fearless, also showed particular gallantry at the same time: both men were to be awarded the Indian Order of Merit.

While the 2/2nd Gurkha companies were advancing on the right, the other Gurkha battalion in the Dehra Dun Brigade, the 1/9th, initially made good progress on the left and reached the south-west corner of

* Havildar – a sergeant in the Indian Army. British Gurkha units adopted British Army ranks after 1947.

The 9th Gurkha Rifles
in France, 1914

Bois de Biez where they began to dig in. But when the divisions on both flanks were held up, the Dehra Dun Brigade was isolated and in danger of being cut off. It was for such a reason that the two battalions were withdrawn to a safer position in the rear.

Unfortunately, as soon as they were ordered back, the Germans took full advantage, moving forward to retake the positions they had so recently lost. Finally, at midday on 12 March, the whole of the Dehra Dun Brigade was withdrawn. That, however, was not the end of the battle because Neuve Chapelle village remained in British hands and the original advance of about a thousand yards, over the two-mile front, was held and consolidated. Stung by these gains, on 12 March the Germans mounted furious mass counter-attacks during which they suffered horrendous casualties. The British made one more plan, aimed at mounting a further assault on the by now heavily fortified Bois du Biez, but fortunately General Sir Douglas Haig, GOC First Army, vetoed the attack. Whose then was the victory? In terms of casualties, both sides lost about the same numbers: in terms of territory, the paltry gains have already been mentioned.

Although it was the Dehra Dun Brigade from the Meerut Division that played a major part in the battle, in the latter stages, the Sirhind Brigade from the Lahore Division moved up into the line, with the 1/4th Gurkhas ordered to relieve the tired and battle-weary battalions, the 1/9th and 2/2nd Gurkhas, in their trenches along the south bank of the Layes stream. It was planned, too, that after dawn on 12 March the 1/1st Gurkhas and the 15th Sikhs would attack and attempt to capture, once again, the north-west edge of the Bois du Biez. Unfortunately a dire lack of co-ordination between the two brigade headquarters resulted in the 2/2nd and 1/9th Gurkhas withdrawing from their trenches before the Sirhind Brigade attacked at first light on the 12th. Not surprisingly, there was appalling confusion when the Sirhind Brigade moved forward in the dark and met the first men of the Dehra Dun Brigade moving back among shell-holes, trenches and wire: the resulting confusion was increased by a steady bombardment by the enemy guns. Delays were inevitable, and when the Allied attack had to be postponed, the Germans seized the opportunity to move up large numbers of men and mount a gigantic counter-offensive, with their leading troops no more than sixty yards from the Allied front-line trenches. The whole British front line burst into flame as every rifle and machine-gun opened up on the German masses and within minutes it was all over: the large-scale counter-attack had been beaten off with heavy slaughter along the entire British front. Once more, there was a moment when an immediate follow-up might well have been successful but with no reserves of artillery shells immediately available, close support for the infantry would not have been possible.

Plans for yet another massive attack were made but as the hours passed, several postponements followed, while behind the trenches the commanders and their staffs struggled to bring a measure of cohesion that would allow such an offensive to be launched. Despite the gallant efforts of the 1/1st and 1/4th Gurkhas, the British attack on 12 March failed – like those before – so the front line remained substantially where it had been on the evening of the 10th.

On 20 March, the Sirhind Brigade was relieved by the Jullundur Brigade and moved back to a rest position. As an example of the brigade's losses, the 1/4th Gurkha Rifles entered the battle of Neuve Chapelle at a strength of 472 all ranks; its casualties during the fighting there amounted to 177. Neuve Chapelle was a battle that was lost by poor staff work and mismanagement: unfortunately the state of affairs was set to

Rifleman Kulbir Thapa, VC, 3rd Gurkha Rifles. The first Gurkha to be awarded the VC, Kulbir won his medal for his outstanding courage near Neuve Chapelle on 25/26 September 1915

continue until the final withdrawal of the Indian Corps after thirteen months in France, when the weary battalions were sent to fight in other theatres of war.

There were to be other battles after Neuve Chapelle was over: on 9 May 1915 came another offensive launched optimistically with the aim of capturing Aubers Ridge, a hill of modest height (on the Western Front, mere hillocks were of greater military importance than mountains as they dominated the countryside). The whole operation came to be called the Battle of Festubert and the six Gurkha battalions who fought in France all have 'Festubert' or 'Aubers', or in some cases both, as battle honours won by their deeds during the fighting there. On that occasion the Allied plan relied on a very short and sharp bombardment, in the hope that, by using these tactics, the Germans would be surprised and would not have time to react. It was an optimistic misconception and, once again, the results were disastrous, as shown by the casualty lists, which were grievous. For example, the 2/2nd Gurkha Rifles, in a short and ill-fated appearance for a few hours, was to lose over a hundred casualties. General Sir James Willcocks, who commanded the Indian Corps, later pronounced: 'I have now come to the conclusion that the best of my troops in France were the Gurkhas.' Nevertheless, those Gurkhas who fought in France later performed far better in the heat of Mesopotamia or Palestine than they did in the wet and cold of the trenches on the Western Front. Sending the Indian Corps to France was an ill-conceived venture and the gloomy casualty figures, 21,000 officers and men in thirteen months, tell the sad story.

One event that must be recorded was the award of the Victoria Cross to the first Gurkha soldier of the Brigade in 1915. In September of that year, Rifleman Kulbir Thapa of the 2/3rd Queen Alexandra's Own Gurkha Rifles, himself wounded, found a badly wounded soldier of the 2nd Leicestershire Regiment behind the first-line German trench and, although urged by the British soldier to save himself, remained with him all day and night. In the early morning of 26 September, in misty weather, he brought the soldier out through the German lines and, leaving him in a place of comparative safety,

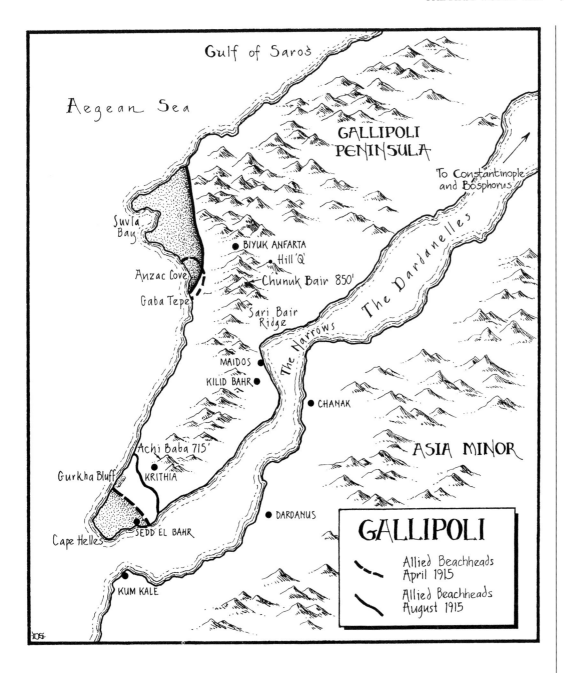

returned and carried two wounded Gurkhas to his own lines, one after the other. Kulbir then went back in broad daylight for the British soldier and brought him in, carrying him most of the way and being at many points under German fire. It is interesting to note that this, the first VC won by a Gurkha, was awarded for saving the lives of his fellow soldiers rather than for killing the enemy during close-quarter fighting with his kukri – which many would have anticipated. Only one other Gurkha soldier was to win the highest British gallantry award in the First World War, Rifleman Karnabahadur Rana, also of the 2/3rd Gurkhas, in Palestine, but there were to be ten Gurkha recipients of

the VC in the Second World War, in campaigns fought in Burma, Italy and Africa.

The reputation that the Gurkha soldier won in the trenches in France under horrendous conditions was to be considerably enhanced by the fighting ability displayed at Gallipoli in 1915. General Sir Ian Hamilton wrote in March 1915: 'Each little Gurkha might be worth his full weight in gold at Gallipoli' and this request, addressed to the Secretary of State for War, Lord Kitchener, initially was granted in the shape of three Gurkha battalions, the 1/5th, 1/6th and 2/10th Gurkha Rifles. These three battalions formed part of 29 Indian Infantry Brigade until later in the campaign, when the 1/4th Gurkha Rifles landed after leaving France, where it had been part of the Indian Corps.

Gallipoli was a most dramatic and tragic campaign, tragic not only because of the severe loss of life but also because from the Allied point of view, priceless opportunities were thrown away after the first landings on 25 April 1915. The morale of the army that set out for Gallipoli was high but, unfortunately, from General Hamilton down to the private soldiers, all lacked both experience and knowledge of combined naval and military operations, so that the Allied superiority at sea was not used to the best advantage. The overall aim of opening up the Dardanelles and defeating Turkey was not to be achieved despite the gallantry shown by the troops on the Gallipoli peninsula.

It is not necessary to tell the full story of the initial landings since the first Gurkha unit, as part of 29 Indian Brigade, did not arrive until five days later. Suffice it to say that while the Allied forces* gained almost complete surprise at certain points, things went awry thereafter when valuable time slipped by and the Turks were given the chance to recover their poise and mount strong counter-attacks. A wonderful opportunity was lost at 'Y' Beach, where a landing force disembarked without meeting any opposition whatever and thereafter sat for eleven hours, greatly outnumbering their opponents in the vicinity of the beach, whilst elsewhere stronger defences were being attacked by other men from the same division, the 29th. To crown it all, 'Y' Beach was later abandoned, although by this time the Turks had pulled back their defenders. Any war inevitably contains a series of 'ifs' but there is little doubt that inept leadership during the first landings threw away an excellent opportunity and led to the drawn-out struggle that followed, a struggle in which the Gurkha battalions were to play their full part.

The first Gurkha unit to land was the 1/6th, commanded by Lieutenant-Colonel the Honourable Charles Bruce who, after the war, was to win renown as the leader of two Everest expeditions. The battalion's landing near Cape Helles went relatively smoothly but in the space of the first nine days, even before anyone in the battalion had a chance to fire a single shot in anger, the 1/6th lost one Gurkha rifleman killed and twenty-one all ranks wounded. On 9 May they moved to take up a position on the extreme left of the Allied line in this sector where they soon displayed great skill in action.

On 12 May came the 1/6th Gurkhas' first major operation when ordered to attack a bluff, some 300 feet high, which the Turkish enemy had converted into a strongpoint: two previous attempts by British troops had been unable to take the feature. After a careful reconnaissance and with close co-operation with the Royal Navy which provided maximum support from their guns, a plan to assault the bluff was carefully prepared by Colonel Bruce. The difficulties were formidable: the side of the bluff was steep, in places almost sheer and in order to make the ascent, the 1/6th had to cross the mouth of a ravine which could be enfiladed by fire from the Turks. Despite the difficulties, with speed and daring the bluff was taken – at a cost of eighteen killed and forty-two wounded. Thereafter, by order of General Sir Ian Hamilton, that feature was known as 'Gurkha Bluff'.

Although no other major engagement occurred in the Cape Helles sector during May, casualties steadily mountd in trenches which now stretched from shore to shore, with raids and counter-raids taking place at an increasing intensity. By the end of the month all the original company commanders of the 1/6th had been killed or wounded. By that time, too, the first two battles of Krithia had been fought without avail, so that the beachhead remained pitifully small: gains were counted in yards and only under the protection of overhanging cliffs could the troops seek rest and relaxation from gunfire and the intense heat. As May changed to June so did the conditions worsen, with the putrid smell of the unburied dead and the flies that swarmed everywhere, tainting the food and spreading dysentery. That disease claimed victims by the score, while lice added to the discomfort of the soldiers.

On 2 June the 1/5th and 2/10th Gurkhas arrived to replace the two Punjabi battalions of 29 Indian Brigade. The brigade commander had asked for the Punjabis to be replaced on the grounds that they might object to fighting against their Turkish co-religionists. One or two commentators have pointed out that this particular suspicion

* The initial landings were made by British, Anzac (Australian and New Zealand Army Corps), and French forces.

about the Punjabi Muslim soldiers was quite unwarranted because in other theatres – such as Palestine, Mesopotamia and Aden – they fought against their fellow Muslims without any obvious inhibitions. Be that as it may, it was not long before the new arrivals were in action in what came to be called the Third Battle of Krithia, the object of which was the capture of Achi Baba, a feature some 700 feet high, and which commanded both the Helles beachhead and the Narrows. After a heavy bombardment had been directed against Turkish trenches with the aim of destroying the wire entanglements, the 1/6th Gurkhas, 14th Sikhs and Lancashire Fusiliers advanced but found that the wire was intact in most places, so that casualties reached alarming proportions as the attackers were held up. The Sikhs, in particular, were badly hit, with only 120 of them surviving out of a total of 500 all ranks who had crossed the start line before advancing.

Later in the day, the 1/5th Gurkhas were called forward in an attempt to succeed where others had been held up. The battalion was ordered to follow the same route as C Company of the 1/6th, but the Turks were not to be surprised twice: the 1/5th were also checked by the unbroken wire until the attack petered out with heavy losses in officers and men. On the steep slopes among the shrub and coarse grass, 130 Gurkhas fell as well as 7 of their British officers, among whom was the battalion commander, Lieutenant-Colonel G.H. Boisragon, VC* – the hero of Nilt – who was shot through the kneecap. Despite such heavy losses, the 1/5th had kept on attacking but each attempt withered before the scorching fire of the Turkish defenders, who had forty machine-guns in the area. One last gallant attempt was made by No.1 Company under the leadership of Major M. R. W. Nightingale, who was awarded the DSO for exceptional gallantry while leading an assault against a strongly defended spur after he had been wounded. 'He reached the crest and was again wounded but coming back a few yards he rallied his men and again led them on. He was wounded a third time but still endeavoured to advance until he fainted.' Those words are from the citation for Major Nightingale's DSO. At dusk the 1/5th Gurkhas was ordered to withdraw; the

odds had been too great despite the gallantry displayed by so many.

The 2/10th Gurkha Rifles had taken its share of duty in the front line until the end of June, when a major task was given the battalion in what was to be called the Battle of Gully Ravine, which took place between 28 June and 2 July. On this occasion three brigades, including 29 Indian Brigade, were ordered to drive the Turks about 1,000 yards back from their position north-west of Gurkha Bluff. The 2/10th followed up the heavy bombardment which the British guns maintained for about two hours and moved under a cliff, with their Gurkha soldiers using all available cover provided by the broken ground and scrub: then the leading company climbed to the top of the cliff and routed the defenders. It was, perhaps, the most successful setpiece attack of the whole campaign, for the battalion helped to take five lines of Turkish trenches.

After that seemingly encouraging start, the 1/6th Gurkhas moved over and extended the line, by which time the Turks had been pushed back about half a mile before being stung into a series of desperate and costly counter-attacks, at a cost of over 10,000 men within a week. These counter-attacks hit each Gurkha battalion in turn, and for eight days and nights the struggle continued, the outcome of local battles often being decided by hand-to-hand fighting in which the Gurkhas excelled, using their kukris with deadly effect. In the 2/10th casualties were heavy and particularly among the British officers until, on 1 July, only three officers, all subalterns, remained with the unit. Under the command of these young men and the surviving Gurkha officers, the battalion held on to all its gains but while repulsing several bitter Turkish counter-attacks, lost 40 per cent of the Gurkha soldiers – all within five weeks of the unit's arrival in Gallipoli.

General Hamilton expressed himself well pleased with the result of the Gully Ravine battle, but by this time 29 Indian Brigade was badly in need of a break from the appalling conditions that prevailed in the peninsula, with the dead lying unburied and rapidly decomposing in no man's land, while the living soldiers were plagued with the heat, flies and dysentery. It was a most welcome relief for the three Gurkha battalions to move back by ship to the Isle of Imbros (now

---

* He had won the VC at Nilt as a subaltern.

Gallipoli – men of the 2/10th Gurkha Rifles sheltering under the crest of Chunuk Bair. The white armband was for identification

Imroz) where, for nearly a month, the men relaxed and reinforcements arrived to fill the sadly depleted rifle companies. While they were there and despite security measures, rumours of another offensive reached the island, although details were shrouded in secrecy. After the initial and, as it transpired, fatal delay, the British Government belatedly promised Sir Ian Hamilton more divisions: so that the arrival of fresh troops would give the army commander one more chance to try and outflank the Turks, this time from Anzac Cove north of Helles. The key to the peninsula appeared to be the main peaks of the Sari Bair Ridge, with features which were soon to be household names in Britain: Battleship Hill, Chunuk Bair, Hill Q. Capture of these peaks would not only turn the Turkish positions that faced the Anzac beachhead, but would have enabled the British to overlook and thus cut off the Turkish forces on the tip of the peninsula at Helles. A night attack on the Sari Bair feature was intended to be the battle-winning blow, launched from the Anzac beachhead. Once more the three Gurkha battalions were to play a notable part, landing at Anzac Cove to support the attack. To 29 Indian Brigade was given the difficult task of leading an assault in the early hours of 7 August against Hill Q, in the centre of the Sari Bair feature.

The nature of the ground made it a forbidding task, with rugged steep spurs rising up from gullies which were covered with dense prickly clumps of scrub. 29 Indian Brigade set off in the dark with inaccurate maps and without having had the chance to reconnoitre the ground beforehand. All told it was a hazardous enterprise, the successful outcome of which depended on the Chunuk Bair peak being captured before daylight on 7 August. At 8.30 pm on the 6th the advance began from the Anzac position and by the early hours of the morning the lower peaks had been reached and the way to the top appeared to be open. However, the lack of any prior reconnaissance by junior leaders began to play an important part as columns were delayed because guides lost direction: in addition, for the Gurkha battalions, the confusion was increased by an inexplicable decision from higher headquarters which halted units before daylight about a thousand yards short of the summit of Chunuk Bair. Undoubtedly an attack in the early hours would have led to a brisk fight; now, after this delay, at 10.30 am the Turkish position was fully manned so that even with naval gun-fire support, the decisive battle was doomed to failure – although fleeting opportunities to gain success were still to occur during the next two days.

As the morning passed so did Turkish resistance stiffen, while casualties mounted and gradually the advance came to a halt. After fighting their way to within 500 yards of the crest, the 1/6th Gurkhas had lost 76 men killed or wounded. There the battalion had to battle hard to hold on to the positions recently won, until reinforcements from the South Lancashire and the Royal Warwickshire Regiments arrived. Serving with the Warwicks was Lieutenant W. J. Slim, soon to transfer to the 6th Gurkhas and who many years later, in the Second World War, was to become famous as the commander of the Fourteenth Army. That day he soon found himself commanding a company of the Warwicks when the other company officers were either killed or wounded. It was his first experience of battle and of fighting alongside Gurkha soldiers who made a most favourable and immediate impression on him. In Slim's opinion, they were superb. He, like many other British and Gurkha officers on that day, was to be severely wounded, which led to him being evacuated. Later the 1/6th were to have better fortune. At dawn on 1 August the accurate naval bombardment continued until 5.30, when shells of all descriptions were hurled on to the Turkish positions, soon to be covered by a mass of smoke, dust and flying clods of earth. Following that was silence.

The words of Major C. J. L. Allanson of the 1/6th have been quoted in many accounts about Gallipoli - not surprisingly, because they make exciting reading.

I had my watch out, 5.15. I never saw such artillery preparation; the trenches were being torn to pieces; the accuracy was marvellous, as we were just below. At 5.18 it had not stopped and I wondered if my watch was wrong. 5.20, silence; I waited three minutes to be certain, great as the risk was. Then off we dashed all hand in hand, a most perfect advance, and a wonderful sight. At the top we met the Turks; Le Marchand was down, a bayonet through the heart. I got one through the leg, and then, for about ten minutes, we fought hand to hand, we bit and fisted, and used rifles and pistols as clubs. And then the Turks turned and fled, and I felt a very proud man; the key of the whole pen-insula was ours, and our losses had not been so very great for such a result. Below I saw the Straits, motors and wheeled transport, on the roads leading to Achi Baba. As I looked round I saw that we were not being supported and thought I could help best by going after those who had retreated in front of us. We dashed down towards Maidos but only got about 200 hundred feet down when suddenly our own Navy put six twelve-inch shells into us and all was terrible confusion. It was a deplorable disaster.

Major C. J. L. Allanson, DSO, 6th Gurkha Rifles, who led the assault on Sari Bair, 9 August 1915

Allanson always maintained that the shells were naval ones but that allegation has been contested. What is certain is that it was the end of this brilliant action: in Allanson's words, 'We all flew back to the summit and took our old positions just below. I remained on the crest with about fifteen men; it was a wonderful sight.' Allanson and his handful of men were the only Allied soldiers ever to reach that point and thus to describe the peninsula that lay below them. For his part in this gallant action, Major Allanson was awarded the DSO.

Once again, the Turks commanded the heights, but the way had been open and for a few minutes an opportunity had existed to strike a decisive blow. That was the last chance in the battle for the Sari Bair Ridge. During the rest of 9 August and the morning of the 10th, the remnants of the 1/6th and 2/10th, with their British comrades, clung to increasingly precarious positions. By this time there was not a single British officer left with the 1/6th so that the senior Gurkha officer, Subedar-Major Gambirsing Pun, commanded the battalion. He had to rely on the regimental doctor, Captain E. S. Phipson, IMS, to act as his interpreter as Gambirsing had no understanding of the English language. By now, both sides were utterly exhausted, and a withdrawal was ordered, so that the Sari Bair feature still remained in Turkish hands. Some 12,000 British and Imperial troops had become casualties in the Sari Bair battle, and Turkish losses were correspondingly high. Sir Ian Hamilton commented in his diary that this effort 'Leaves us with a fine gain of ground although minus the vital crest. Next time we will get them.' There was to be no next time – the chance had been lost for ever.

The Battle of Sari Bair was the last major offensive of the campaign and from then on, the three Gurkha battalions settled down to a routine of trench warfare, of patrolling, digging and reliefs in the line. As a consequence it was an opportune moment for the 1/4th Gurkhas to arrive as reinforcements for the Indian Brigade. The battalion had been sent to Gallipoli from France without any significant break between active service in the two major campaigns – apart from a brief stay on the island of Imbros, where it was inspected by Sir Ian Hamilton who noted in his diary: 'A superb battalion – 1,000 strong!' The 1/4th's role after landing in Gallipoli was to take more than its full share of manning the forward trenches. The experience gained in France enabled the officers and men to adapt themselves quickly to the new conditions. Like their Gurkha comrades in the other three battalions on the peninsula, they soon found that there was no real respite from danger because their casualties when 'resting' were almost as high and occasionally even higher, than when in the front line, since all beachheads were under constant small-arms and artillery fire, directed by Turkish observers on the high ground. It was not long either before the 1/4th's soldiers began to fall victim to the heat, flies, contaminated water and poor food so that dysentery ran rife in the battalion – as it did in the other units of the Indian Brigade.

As winter approached so the weather deteriorated in a dramatic fashion, and between 26 and 28 November the first major storm caused much damage to the shipping as well as to transport, boats, infrastructure and piers on the beaches. A torrential thunderstorm led to a torrent of water sweeping down from the hills which flooded the trenches and swept all before it. Under such terrible climatic conditions both sides took refuge on the top of their trenches, in full view of each other, and for a short time hostile intentions were forgotten. That was followed by a blizzard of sleet and snow that raged for two days; Allied casualties from frostbite and exposure eventually reached over 10,000, with several men being frozen to death. The 2/10th was the worst hit with nearly 430 cases of frostbite, while the 1/4th, no doubt profiting from its traumatic experiences during the previous winter in France, suffered less than the other Gurkha battalions.

The end of the Gallipoli adventure was approaching. After seeing for himself the conditions during a personal visit to the Dardanelles, Lord Kitchener ordered a general evacuation. Prior to this, however, the 2/10th – which had suffered the heaviest casualties – was relieved and embarked for Mudros and eventually sailed on to Alexandria. Of the original party, some eight hundred strong, that had set out for the Gallipoli campaign in May 1915, only one British officer and seventy-nine Gurkha soldiers returned with the battalion some six months later; the rest were reinforcements that arrived subsequently.

C Company, 2/9th Gurkha Rifles, crossing a pontoon bridge in Mesopotamia

However, it was not to be General Sir Ian Hamilton who commanded and planned the final evacuation. He was sacked by Lord Kitchener in October with the words: 'The War Cabinet wish to make a change in the command which will give them an opportunity of seeing you.' In such classic fashion was Ian Hamilton relieved of his command, a victim in many ways of the British Government's prevarication and vacillation at the beginning of the campaign. In another respect, he suffered from the incompetence of some of his subordinates in whom, at times, Hamilton placed an implicit faith, only to be let down at crucial moments.

The final evacuation was planned and organised by the new Commander-in-Chief, General Sir Charles Monro, but controlled by Lieutenant-General Sir William Birdwood, formally the Anzac commander. As an operation it was carried out with a degree of skill unequalled during the whole of the campaign, a truly ironic ending to the tragedy. The final evacuation of the Anzac and Suvla beachheads was completed during the night of 19/20 December but before that time, the first elements of the Indian Brigade had left. The rear parties from the three remaining Gurkha battalions, the 1/4th, 1/5th and 1/6th, were left manning the trenches until they too slipped away without the Turks realising that their foes had disappeared into the night – apart from one unfortunate Gurkha corporal who was captured as a result of being separated from his comrades. Early next day, the Turks

attacked the Allied lines, whereupon they were pounded by Allied naval guns until they were driven back from the Anzac position. Only then did the Turks realise that their adversaries had abandoned their trenches and strongpoints during the previous night. The Gallipoli campaign was over, but it is interesting to note that General Sir Ian Hamilton's secretary was to write, when sending a Christmas card to the 1/6th Gurkhas: 'It is Sir Ian Hamilton's most cherished conviction that had he been given more Gurkhas in the Dardanelles then he would never have been held up by the Turks.' For the Gurkha battalions a heavy price had been paid, however: 25 British officers and some 730 Gurkha officers and men were killed in action on the peninsula, with many of them having no known grave, although their names are engraved on the regimental rolls on the Gallipoli Memorial, which now stands on the cliffs overlooking the beaches at Cape Helles. To that dreadful toll must be added the 1,500 Gurkhas who were wounded, while as many again fell victim to disease and frostbite which led to their being discharged and sadly, in many cases, left them disabled for the rest of their lives.

Units from the Gurkha Brigade were to meet the Turks in battle during other campaigns in the Middle East; on the river road to Baghdad in Mesopotamia, over hill and valley towards Jerusalem in Palestine, and in Egypt when defending the Suez Canal against Turkish attacks. One or two of the Gurkha battalions

Gurkha stretcher bearers carrying a dead comrade

which fought in France or Gallipoli also took part in the long-drawn-out campaign in Mesopotamia or participated in General Sir Edward Allenby's successful operations against the Turks in Palestine. By the end of the war the soldiers from Nepal and the soldiers from Turkey had faced each other in many battles and there was considerable mutual respect for each other's fighting prowess – even if there was little affection.

Chronologically the action against the Turks in the Suez area came first when they launched a major attack near the Great Bitter Lake. This assault was thwarted by a mixed force of Indian Army troops, with considerable help from the naval guns of nearby ships. The 1/6th and 2/10th Gurkha Rifles took part in this battle when, in the early morning of 3 February, the Turks attacked. Machine-guns mowed down the

leading men and the attackers were beaten back to the east bank of the canal. Subsequent assaults were hammered by accurate gunfire from Allied warships, a bombardment that won the day for the British because many Turkish guns were hit and put out of action. By the night of the 3rd the attackers had been defeated whereupon the main Turkish force withdrew. Unfortunately for the British, their commanders at the time overestimated the threat posed by Djemal Pasha's forces and even when they retired across the Sinai Desert, General Sir John Maxwell, commander of the British troops in Egypt, did not believe that their retreat was a permanent one, thus missing an excellent opportunity to harass the Turks as they withdrew.

The most recently raised Gurkha battalion, the 2/7th Gurkhas, had their first baptism of fire at El Kubri. Three days later came another chance for them to show what they could do on active service, the first since the battalion's raising in 1908. On this occasion, detachments were sent on a mission shrouded in secrecy for which they embarked on HMS *Minerva* on 10 February 1915. A gang of Arab raiders, sponsored and urged on by the Turks, was threatening the village of El Tur on the Gulf of Suez. A plan was made to land the troops south of the village in order to cut off the raiders, but

3/3rd Gurkha Rifles in Palestine, 1917. The rifleman at left is manning a Lewis light machine-gun

because of rough seas this had to be abandoned. Instead, *Minerva*, without lights, had to move in close to the coast in the darkness. It was a difficult task for the Gurkhas, indifferent sailors to say the least, who had to climb down into open boats on the choppy sea. This was achieved in silence although several of the men were desperately seasick before the landing was accomplished. The landing party set out on compass bearings towards the Arab village, some nine miles away. All went well until the final assault was launched at six o'clock in the morning of 11 February. As the first troops moved into the village, firing broke out and the clearing of isolated groups of the enemy lasted until midday. By noon, the operation had been completed: the Arab raiders had lost some sixty dead, with over a hundred prisoners of war being in the hands of the 7th Gurkhas. The price the battalion had to pay was one Gurkha soldier killed. He was buried with full military honours, which included a firing party from the Royal Marines and with all HM ships in the vicinity flying their flags at half-mast. Not surprisingly, the regimental historian commented that, 'It is improbable that any Gurkha Rifleman has ever been, or ever will be again, attended to his grave with so much honour.'

Meanwhile the threat to the Suez Canal had lifted: Djemal Pasha had thrown away the best chance he was ever to have of disrupting traffic through the canal, so that the Allied units which remained in Egypt were able to continue their training for operations elsewhere. To some it was just the prelude to the severe testing they were to undergo at Gallipoli or in Mesopotamia and, eventually, in Palestine.

The Mesopotamian campaign which began in November 1914 was a sideshow when compared with the large-scale operations on the Western Front. Nevertheless, victory was vital for both sides; Muslims in Persia, Afghanistan, and in India itself, watched events in Mesopotamia with the greatest of interest. If the British had been defeated there would have been far-reaching consequences throughout the East: conversely, a quick British victory would have ended all Turkish and German ambitions in that part of the world.

The contestants were fighting in the most difficult country imaginable. A flat desert of barren earth, without trees and with the minimum of landmarks; nowhere was impassable but the scarcity of water tied armies to the main rivers. Rivers provided

The Arch at Ctesiphon, on the Tigris upstream of Kut – the limit of General Townshend's advance water and were the only means of transporting armies across a bleak and inhospitable land. Everything conspired to make a soldier's life one of discomfort; excessive heat in the summer, bitter cold in the winter, stifling sand which got into everything and a plethora of flies by day and mosquitoes by night. To fight in such a country required good administration, quick and efficient medical support and the basic necessities of life to make existence tolerable. Unfortunately for the British and Indian troops, such a state of affairs did not pertain for a considerable time. All necessities were in short supply, like tents to shelter the wounded and warm clothing for the nights and the winter; the list of major deficiencies was a long one so that the sick and wounded had to accept conditions which, in many respects, were similar to those endured during the Crimean War.

Britain's first aim in Mesopotamia was to secure Basra so that any Turkish attempts to disrupt the oilfields of the Persian Gulf could be prevented. This was duly achieved by late November 1914. From the start the Government of India controlled the theatre with responsibility for all the logistic supply and it was not long before an independent line from the one advised by Whitehall was being taken. General Sir John Nixon arrived from Delhi to command, with instructions to obtain and thereafter retain complete control of Lower Mesopotamia 'and such portions of neighbouring territories as may affect your operations'. Such an open-handed directive was to lure him on until the capture of Baghdad became an obsession: it was not

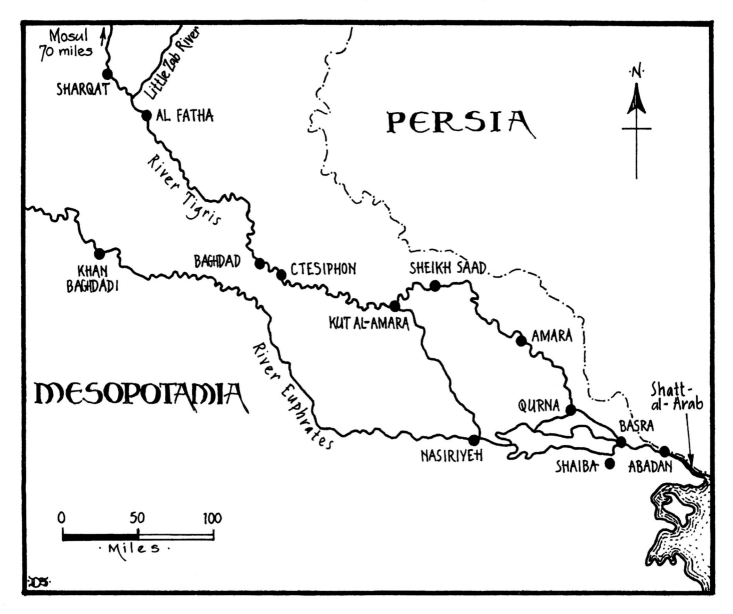

long before he had the complete support of the Viceroy of India, Lord Hardinge, when early successes seemed to promise an easy victory with far-reaching political rewards.

Of the fourteen Gurkha battalions that were to serve at one time or other in the campaign in Mesopotamia, the 2/7th were the first to arrive, fresh from their successful foray from HMS *Minerva*. The last battalion to be raised in the Gurkha Brigade, they were to be faced with a most traumatic experience when nearly all the battalion was taken into captivity at Kut al-Amara, but prior to that they were to enjoy successes and earn a high reputation in battle. When the Turkish forces retreated after their defeat in the Battle of Shaiba, it was impossible to follow them up through the flooded countryside so that the newly arrived commander of the 6th Indian Division, Major-General Charles Townshend, was ordered to organise and command an amphibious operation. Whilst this was under way, the Turks quickly abandoned positions and hastily retreated up the River Tigris. This challenge was met by Townshend; with himself in the van, the enemy was chased up the river and in four days a mere handful of British soldiers and sailors had captured over 2,000 Turkish prisoners.

The 2/7th was part of a river flotilla sent out to capture Nasiriyeh, which was considered by General Nixon to be the most likely base on the River Euphrates from which the Turks might be able to launch a counter-offensive against Basra. In practice it was no pleasure trip as boats had to be dragged across swamps, sometimes by as many as 300 men, where the steamy heat in the marshes and mosquitoes claimed victims by the score from heat exhaustion and malaria. Nevertheless, the force pushed on and threw back the Turkish outposts until their last-ditch position was reached, some five miles down river from Nasiriyeh. After a long approach march by night, the decisive battle was fought on 24 July. After all their tribulations and sickness, the 2/7th 'looked forward to the approaching battle; we were confident.' Even so for a few minutes the battalion's attack appeared to lose momentum as the struggle swayed one way and the other. At this stage a young NCO, Naik (Corporal) Harkaraj Rai, at the head of his section, charged the Turkish trenches. With drawn kukris the Gurkhas leapt the parapet into the trench and killed thirteen of the enemy. Immediately, the remaining sub-

units around them took up the charge and the battlefield belonged to the 2/7th. An eye-witness wrote that 'the appearance of the men was striking; they looked conquerors every inch, ready for everything.' Naik Harkaraj was awarded the IOM and later, after a most distinguished service, became an Honorary Captain. The 2/7th had won the regiment's first major battle honour and, prior to 'Options for Change', Nasiriyeh Day was always commemorated as a regimental holiday by the 7th Gurkha Rifles.

This latest success appeared to stimulate the Viceroy in India because, shortly after the Nasiriyeh battle was over, he was urging the Secretary of State for War in Whitehall to accept the necessity of a further advance up the Tigris to Kut. In the field, General Nixon had come to a similar conclusion and had decided that the best strategic centre was Kut, since it was situated at the junction of the waterway that connects the Rivers Tigris and Euphrates. Baghdad was only 100 miles away and although Nixon did not admit publicly that the capture of the capital was his real objective, there is little doubt that it was there at the back of his mind. The regimental historian of the 7th Gurkhas commented: 'The opening chapter of the Mesopotamia campaign had shown how each objective gained made a further objective appear desirable – even necessary.' As a consequence, in the autumn of 1915 Townshend was authorised to occupy Kut and began concentrating his force for the advance, due to start on 12 September.

In extremely hot weather, 110°–120° F, the advance began and despite the heat, the troops' morale was high; they were looking forward to another victory. The Battle for Kutal-Amara, as it was later known, was won with remarkable ease as surprise was obtained during the approach marches to the Turkish positions, the advance being made at night, and the small town was evacuated by the Turks on 6 October; by this time Townshend's vanguard had pursued the enemy upstream, where it was learnt that a large force was occupying a well-prepared position astride the river at Ctesiphon.

Once again, there was a major disagreement between those who wished to push on, led by General Nixon with strong support from the Viceroy, and those who were opposed to any occupation of Baghdad – like Lord Kitchener in Whitehall. After much vacillation, the British War Cabinet was swayed by the fact that victories had been achieved with ease up to that time and, moreover, reinforcements from France were arriving in the shape of the 3rd Lahore and 7th Meerut Divisions. Nixon was therefore instructed to go on. One of the reasons for the disaster that followed was Nixon's underestimation of the fighting ability of the Turkish troops. While he was right to doubt their senior officers' strategy and tactics, he was quite wrong to underestimate the fighting spirit of the tough Turkish soldiers, many of whom were fresh while his own troops had campaigned throughout the very hot weather and were badly in need of a rest. In fairness to General Townshend, who was blamed for much of the disaster that followed, it must be recorded that he considered his force to be inadequate for the task of capturing Baghdad, but he was overruled by Nixon and, in public, accepted his new directive. In his diary Townshend wrote: 'The British troops can be relied on as before but the Indians now shake and are unreliable.' As far as the Gurkha conquerors of Nasiriyeh were concerned, such a verdict was unfair, inaccurate and ungenerous – as events were soon to prove at the Battle of Ctesiphon.

In ancient times Ctesiphon had been a magnificent royal city, but in AD 637 it had been destroyed by Omar, the second Caliph of Islam, and his Arabs, so that all that remained was the Arch, a fragment of the palace rising some 95 feet above the desert and the high wall which was formed by two narrow mounds at right angles. The Turkish position on the left bank of the river followed a line of low mounds. A continuous stretch connected fifteen closed redoubts and the two very strongly defended ones at the northern end were called Vital Point by Townshend. The strong Turkish force was led by General Nur-ud-Din and unbeknown to Townshend, the Turkish Army had a reserve division nearby; this extra strength meant that Nur-ud-Din began the battle with superior numbers, as well as a card up his sleeve.

With 18,000 men and 52 guns, the Turkish commander had strong grounds for optimism when Townshend's force, of about 13,000 men, began their attack in four columns during the night of 21 November. The 2/7th were with Column A under Major-General Delamain and their task was to make the decisive frontal attack on Vital Point. This entailed crossing some 5,000 yards of open desert before attacking their objective. All went well until the Turkish wire was met; a way was cut through but by this time casualties were increasing. Attack and counter-attack followed and the British casualties increased after an uneasy night during which the opposing generals then took stock of their positions. Dawn came, heralded by a severe sandstorm; then followed a strong Turkish attack on the low mound near the historic Arch of Ctesiphon. This position, later to be called Gurkha Mound, was defended by some 300 men from the 2/7th and about 100 soldiers from the 21st Punjab Regiment. A desperate struggle ensued with the small detachment, vulnerable and exposed, coming under attack from a complete Turkish division which virtually surrounded the mound. Throughout the day the Turks tried to seize the post but by early evening they gave up the attempt. The magnificent little force inspired the Turkish historian into paying this tribute to their exploits on Gurkha Mound:

I must confess to a deep hidden feeling of appreciation of the deed of that brave self-sacrificing enemy detachment, which for hours, although only 400 strong, opposed and finally drove back thousands of riflemen of the 35th Division.

Although the Turks were driven from the field, General Townshend had to fall back because his division had been badly knocked about and was now incapable of taking any offensive action whatever. Unfortunately, as soon as the British started withdrawing on 25 November, the Turks turned round and began harassing them as they retreated, eventually to Kut, where they arrived on 3 December 1915 after completing an eighty-mile retreat. The wounded had been sent on ahead and throughout the day they travelled in bumpy transport carts, each one taking three lying-down cases and three sitting up: it was a journey that greatly added to their suffering. Having reached Kut, the British force found that the town, with a population of around six hundred, had little or no sanitation and was filthy beyond description. The peninsula of Kut al-Amara was roughly two miles long by a mile broad. On 3 December Townshend stood to watch the exhausted men file past him into Kut and in his diary he wrote: 'Courage and firmness in adversity were not wanting in the Sixth

Division.' The seven-and-a-half-day retreat was one of the most arduous in the history of the British Army and Townshend's praise for his tired and depleted force was well deserved. It was then to his army and to the world that he declared: 'I mean to defend Kut as I did Chitral'* and his decision was greeted with approval by General Nixon. The latter promised that reinforcements would soon be fighting their way through to relieve Kut but as the Turks began to close in, it became apparent that with little food, insanitary conditions in the dirty town and the troops already exhausted, Townshend's defensive preparations could not match his brave and optimistic declaration. There was no alternative but to dig in, build defences, tighten belts and to defy the Turks who were now in position around the town.

While Townshend was holding Kut a relieving force under Lieutenant-General Sir Fenton Aylmer, VC, was advancing up the Tigris and among his troops were two Gurkha battalions, the 1/2nd and 1/9th. Throughout the winter they tried to batter a way forward in an attempt to relieve the garrison. Unfortunately, the weather was at its worst with heavy rain turning the earth into thick mud which made movement forward slow and tiring; nor did grave deficiencies in basic organisation help the British advance. In an attempt to save time, General Aylmer decided to move across country on the south side of the Tigris to the Dujaila Redoubt, a strong Turkish position about eight miles east of Kut, where he then intended to wheel round and cut the enemy's communications, while another part of his force advanced directly towards Kut. His hope was that Townshend's defenders would be able to fight their way out and help them in the final battle. At first, all went well and with the advantage of surprise, Aylmer and his men appeared to be on the brink of success. Then there was an inexplicably long delay while they waited for the artillery to come up, by which time the Turks were fully on the alert and the redoubt had been reinforced, ready for the battle.

On 8 March 1916 the battle was joined at the Dujaila Redoubt. Fierce hand-to-hand fighting took place between Turk and Gurkha but the defenders had superior numbers and aided by well-sighted posts eventually triumphed. The 1/2nd, fighting their first action in Mesopotamia, lost 80 all ranks killed and 100 wounded, while the 1/9th also suffered severely, particularly among the British and Gurkha officers – among them the Colonel and the Subedar-Major. This setback was to be the final blow to the chances of Kut being relieved and in the town itself, the news of Alymer's defeat was received in silence. On the next day, by now very short of water and totally exhausted, Aylmer's forces withdrew eighteen miles, the wounded suffering greatly throughout a long hot day which seemed to have no ending. Meanwhile, in Kut, rations had to be further reduced, which meant that the transport animals had to be slaughtered to provide horsemeat. While many Indian troops, on religious grounds, refused to eat the meat and grew weak and ill, the Gurkhas, like their British comrades, ate it willingly. Attempts to drop food to the garrison by aeroplane did not prove successful so one more bid was made to bring supplies and food through the blockade. The river steamer, *Julna*, crewed by some volunteer Royal Naval officers, came within a stone's throw of success: then, almost before the eyes of the besieged garrison, the ship ran against a cable across the river and drove on to a sandbank, where the gallant venture died under the pounding of Turkish gunfire.

Early in April 1916 a fresh attempt was made to reach the beleaguered garrison. The relieving force was now under the command of Lieutenant-General Sir G. F. Gorringe. The right column advanced on Hanna on the south bank, before crossing the river and attacking the enemy at a place called Bait Isa. The battle that followed was another fierce one with heavy casualties on both sides. The Gurkha units played their full part, with the 1/9th leading the assault and the 1/8th being among the first British troops to reach the first line of the Turkish trenches. Despite the efforts of the whole force, the attack eventually faded out until a truce was agreed so the many wounded could be evacuated, the Turks under the Red Crescent and the British under the Red Cross.

No further attempt could be made to save Kut, as General Gorringe's force had suffered over 21,000 casualties in the vain attempt to

---

* Chitral was a fort on the North-West Frontier of India. In 1895, Townshend had commanded the garrison there with great skill, driving off repeated assaults by tribesmen until finally relieved.

save the 10,000 men besieged in Kut. On 29 April 1916, after destroying all his guns and military stores, General Townshend was forced to surrender. It was a sad ending to a brave adventure; the surrender of Kut set the whole world agog and 'shook the Empire'. Into captivity went men of the 2/7th Gurkha Rifles, with the British officers being parted by their Turkish captors from the soldiers they had led with such gallantry. For all of them lay ahead a long, uncomfortable period of captivity in primitive Turkish camps and prisons. In adversity the conduct of the 7th Gurkhas was as steadfast as it had been in battle and won the respect of the Turks and the Germans because, although separated from their officers, the NCOs ran the battalion on normal regimental lines and thus discipline was maintained. The Turks were not cruel by deliberate intent but showed a complete lack of interest in the fate of their captives, and such an attitude was to cause thousands of deaths. However, for the 2/7th it was not the end of the war when they disappeared into prison camps because that battalion – which had won such honour at Gurkha Mound – was re-formed with fresh drafts from the Gurkha Brigade and, by a strange coincidence, first went into action near the place where the original battalion had first joined 6th Division. Some twenty-seven years later, after the 2/7th had been captured in Tobruk, regimental history was to be repeated when the battalion was re-formed and continued the fight against the enemy of that time, the Germans.

The fall of Kut led the War Office to take over direct responsibility for the Mesopotamian campaign and a great improvement was soon felt. An energetic, able commander, Lieutenant-General Sir Stanley Maude, soon tackled much of what had been wrong before and by the end of December 1916 his army had secure communications, while transport resupply had been reorganised so that his troops were poised to open the road to Baghdad – via Kut. Preliminary moves soon showed that only hard fighting would drive the Turks from their positions south of and around the junctions of the Rivers Tigris and Hai, on the opposite bank to Kut. In an initial skirmish, Major Scott, commanding C and D Companies of the 2/4th Gurkhas, drove the Turks from the Dahra Bend, as a result of which his battalion took more than 350 prisoners.

The chance of a decisive battle offered itself in late February 1917 when 37 Brigade was given the honour of leading what was considered by many to be a forlorn hope. The plan was to cross about six miles up river from Kut at the Shumran Bend, with the aim being the possible capture of Khalil Bey's whole force. Rowed by men of a British regiment, two Gurkha battalions, the 1/2nd and the 2/9th, were to cross in boats, each of which carried about a dozen men plus the rowers. The crossing was not easy as the Tigris was swollen and the current was running at five knots. Under a storm of bullets at point-blank range, those who survived the initial crossings landed and closed with the Turks in their positions by the river bank, and after a bloody struggle overcame them. Generous tribute must be paid to the men who did the rowing, soldiers from the Hampshire Regiment and the Royal Engineers, because theirs was a most unenviable task when fire was directed on them, whichever way they were rowing. It is not surprising that at first only about eleven boats of the 1/2nd actually reached the far bank. The current of the river caused several boats to land right under the Turkish defences, where boats sank or the occupants perished under a hail of bullets. Some boats were stranded on the enemy's side of the river, while soldiers waiting to cross could only watch in anguish and dismay.

Meanwhile, the first tow of the 2/9th, under the command of Major Wheeler, crossed in thirteen boats, three of which drifted down-river out of control. Led by Wheeler, the first party rushed the nearest Turkish position which they took, only to be counter-attacked by some thirty or forty of the enemy. Wheeler and a subaltern, Second Lieutenant Russell, together with three Gurkhas, charged the advancing Turks and dispersed them, although both officers were wounded. Despite that, Wheeler remained in command, inspiring his men while consolidating the small bridgehead. For such gallantry, Major Wheeler was to be awarded the VC while Russell was granted the DSO.

For the 1/2nd, it was to be a close shave, too, when only fifty-six men under two subalterns managed to cross where they clung to a small bank, holding the Turks at bay for some time. As reinforcements could not reach them, the decision was taken to abandon the 1/2nd Gurkhas' ferry point, a wise move as it turned out and one that was to prove the turning point in a struggle full of hazards. In the end, the ferry point used by the Norfolks was the one that was not only held but enlarged, and it was through there that the rest of the two Gurkha battalions passed to help enlarge that bridgehead. Later General Maude was to say: 'Our troops have by unconquerable valour and determination forced a passage across a river 350 yards wide in the face of heavy opposition.' Both Gurkha battalions suffered heavy casualties and subsequently were awarded 'Tigris' as a battle honour, thus commemorating the brave feat of arms when they crossed a dangerous river against a determined enemy.

Even then the fighting was not over because for two more days the Turks fought on from prepared defences but were eventually forced to fall back; by the night of 25 February it had become a full retreat and the way to Baghdad was open at last. On 11 March Baghdad was entered by the Buffs, followed by the 2/4th, without any opposition being offered – and General Maude ceremonially received the keys to the city.

However, the campaign in Mesopotamia was not yet over because the Turks still had a force near Mosul. The continued advance up the River Tigris, at the height of the summer, was an arduous one, with the British Imperial force being taxed severely by problems of movement, resupply and evacuation of the sick and wounded. As one regimental historian was to write: 'Officers and men succumbed to heat exhaustion, not in ones and twos but in scores. The want of water was acute.' One battalion lost 250 officers and men as victims of the heat which meant, for a time, that the unit was powerless to carry out its tasks. Eventually battle was joined at Ramadi on 27 September 1917 when 15th Division went into action. The attack was carried out by 42 Brigade which consisted of three battalions of Gurkhas, the 1/5th, 2/5th, and 2/6th, with the redoubtable support of the 1/4th Dorsets. Before dawn, 42 Brigade's attack was launched and at about 6am the 2/6th was ordered to recapture the enemy trenches with the 1/4th Dorsets. The Turkish soldiers fought with spirit but in the end most of them were captured, while the 2/6th lost three killed and eighty-two all ranks wounded in this, the battalion's last major action in the Mesopotamian campaign.

A bitter blow to the British cause in Mesopotamia occurred in November 1917 when General Maude died from cholera at Baghdad: his great energy and determination had transformed the whole campaign; he had instilled confidence into the army, thus giving officers and men a sense of purpose and, most important of all, producing success that had previously eluded his predecessors in Mesopotamia. Never again were the Turks able to threaten the Persian Gulf or have the heart or resources to mount a dangerous offensive. Nevertheless, operational tasks continued for all the Gurkha battalions, such as guarding the long lines of communication against marauding Arabs which proved to be an unexciting and a most uncomfortable task, albeit a very necessary one. The last major action in Mesopotamia in which any of the Gurkha battalions took part was in October 1918, after the summer heat had died away. By this time General Sir Edmund Allenby had begun his great offensive in Palestine and it was hoped that the coup de grâce could be administered in Mesopotamia at the same time. Preparations were carried out by HQ I Indian Corps, assembled in the Tekrit area, south of the Turkish main defences at Sharqat. The Turks had other divisions held in rear of their main position, so the British plan had to rely on speed as any delay would have enabled the enemy to bring forward and concentrate a considerable force against the attackers. Three battalions of the Gurkha Brigade took part in the ensuing battle for Sharqat: the 1/7th and the 1/10th, both composed of Rais and Limbus from East Nepal, and the 1/8th, mainly composed of Magars and Gurungs from the west of the mountain kingdom.

Initially the British outmanoeuvred their enemy, compelling the Turks to evacuate the whole of their forward position and pull back to their second line on the right bank of the Tigris. By 24 October, the 1/7th, in its first operation on active service during the First World War, came under fire, losing one man killed and twenty-one wounded in a brush with the Turks, after which all ranks were commended for their steadiness under fire. This was to be but the prelude to a forced march of thirty-six miles in twenty-six hours which brought the 1/7th to the cavalry's aid in the rear of the Turks. Major-General Sir William Marshal, the C-in-C, wrote:

During the night 28/29 October the Turks made repeated efforts to break through to the north but each time were repulsed. In this fighting, the Guides Cavalry and the 1st Battalion 7th Gurkha Rifles distinguished themselves by their staunchness.

Meanwhile, on the other flank, the 1/10th and 1/8th faced a daunting series of marches and conflicts, advancing over a series of ridges, often under hostile machine-gun fire, making the going extremely difficult. A succession of small Turkish outposts held them up, each of which had to be cleared before the general advance could continue. Spurred on by the news that their comrades in the north were fighting desperately to prevent the Turks from escaping, the two Gurkha battalions did not hesitate when they came up against the enemy's advanced elements and, despite heavy artillery fire, they continued to press forward. By now, however, the Turkish commander, Ismail Hakki Bey, knew that his army was completely hemmed in, with no possible chance of escape; at daylight on 29 October white flags began to appear all along the Turkish defences: at last, the long war in Mesopotamia, which had cost the British Imperial forces over 30,000 dead, was over. The battle honour 'Sharqat' had been won by the three Gurkha units which had participated, in recognition of strenuous marches on limited rations and little water, as well as a reward for their physical toughness and courage, which was more than equal to that shown by the Turkish soldiers. The 1/10th for example, after advancing over sixty miles in six days with minimum food and water, was close to exhaustion but a skilful use of ground enabled them to close up to the Turkish enemy near Sharqat before the white flags appeared, signifying that the fighting was over. At Sharqat, over 11,000 Turks surrendered and casualties among the Gurkha battalions were heavy: the 1/10th alone suffered 110 all ranks killed or wounded in battle.

Elsewhere in the Middle East, a virtual stalemate prevailed in the Suez Canal area and on the Gaza front until, in June 1917 a new army commander, General Sir Edmund Allenby, arrived. His predecessor, General Sir Archibald Murray, had tended to be over-cautious, once invoking Kitchener's taunt: 'Are you defending the Canal or is it defending you?' Allenby's arrival

was soon to inject a new offensive spirit into the army.

Six Gurkha battalions were to take part in the campaign, under command of four different divisions, among them the 4th Battalion of the newly-formed 11th Gurkha Rifles; four battalions of this regiment were raised in the Middle East during May 1918, to allow every available British unit to move to France for the final offensive on the Western Front.

During the early summer of 1917 no major actions were fought in Palestine, but for the Gurkhas their first few weeks of duty on the plains, and especially near the Auja River, introduced them to a different type of mosquito and within a short time, literally scores had become victims of an extremely virulent type of malaria.

By the middle of September 1918 there was much tension and excitement as Allenby kept the Turks on tenterhooks. While threatening to move inland around their left flank, secretly he had massed overwhelming strength against their right on the narrow Plain of Sharon, adjoining the sea. On 11 September when the attack began, during the fighting at El Kefr, the leading companies of the 2/3rd came under severe pressure and were held up by an enemy machine-gun which was playing havoc with them. It was here that Rifleman Karnabahadur Rana, at the head of a small group, crept forward with a Lewis gun in order to engage the enemy machine-gun. After the No. 1 of the Lewis gun had been killed, Karnabahadur took over and despite being the main target of enemy fire, knocked out the Turkish machine-gun and kept the Lewis gun in action for the rest of the engagement. This gallant action, which was recognised with the award of the VC, eventually enabled his company to move forward and reorganise.

The attack on 19 September was the first decisive blow in the Battle of Megiddo, which was to lead to an overwhelming victory for General Allenby and his army. As the 2/7th moved up into position before first light, the part they had to play seemed small but as events turned out, it was to have far-reaching effects. At 4.30 am pandemonium broke out as the front erupted with fire and the companies went off into the darkness, trying to accomplish a flanking 'wheel'. In spite of the noise and confusion, most of the battalion reached its objective and went through the wire to take the last line of the

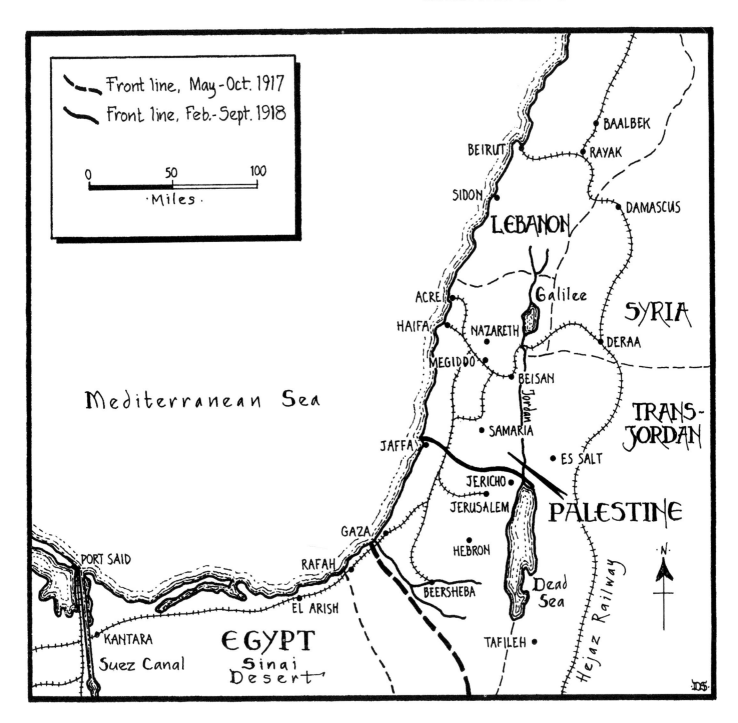

Front line, May-Oct. 1917
Front line, Feb.-Sept. 1918

0   50   100
·Miles·

enemy trenches. At that time, Turkish machine-guns opened fire from a village some distance away, so the battalion moved out to clear them away. The regimental history states that for a time, the 2/7th appeared to be on its own; their commanders received no orders nor did they know anything about the situation on either flank. Nevertheless, they kept advancing until friendly units could be seen on their left.

In a day of confusion, it was difficult for the infantry who took part in the battle to realise that their advance had pushed the Turks back to the hills, thus enabling the cavalry to sweep to the north, at great speed. It was hard going and particularly tough on the footsore infantry. The Gurkhas, like their British counterparts, outmarched their supplies and went hungry: the pace was terrific and there was no relief. On they went to the north-west, past Jezreel and Nazareth to the Sea of Galilee. On 31 October 1918 the whole army learnt that the Turks had surrendered: the war in Palestine was over.

The most spectacular role in the Battle of Megiddo undoubtedly belonged to the cavalry which, in the space of some 38 days, rode 350 miles while fighting some brilliant actions on the way to Aleppo. The Gurkha battalions showed that their men were courageous and efficient soldiers, a reputation that was to be maintained and even enhanced by the deeds of their sons and nephews in the Second World War.

The spirit and achievements of the Indian Army Gurkha Brigade during the First World War were embodied in the distinguished personalities among its Viceroy's Commissioned Officers (Gurkha officers). General Tuker cites an outstanding example. He was Lieutenant Bhim Sing Thapa, whose father and grandfather had served before him during the Indian Mutiny and in Bhutan, Afghanistan and Burma, and whose sons served after him – all in the same regiment. Bhim Sing himself fought in Waziristan, France, Sinai and Palestine, winning the Military Cross, the Indian Order of Merit and four Mentions in Dispatches. In General Tuker's words: 'This is a record substantial enough to be noticed in a history of the Gurkhas of Nepal.' On such men has the Gurkha Brigade depended in peace and in war. Each regiment can boast magnificent Gurkha officers, of which Bhim Sing Thapa must be an outstanding example. Twenty-two years later, in the Second World War, their courage, loyalty and leadership were to be fully tested once again; rarely did they fail to respond to the highest traditions of the Gurkha Brigade.

5 THE INTERLUDE

ALTHOUGH the Great War ended in 1918, it was to take three more years before the last of the Gurkha battalions returned to India. Most of the world may have been at peace, but for some battalions of the Gurkha Brigade, it meant operational moves up to the North-West Frontier to meet and defeat a widespread Mahsud rising in 1919. As already stated, the fact that the wartime Gurkha battalions had not been disbanded was very much due to Nepal's Maharajah, Chandra Shamsher Rana, who had forecast that there would be violence along that sensitive frontier. Britain owed much to him and as a mark of official gratitude, he was made a full general in the British Army, while to the nation of Nepal Britain made a gift of 1 million rupees, to be paid annually in perpetuity.

Events in Afghanistan and on the North-West Frontier added to the sense of turmoil within India itself, especially when the Indian Army was in the throes of demobilisation. The Third Afghan War began after Amir Habibulla of Afghanistan had been assassinated, only for his third son – who took over as Amir – to reverse his father's policy and throw in his lot with the revolutionary movement in Waziristan. One or more battalions from each regiment of the Gurkha Brigade participated in the short campaign, following which they were granted 'Afghanistan 1919' to add to an impressive list of First World War battle honours. Even when the Afghan War was over, many of the tribesmen in the Waziristan area were still up in arms so that Gurkha soldiers were to spend several tours on active service in that troubled spot before the outbreak of the Second World War. Soldiering there proved to be an excellent way of keeping all ranks up to the mark in peacetime, with junior leaders being given the chance to command men against a 'real' enemy while fortunately, casualties were light. Undoubtedly, events on the Frontier fanned the hot air of revolution in the big cities throughout the continent of India until

Signallers of the 1st Gurkha Rifles with heliograph and semaphore flag on the North-West Frontier in the 1930s

Evacuating casualties,
North-West Frontier,
in the late 1930s

The 1st Gurkha Rifles on
the march on the Frontier,
just before the outbreak
of the Second World War

the Amritsar massacre occurred, an event which caused nationwide controversy in both Britain and India at the time. Brigadier-General R.E.H. Dyer pulled a party of 1/9th Gurkha soldiers off a train and ordered them to fire on a crowd of some 20,000 people, gathered in the garden of Jallianwala Bagh. The film *Gandhi* (1982) showed those Gurkhas in the worst possible light. Without attempting to defend General Dyer, the facts were that the majority of those who died (about 240) were not killed by the rounds fired at them by the troops, but perished during the panic-stricken stampede in an attempt to escape through a single narrow exit. Be that as it may, the young Gurkha soldiers, until recently recruits, were but obeying orders when they opened fire at the crowds in the garden at Amritsar.

Peace in India did not mean just routine soldiering or participation in military and sporting competitions or extolling the exploits of officers at polo or as big-game hunters. Such topics appeared in all regimental diaries after 1918 so let us examine what conditions were like for the

Gurkha soldiers, the regulars from Nepal, those who continued serving the British Raj after the conflict was over. Prior to 1921, a Gurkha rifleman received 11 rupees a month, so the increase to 16 rupees a month* was a welcome rise, even though still a paltry sum for men who were earning their living as mercenary soldiers. We must remember, too, that every man was – and is to this day – a volunteer. The warrior class stands high in the Hindu caste system, so that men were not driven to enlist by unemployment or an inability to live amicably within their own village environment. Indeed, the Gurkha soldier was and is honoured and respected in his village, both while serving and later, when on pension. Competition to be enlisted has always been intense, even in the Second World War when there were over fifty battalions of Gurkha soldiers serving the British Crown.

With peacetime came a wide variety of recreational pursuits, and the fact that the ten regimental depots were in Himalayan hill stations meant that big-game shoots were relatively easy to organise. Mountaineering in the Himalayas achieved a considerable boost when Brigadier-General Charles Bruce, who had commanded the 1/6th at Gallipoli, was appointed leader of two Everest expeditions (in 1924 he reached a height of 27,000 feet on that mountain, without oxygen). Following his example, the Gurkha Brigade thereafter produced excellent mountaineers,

British officers and Gurkha soldiers, as they continue to do today, albeit from a sadly truncated force.

Between the wars, Gurkha soldiers took a great interest in sport and especially in football. The annual competition for the Gurkha Brigade Cup was intense with encounters being fiercely contested, with no quarter being asked or given but without descending to gamesmanship or dirty play. The 7th claim that their two battalions won the coveted trophy more times in the 1930s than the other regiments – a claim that has not been checked out by the unbiased author of this book! Boxing would seem to

A group of Gurkhas on the North-West Frontier in the 1930s

The Frontier - a section of Gurkhas with a Lewis gun carried on a mule

* Less than £2 a month.

The CO of the 2/7th Gurkha Rifles rewards a Gurkha, who is holding a large ceremonial kukri, for successfully beheading a buffalo with a single stroke at the festival of Dashera. This photograph was taken in the early 1950s

efforts on active service. Festivities over, on the eleventh day it used to be traditional for the whole battalion to set off on a route march, thus bringing all ranks down to earth with a bump.

Another main annual festival celebrated by the Gurkha Brigade is Diwali, the Hindu festival of light, which takes place in October or November. This colourful festival lasts five days and each day has a special name and a special object of worship. Groups of merrymakers go from house to house singing, following which their hosts offer them food and drink and the madals (drums) keep beating out their repetitive throbbing rhythm until morning breaks. It is the one time in the year that gambling is allowed throughout Nepal and thus in the Brigade of Gurkhas. The great Maharajah Jangbahadur Rana was the ruler who forbade gambling at other times in the year because, given the chance, the Gurkha villagers would sit down all day and indulge. Many stories were told by old soldiers about fortunes lost and won in their villages during Diwali, with animals, livestock, complete farms and even wives being won and lost on the throw of a dice. Not surprisingly, in the old Indian Army Gurkha Brigade – and in today's Brigade of Gurkhas – strict control was and is exercised, with the sale and drinking of alcohol being confined to certain hours and always under supervision.

From festivities to fitness and the special type of fitness which was necessary when the Gurkha Brigade carried out picketing duties on the North-West Frontier,* duties that entailed withdrawal at speed using whatever cover there was while the picket scampered down to rejoin the main column below. The Gurkhas were in their element, possessing the ability to descend in great crashing bounds, leaning forward down the slope with their legs going as fast as in a sprint; it was something that even the Pathan tribesmen could not surpass. To that end, it was not surprising that the Gurkha Brigade started to hold annual 'khud races'. The regimental history of the 5th Gurkha Rifles describes a typical khud race:

The men, bare footed, dressed in singlets and shorts. The race was run over a steep and rocky hillside, so

have been an unlikely sport for Gurkhas until the 8th Gurkhas introduced it in their Regimental Centre at Quetta, where it caught on very quickly: in 1944, one of their young NCOs, seventeen-year-old Naik Lalbahadur Thapa, was to win the All-India Flyweight Championship, the first Gurkha soldier ever to achieve such a distinction.

In peace and whenever possible on active operations, each Gurkha battalion celebrates the main Hindu festival of Dashera (Durga-Puja) with great gusto and fervour. It is the one time in the year when the natural self-discipline of the Gurkha soldier occasionally lapses – or is allowed to lapse by their indulgent officers, who join in the celebrations with enthusiasm. In peacetime, between the wars, the Dashera festival lasted ten days, with much merrymaking and religious sacrifices, dedicated to ensuring that if the unit was ever called upon to do battle in the oncoming year, the goddess Durga would be with them, adding her strength to their

---

* Picketing involved small bodies of troops taking up positions on high ground while the main column advanced along the valley. The most dangerous moment came when the pickets had to withdraw from their vantage points.

'Steady up; fast down.'
Men of the 5th Gurkha Rifles taking part in a khud race

precipitous even in the downhill portions that the ordinary plainsman would need to use his hands. Not so the trained Gurkha, who dropped full speed from one rock to another eight feet below, to land on one leg and bring the other forward to continue unchecked his headlong career.

Between the wars great runners were produced by the various regiments: as a prime example, the 1/3rd's Budhiparsad won the 5th Gurkha Challenge Cup for seven years in succession. Both the 5th and the 6th while stationed in Abbottabad boasted runners who were famous for their exploits in khud races held before 1939.

It should not be thought that during the inter-war years in the Gurkha Brigade, or in the Indian Army as a whole, life was little work and mostly play, because that would be completely untrue. Each battalion carried out regular tours of duty on the North-West Frontier, where the bullets used were real. Such training, for the young officers, NCOs and men, was to prove invaluable when the Second World War broke out. The North-West Frontier was a hard school and one that taught basic military virtues, even though the detailed tactics and techniques were to prove of little value when fighting the Japanese in the jungles of Burma or the Germans in the Western Desert.

Natural disasters ocurred too, and in January 1934 Nepal experienced her most devastating earthquake of modern times when several thousand houses were destroyed, and severe damage done to many historic buildings in Kathmandu. Some months before, two aircraft from Lady Houston's aerial expedition had flown over the country and around the summit of Everest, the first planes ever to do so. As a consequence, the more superstitious people were convinced that the gods, who dwell among the mountain peaks in the Himalayas, were furious at the violation of their sacred homes so that the country of Nepal had been shaken in anger. As a result, the Maharajah forbade the flying of aircraft over Nepal until the Second World War broke out.

Little more than a year later, another violent earthquake was to strike, this time at Quetta, in north-west India, when, in the early hours of the morning of 31 May 1935, the earth heaved in violent convulsions for thirty seconds – but in those thirty seconds the city fell into ruins and several thousand people were killed. Although the Quetta earthquake was the one that caught the attention of the world, the one in Nepal had far greater consequences for the two eastern Gurkha regiments, the 7th and 10th, whose Rais and Limbus have their homeland in that part of the world. Terraced fields were destroyed and whole villages – men, women, children and cattle – were swept down into rivers whose banks had disappeared. In those days communications were primitive in the extreme so that

Men of the 8th Gurkha Rifles searching for survivors in Quetta after the earthquake of 30/31 May 1935

rumours spread and although the disaster was not as bad as had been anticipated, both regiments had many men whose homes had suffered damage or whose relatives had perished in the earthquake.

In the 1935 Quetta earthquake, the two battalions of the 7th were fortunate because, although stationed there at various times, both units were out of the cantonment* when the violent tremors began. The 2/8th were there, however, and under the leadership of their commanding officer, Lieutenant-Colonel Geoffrey Scoones, quickly organised rescue teams because the battalion lines had not suffered badly, whereas affairs in the city were extremely pressing. The Gurkhas toiled all through the night and did some magnificent work while rescuing Indians trapped among the ruins. One Gurkha rifleman, Harkbir Thapa, saved many lives because he had an unusually acute sense of hearing and using this gift to the full, several people were located under ruins of collapsed buildings, and he also insisted on going

among the unstable rubble to effect rescues. For his gallantry the rifleman was awarded the Albert Medal.

During the 1930s, the whole Gurkha Brigade, twenty battalions from the ten regiments, had become well-trained units, all with experience gained in skirmishes against the tribesmen on the North-West Frontier. During those last few years of peace, certain British officers were obtaining valuable experience while commanding Gurkha units, experience that was to stand them in great stead when, after 1939, promotion to higher rank usually followed. One who was to become most famous was Lieutenant-Colonel W. J. Slim who transferred from the 6th to command the 2/7th. Some of his chief lieutenants, as corps and divisional commanders in Burma, were from the Indian Army Gurkha Brigade: Geoffry Scoones; W. D. A. (Joe) Lentaigne; Bruce Scott; D. T. (Punch) Cowan (later to become one of the most experienced divisional commanders in the whole Burma campaign); Douglas Gracey. In the Middle East and Italy, generals who won renown included Francis 'Gertie' Tuker; A.W. Holworthy; 'Os' Lovett and Charles Boucher: all were to reach the rank of major-general or above before the Second World War was over.

Although Nepal's contribution in the First World War had been a magnificent one, it was to be surpassed during the six years that followed 1939, when the Gurkha Brigade was expanded to forty-five battalions and ten training centres: nearly a quarter of a million of Nepal's young manhood rallied to the cause of Great Britain. Once again their soldiers were to see action in many parts of the world – in Burma and Malaya, Persia, Iraq and the Middle East, Cyprus, Italy and Greece, as well as standing firm on the North-West Frontier and helping to maintain law and order in the cities of India.

* In India, a permanent military station, including the troops' living quarters.

6 THE SECOND WORLD WAR

Iᴺ Nᴇᴘᴀʟ, the Ranas were gradually losing their hold over the country, although they managed to cling to power until the early 1950s. In 1939 the Maharajah was Judha Shamsher who held the post until he voluntarily retired in 1948. Well before that time, his sons had been installed in responsible positions in the government and in posts of influence. Judha was the last of the Rana Prime Ministers to exert absolute power in his own country. He was quick-tempered and inclined to be impulsive but, on the other hand, he was a hard worker and had regular contact with applicants who petitioned him for his support or appealed against certain decisions of his officials. Much as he admired the British, Judha was convinced that the Westminster style of democracy could not succeed in a backward country like Nepal which lacked universal education or even adequate communications. As a consequence, Nepal remained a primitive and isolated kingdom under his rule and it was by deliberate intent that no motor road connected Kathmandu with India until the end of his days as Prime Minister. It used to take 120 porters 8 days to carry a motor car from the roadhead at Bhimphedi over the hills into the valley of Kathmandu. Once there, the car could only travel around the valley because no roads penetrated into the hills which encircled the city and its surrounding fertile plain.

Whatever defects Judha Shamsher might have had, he was a Gurkha and having pledged his friendship to Britain, he did not hesitate when the Second World War broke out in September 1939. Without being asked, he made a spontaneous offer of eight Nepalese Army battalions to assist in the

The first car to arrive in Nepal. As, at the time (the mid-1930s), there were no roads linking India with Kathmandu, it had to be carried all the way by relays of porters

internal security of India, an offer that was to be accepted after some delay. Thereafter, the so called 'phoney war' during the winter of 1939 lulled the Allies into complacency, so no other requests for support were made until mid-1940 when Great Britain, her Empire and Dominions, had been left to fight alone against her powerful foe, Germany. At a time when the rest of the world felt that Britain might be forced to surrender, the British Minister in Kathmandu went for an audience with Judha in order to ask permission to allow Gurkha units to go overseas and also, of more importance, for the Indian Army to increase the number of its Gurkha battalions from twenty to thirty. He went there in trepidation, but permission was granted without any hesitation whatever. It was then that Judha gave this classic example of friendship and staunchness: 'Do you,' he demanded of the Minister, 'let your friend down in a time of need?'

'No sir, but there is often a difference between countries and individuals.'

'There should not be. If you win, we will win with you, if you lose, we will lose with you.'

The speed with which Judha gave his sanction was heart-warming, especially at a time when British morale was not at a high level. That was not to be the end, however, because further requests followed and each time, without hesitation, the Maharajah gave his permission. Moreover, in September 1940, when London was burning from the Blitz, Judha gave another example of his staunch generosity. Hearing that the East End had been a target for the Luftwaffe, he ordered his Government to give the equivalent of 25,000 rupees in sterling to the Lord Mayor of London to be used to help the people in that distressed area.

Thereafter the swift expansion of the peacetime Gurkha Brigade, which more than doubled its size in a matter of months, inevitably placed an enormous strain on the small band of regular officers and senior Viceroy's Commissioned Officers (Gurkha officers). With many of the regular officers being required to fill staff jobs in newly formed headquarters, in ever-increasing numbers their place was taken by wartime Emergency Commissioned Officers (ECOs), the majority of whom had never been east of Suez before and lacked any real experience of military life. After six months' training at an Officers' Training Centre in India, they were posted to a Gurkha training centre to meet, for the first time, recruits from Nepal who had never left their country before and certainly knew nothing about the white officers now appointed to train them and, in time, to lead them in battle. Those ECOs when they reported for duty, proudly and self-consciously aware of a single black pip on each shoulder, soon learnt that they had to rely very much on the Gurkha officers until they were able to speak the language and to understand more about the men under their command. The Gurkha officers formed the vital connecting link between the senior NCOs and the British officers and in wartime, several of the more senior ones were called back from pension or asked to serve beyond their normal tenure of service in the regiment.

Each Gurkha training centre owed much to these senior Gurkha officers who had come back from pension at a time of need. It was they who licked into shape the newly arrived recruits when they reached the centre, the majority of whom had never before seen a train or motor car or even worn a pair of boots. Completely unspoiled, they showed the basic qualities of the Gurkhas, with their love of life and a natural warm sense of humour as well as an unconscious but fearless pride in their race. In seven hard months those young boys became fully trained soldiers: it seemed impossible but the impossible was being achieved in each of the training centres. While they were changing, so, too, were the British officers, as they learnt Gurkhali or played games with the men, or met the Gurkha officers socially after parade and gradually discovered more about the men they were aspiring to lead in battle. The shy, unspoilt boys changed into seasoned riflemen, expert with their weapons and trained in the many complexities of warfare that were to face them in the jungles of Burma, the deserts of North Africa or in the mountains of Italy.

Battalions from the ten regiments set out on the first of many journeys in the spring of 1941, journeys that would take them during four or five eventful years to South-East Asia, the Middle East, North Africa, Italy and Greece: once there, they were never to be far from the centre of the stage. Now the world outside India and Great Britain heard about the warriors from Nepal, with one American editor writing in 1943: 'Why have I not been told of these Gurkhas before?'

In a comparatively short account like this, it is manifestly impossible to follow the fortunes of so many battalions in the varied theatres that the British and Indian Armies fought in during nearly six years of war. Battalions from seven of the regiments had the grave misfortune to lose many of their officers and men into captivity: in the Western Desert, the 3rd, 4th, 7th and 8th (all four units being reformed thereafter). Likewise, in Singapore, three battalions formed part of General Percival's army which, in February 1942, was forced to surrender by the Japanese. Four battalions marched with Wingate's Chindits in Burma while many Gurkhas volunteered to join the Gurkha Parachute Battalions. The 5th Royal Gurkha Rifles won four out of the twelve Victoria Crosses awarded to men of the Gurkha Brigade in the Second World War. Finally, the 10th Gurkhas surpassed all other Gurkha regiments in the total time spent in action against the Germans and Japanese and in the number of gallantry awards won by its four battalions. Indeed, its casualties, at a total of 1,012 dead and 1,958 wounded, was exceeded in the whole Indian Army only by those of the 5th Royal Gurkha Rifles.

What follows is an account of what befell some of those units which fought in the Middle East and Europe before returning to the Far East, where twenty-six Gurkha battalions took part, at one time or another, in the long-drawn-out campaign waged in Burma against the Japanese. On 4 May 1941 unrest in Iraq led to the newly-promoted Major-General W. J. Slim taking command of the 10th Indian Division and under his leadership the government of Rashid Ali, accused of being pro-Germany, was defeated even though there were Germans still in key posts in neighbouring Persia (now Iran), where the Shah disregarded requests from the Allies that he should expel these technicians. As a consequence, in August a British force moved into Persia from the south and the Russians from the north. By this time the 1/2nd, 2/7th and 2/10th had arrived and were revisiting places that had been familiar to their fathers during the First World War, but this time there was no formidable enemy like the Turks to fight, and active operations were soon over without a real scuffle. The Persian Army, relieved that no bloodshed was necessary, welcomed their adversaries with dignity and even with a military band in one place. Peace soon reigned around the Persian Gulf.

Two Gurkha battalions remained in that part of the world, initially as part of 10th Indian Division, and did not see any major active service until moving to Italy in 1944. Meanwhile, the 1/2nd, 2/7th and 1/9th moved to join 4th Indian Division, now commanded by Major-General 'Gertie' Tuker (late 2nd Gurkha Rifles). By the end of the war, all three battalions had added several battle honours to their respective regimental lists.

In February 1941, General Erwin Rommel arrived with his Afrika Korps in the Western Desert, and the Germans, with their Italian allies, drove the British back to Egypt. Despite a long siege, Tobruk was held, thus denying the vital port to Rommel, which forced the German general back to his starting line. However, this was to be a temporary rebuff only, and in May 1942 Rommel was to strike once more. By that time the 2/7th had joined 11 Indian Infantry Brigade in 4th Indian Division, the famous 'Red Eagles', which had won great fame in actions fought since 1940 in the Western Desert and East Africa. At this time, the division was to be widely spread throughout the Eastern Mediterranean, with 11 Brigade being its only brigade remaining in North Africa.

Rommel's offensive had been foreseen by the British and even the date of it, 26 May, had been known at the higher echelons of command. But although Eighth Army in the field was numerically superior to Rommel's force and possessed more tanks, the British generals lacked experience in handling large armoured formations; moreover, the tanks' puny 2-pounder guns were totally ineffective against the German armour.

On 1 June, the 2/4th Gurkhas, serving in 10 Indian Infantry Brigade (5th Indian Division), received an urgent message to move at once to Point 180 in the desert, ten miles east of the Knightsbridge Box. As they moved, the news was exciting for all ranks of the unit as they realised that they were going into action at last; but, sadly, for many, this was going to be of a short duration only. After digging in and being prepared, at all costs, to hold Point 180, away from their perimeter chaos reigned.

It was some time before we realised that no one who left our position ever did return. The outside world was

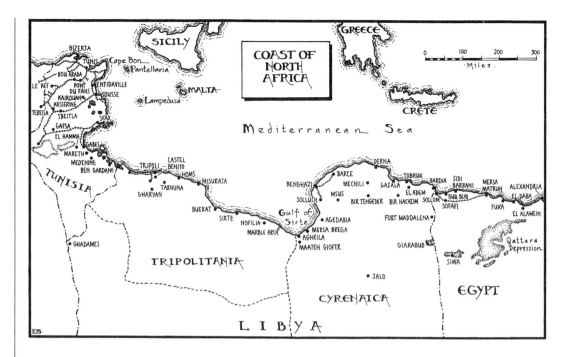

dead and we were isolated but did not know it. No reply came to our signals … we did not know then that Brigade Headquarters were no more, that Divisional Headquarters had gone, that the Brigadier and CRA* who had lately left us were prisoners.

The units nearby were overrun, in turn, by the Germans until the 2/4th itself was completely surrounded and despite all their efforts, an overwhelming force of German tanks gradually closed in on them. The Gurkhas' 2-pounder anti-tank guns were too light, and the men watched, with horrible feelings of frustration, as their shells ricocheted from the armour of the German tanks as they came steadily on. Company by company was overrun and after 48 hours without food or sleep, surrounded and isolated, those officers and men who remained could do no more and were finally overpowered on 6 June. In the words of the regimental history:

As the sun went down we were lined up to be led off into captivity, the British separated from the Gurkhas and the Gurkhas from the rest. The darkness descended on us – in prelude and in presage of the months and years of tribulation to come.

Such was the battle of the Cauldron as far as the 2/4th was concerned. The battalion was re-formed, however, and, as part of 10th Indian Division, took its full part in the 1944/5 Italian campaign.

Similar misfortunes, in varying degrees, befell the 2/3rd and 2/8th, both of which were rushed to the Western Desert when Rommel threatened to break through to the Nile in the summer of 1942. The 2/3rd formed a battalion 'box', only for C Company and half of D Company to be overrun, with about 200 men being taken prisoner; many of these managed to rejoin the Allies when the Germans later retreated from Tobruk.

The 2/8th Gurkhas saw its first action on 28 June 1942 in a most confused battle which ended in remnants of the unit eventually reaching El Alamein by the end of the month. Some of those who escaped did so after dramatic adventures. As an example, Captains Ross and McKenzie escaped on foot and finally reached the British outposts on 4 July. The 2/8th eventually joined 43 Gurkha Lorried Infantry Brigade, and saw much action in Italy during 1944-45.

In Tobruk a similar story had been enacted when the incessant rumbling of guns steadily grew closer as Rommel's Afrika Korps broke through the British Eighth Army. Unlike the last siege in 1941, when Tobruk had been held for months on end, this time the Royal Navy could not guarantee that it could resupply the garrison in the event of a long siege being repeated. By June 1942 Tobruk was not prepared for defence and there was

---

* Commander Royal Artillery, at divisional level.

a thirty-five mile perimeter to hold, of which 11 Indian Brigade was responsible for a sector over thirteen miles long. As a consequence, only the outer perimeter could be manned and that by men in isolated section posts. In short, 11 Brigade had everything in the shop window with nothing in reserve. The 2/7th's diarist was to write: 'The destiny of Tobruk was once more in the hands of the Almighty with a conviction that all ranks should fight to the last rank and last round,' while, back in London, Winston Churchill was adamant that Tobruk could be held and once more become a thorn in Rommel's flesh. Grave deficiencies in its defences had not been revealed to Churchill or the British Government, nor had they been made aware of the very different circumstances that now prevailed at Tobruk.

On 21 June the Germans struck, launching a powerful attack against the 2/5th Mahrattas, who were bombed by Stukas and pounded by German 88-mm guns before being attacked by a whole brigade. One by one, the Mahrattas lost company after company until the last few soldiers were forced to surrender; without any unit being able to move to their support, because the long perimeter forced all the defenders into putting everything forward 'in the shop window'. Inevitably this breach in the defences was exploited with speed and determination by Rommel who split the British posts in half and overran many of the artillery positions.

The GOC 2nd South African Division, General Klopper, who was also in overall command at Tobruk, originally planned to try and break out through the encircling Germans but he was dissuaded from this by his own South African subordinate commanders. When it was reported that the artillery had run out of ammunition and their supplies almost exhausted, Klopper reluctantly ordered a surrender. Such an order did not reach either the 2nd Queen's Own Cameron Highlanders or the 2/7th Gurkhas, nor did they know that at 6.30 on the morning of 21 June, white flags would be raised by the South Africans who were fighting alongside them. Communications had broken down and to keep the overall situation in perspective, it is wise to remember that the distance, even between the 2/7th and the Camerons of 11 Brigade, was nearly six miles.

During the night of 20/21 June, the 2/7th was attacked and battalion headquarters was forced to move and seek protection with C Company. After dawn on 21 June the Germans began attacking the rifle companies in turn: each fought to the last before being forced to surrender. One officer who took part in the action was to write afterwards about the men who, prior to the battle, had been full of confidence: 'After they had

Four Gurkhas of the 2/7th Gurkha Rifles who, after the fall of Tobruk, set out on foot to regain Allied lines in Egypt. Their journey took them thirty-six days

fought it out against overwhelming odds, and had lost, the stunned expression on their faces was a sight that few who saw it will ever forget.'

By now, the 2/7th's commanding officer had realised that the situation was hopeless and having ordered a small party to try and break out, he decided to surrender. For the second time in its history, the 7th lost its 2nd Battalion into a prisoner-of-war camp. An even more remarkable coincidence was that official permission, once again, was given for a new 2/7th to be raised: from the survivors, a few of whom managed to rejoin Eighth Army after crossing miles of desert and experiencing adventures galore; from the officers and men who had been 'left out of battle' in reinforcement camps or on courses; from drafts of men posted in from other battalions of the Gurkha Brigade; in such a way did the new 2/7th once more become part of 4th Indian Division when it fought in the Italian campaign during 1944.

Due honour must be paid to the 2nd Camerons, who, like the 2/7th, continued fighting after the official surrender, until on the morning of 22 June, led by their pipers, those that remained of the Scots battalion marched into captivity. Appropriately, too, this battalion was also re-formed and later fought alongside the 2/7th in 11 Brigade against the Germans in Italy.

Fortunately, the Gurkha Brigade still had other battalions in 4th Indian Division and it was not long before they were to win great renown in battle. After the fall of Tobruk, the 1/2nd moved back from Cyprus to rejoin 7 Brigade in Cairo, thus once more coming under command of 4th Indian Division. However, on 28 August 1942, even before the 1/2nd had moved forward from Cairo, the blackest day in the history of the regiment occurred. Almost the whole of Headquarter Company was wiped out in one second when a Royal Engineer instructor inadvertently inserted a detonator into a live mine and pressed the plunger. Sixty-eight officers and men who had been watching the demonstration were killed outright, and another eighty-five were severely injured. Unfortunately, too, nearly all the victims were specialists, signallers, mortar men and drivers. In no battle had the 2nd ever lost so many killed and wounded in a single day's fighting, let alone in one disastrous second. It meant that the battalion had to move forward into the desert minus most of its specialists. Fortunately, a month's grace was granted before the El Alamein battle was launched so that replacements arrived from other battalions in the Gurkha Brigade, as well as from the 2nd's training centre in Dehra Dun.

On 23 October 1942 the Battle of El Alamein began, opening with the fire of

North Africa –
a 6-pounder anti-tank gun
in action, manned by Gurkhas

1,200 guns until the final rout of the Axis armies, some twelve days later. Both the 1/2nd and the 1/9th were part of the 4th Indian Division but neither unit had a spectacular role to perform at the beginning of the battle. Indeed, once the Axis forces began a headlong retreat, exhilaration at the victory soon turned to disappointment as far as 4th Indian Division was concerned, as it was ordered to stay behind and 'clear the battlefield'. The main reason for such an order was because the strain placed on the available transport meant the temporary grounding of some formations; it was to be four months before 4th Indian rejoined the front-line troops. Needless to say, their live-wire commander, General 'Gertie' Tuker, used every day of this period to perfect the training of his division until his efforts had produced a formation that was to become one of the most efficient in the whole of the Eighth Army. When they did rejoin, General Sir Bernard Montgomery's forces had reached Tunisia with its barrier of mountains and salt marshes, where Rommel was preparing to fight on the Mareth Line, a series of fortifications which led inland to the Matmata Mountains.

At Wadi Akarit early in April, General Tuker persuaded General Montgomery to let the 4th Indian Division undertake a task of vital importance in the battle, with his troops being ordered to seize a key feature of the Fatnassa Heights, which would open a corridor for the main thrust behind the Axis defences. On the night of 5 April 1943, in silence, the 1/2nd and the 1/9th scaled the slopes, located the main gun positions and moved in, wielding their kukris with deadly effect. It was not long before the German garrison fled across the plateau. Prior to this victory, Tuker himself had said to a friend about the undertaking: 'Perhaps I have asked too much of them and have set them a task beyond human accomplishment.' His doubts were set at rest during that night; by dawn on the 6th, all the important features were in British hands and the next brigade passed through. It was during the battle that an outstanding display of leadership was shown by Subedar* Lalbahadur Thapa, then the second-in-command of D Company, the 1/2nd. At the head of a handful of men, he scaled the vital passage leading up to the top of the most important feature; there several enemy posts were dealt with by Lalbahadur and the rest of his men. When they reached a point just below the final crest, the subedar, now with only two riflemen in support, killed several enemy before the remainder fled. The gallantry of the Gurkha officer led to the capture of the feature, and his bravery was recognised with an immediate award of the Victoria Cross.

Then followed the relentless struggle on the bare rocks of Djebel Garci when a fierce German counter-attack was resisted for three days and nights. It was here that officers and men from the 1/9th distinguished themselves in the fighting that was carried out at close quarters, with the Gurkhas wielding their kukris and using grenades until the Germans, shaken by the ferocity of their foe, broke and fled. On D Company's front alone, forty-five dead and wounded Germans were left behind. Nevertheless, the overall casualties in 5 Indian Brigade led to General Tuker deciding that a continuation of the slogging match would only invite more casualties: instead the enemy would be allowed to wear himself out in costly counter-attacks, with the British artillery exacting a heavy toll. As a result of Tuker's representations, the plan for the next phase of the battle was changed and the main thrust of the attack was shifted to the narrow coastal plain north of Enfidaville, while the Garci operation was abandoned.

Final victory in Tunisia was approaching and it was fitting that 4th Indian Division with some officers and men who had borne the burden since the end of 1940, was there at the finish. The Axis forces in Tunisia formally surrendered on 12 May and by 6 pm all organised resistance had ceased, with 220,000 prisoners crowding into cages. Africa was at last clear of the foe. The 1/2nd Gurkhas stumbled upon the headquarters of General von Arnim, the Commander-in-Chief of all Axis forces in Africa. He had earlier sent a message offering to surrender and the 1/2nd thus found upwards of 1,000 Germans fallen in, 'immaculately clad, clean shaven, with accoutrements polished as if for a ceremonial,' ready to surrender. Thus ended the task that 4th Indian Division had begun at Sidi Barrani on a cold December morning, some 29 months earlier.

* Subedar – senior Viceroy's Commissioned Officer in the Indian Army, usually second-in-command of a company.

Monte Cassino – the Abbey from Snake's Head, 1944

At first, following the Axis surrender in Tunisia, it appeared as if the division would not be used immediately; indeed, it did not take part in the invasion and capture of Sicily later that summer. General Tuker lobbied hard for his men to return to the Eighth Army until his efforts resulted in the division landing in Italy at the end of the year, by that time including a re-formed 11 Indian Brigade

in which the reborn 2nd Camerons and the 2/7th renewed strong links that had ended when their predecessors had been captured in Tobruk. Tuker's division now contained three Gurkha battalions; the 1/2nd (7 Brigade), 2/7th (11 Brigade) and 1/9th (5 Brigade), and it was not long before the whole division moved from the Adriatic front to south of Cassino, where they joined the American Fifth Army.

These were not the first Gurkha units to fight in Italy because during September 1943, the 1/5th Gurkhas, as part of 8th Indian Division, had landed before moving north where they saw action south of the mouth of the River Sangro. By late autumn the weather had broken and heavy incessant rain meant that there was mud everywhere. It was not long before the 1/5th was in the throes of heavy fighting when Eighth Army reached the swollen River Sangro which, by then, was in flood and in places 300 yards wide. On 27 November, the 1/5th crossed with the aim of storming the village of Mozzagrogna, which they took but only after some desperate fighting. Indeed, the position worsened until the Gurkhas were told to pull back so that a massive artillery barrage could be brought down on the village. Being in close contact with the Germans, such a withdrawal was not easy and tragically the artillery barrage

Cassino – the Abbey with, on the left, Hangman's Hill and, on the far right, Castle Hill, Point 193

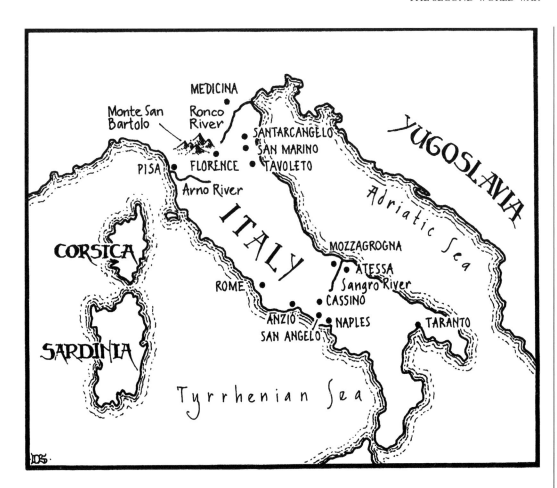

caused more Gurkha than German casualties. Having to give way through no fault of their own, it was not surprising that the men were bitter at handing back parts of the village they had won by such hard fighting. Eventually a combined attack by British armour and the 1/12th Frontier Force Regiment recaptured the village after a ding-dong battle had ensued. By 1 December the last desperate German counter-attack had been resisted and the Sangro was in the hands of the Allies. In this fiercest of battles, the 1/5th lost 3 British and 4 Gurkha officers and 129 other ranks.

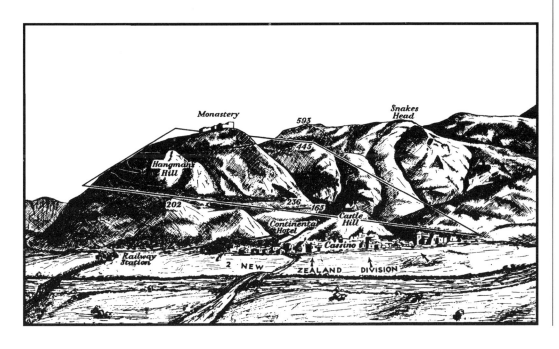

Cassino – a sketch map of the battlefield

For the Gurkha battalions in Italy, the next major battle was to occur at Cassino. Here 4th Indian and 2nd New Zealand Divisions were ordered to move across to join the US Fifth Army and together form the New Zealand Corps under command of Lieutenant-General Sir Bernard Freyberg, VC. By the time they had arrived, in January 1944, the German defence system was firmly hinged on the mountains north-east of Cassino, and linked to key strongpoints around Monte Cassino itself. The road to Rome, Route 6 (also known as Highway 6), curled into and around the town of Cassino which nestled below the beautiful abbey (or monastery)* on the mountain above. From their observation points on Monte Cassino and to the north-east on the high peaks of Monte Cairo, the Germans had a complete view of the battlefield which lay before them. Prior to the Allies reaching that area, the Germans had been quick to devise and construct defences which included machine-guns, mines and a series of well-sited guns and mortars. Cassino was as nearly impregnable as any defence could be; it needed only fanatical crack troops – like a German parachute division – to ensure that its capture would pose terrific problems. And the 1st Parachute Division duly took over its defence at the same time as Freyberg's corps prepared to launch the first attack.

Ironically, air superiority influenced the Allied generals into carrying out direct assaults against the famous abbey, although fully appreciating the strength of defences round that building. Assured by the American Air Force general in the theatre that the air forces 'could whip out Cassino like an old tooth', General Sir Harold Alexander agreed to the New Zealand Corps carrying out two frontal attacks, after the gallant US 34th Division had clawed its way, at great cost, up to the high ground to the north-east of the abbey. Unfortunately 4th Indian Division entered the battle without General Tuker who was struck down by a chronic tropical illness: he was not to return to command the division that he had led with such flair and success in the past. This was a sad blow because without Tuker's voice in dissent, a direct attack, which substituted heavy support by fire for tactical surprise, was adopted by Freyberg.

Even taking over the American positions around Point 593 proved to be extremely difficult. One US regiment, the equivalent of a British brigade, had less than 200 men in the forward position. 'Of this number 50 were so exhausted that it was necessary to carry them out on stretchers. The dead were strewn everywhere, 150 of the enemy being counted on a single enemy front.' That quotation illustrates the ferocity of the fighting that had just taken place and was to continue unabated after the arrival of the Indian Division.

On 15 February 1944 the aerial bombardment of the abbey began. The ethics of the decision to bomb the building have troubled historians over the years, but this is not the place to examine the pros and cons. All that can be said is that the bombardment was not correlated to any ground assault or timed to assist the forward movement of troops so that, militarily, the bombing was a failure. The decision was taken to treat the capture of Point 593 as a separate operation and only to begin the main attack on the abbey after that feature had been secured. This objective was left to the 1st Battalion, Royal Sussex Regiment, but by the time they attacked, the Germans were ready for them: Spandau (machine-gun) fire and showers of grenades greeted the British soldiers as three companies flung themselves at the objective, one after the other. By a supreme effort, the leading elements did manage to reach the summit of Point 593 only to be cheated of victory when the Germans fired three green flares, the prearranged signal for a Sussex withdrawal. Unfortunately the ruse was discovered too late and the battalion fell back after having lost seven officers and sixty-three men. By now it was appreciated that a much larger striking force was necessary: the next attempt committed nearly every unit in 4th Indian Division in one role or another.

The first phase would be another Royal Sussex attack on Point 593; two hours later, the 1/2nd and 1/9th would advance on the left and storm the abbey: from there they were to continue until they had gained control of Highway 6. At the same time, the New Zealand Division would smash a way through the lower Rapido Valley, attack the

* Although the term 'monastery' was used in some accounts, for consistency 'abbey' has been used throughout in this one.

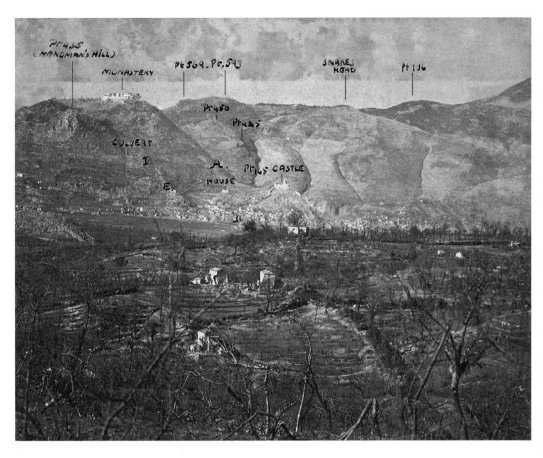

Cassino – part of the original photograph used as a battle map by the CO of the 1/9th Gurkha Rifles, with objectives and locations pencilled in

town and effect a junction with the two Gurkha battalions. Two companies of the 2/7th were attached to the 1/2nd to act as porters, carrying ammunition and stores behind their fellow Gurkhas to the objectives which, it was hoped, were soon to be wrested from the defenders.

The attack was scheduled to begin at 4 am on 18 February and at the appointed time, the Gurkha companies topped the ridge in front of them and advanced toward the abbey, less than 800 yards away. Pandemonium broke loose as devastating fire was opened by Spandau groups on the right, from machine-guns on the crest of Point 593, and from posts sited under the walls of the abbey itself. The leading Gurkhas made a dash for the nearest scrub only to leap into a deathtrap because the scrub was thorn thicket, and sown with mines and booby traps. The 1/9th's first objective was Point 444, a ridge less than 300 yards from the rear walls of the abbey. Initially on the left, a part of the German position was taken but murderous crossfire soon pinned down both the leading companies and although more troops were sent forward, the advance came to a halt after the 1/9th had suffered ninety-four casualties.

Meanwhile the 1/2nd likewise met death from mines and booby traps until B and C Companies were left with more than half their number out of action. The other rifle companies were to fare little better while the CO, Lieutenant-Colonel L. J. Showers, fell, shot through the body, and other officers and men were hit until just under 150 all ranks were killed or eventually declared missing or seriously wounded. By nine o'clock next morning it was clear that the attack had failed, while on the Gurkhas' right, the Royal Sussex had been unable to take Point 593. Heroism had not been enough to overcome well-planned defences, manned by first-class fighting men. The porters provided by the 2/7th had also suffered many casualties while trying to perform the thankless task of carrying heavy loads up the rough tracks under incessant mortaring and shelling. Afterwards they complained that they had to suffer punishment without being given the chance to fight back!

For the next few days defenders and assailants in the forward areas were often so close to each other that supporting fire could not be called by either side while below, in the town of Cassino, which was now completely battered, the New Zealanders

A rifleman of the 3rd Gurkha Rifles meets an American GI in Italy

had fought with the utmost gallantry but had also failed. The first attack by the New Zealand Corps had been repulsed with heavy losses.

Thereafter, the weather took a hand and a period of frustration followed which lasted nearly three weeks, three weeks which saw several delays and postponements. Fierce rain, snow and sleet made life miserable for the soldiers of both sides: for the tired, wet troops, relief was impossible while the forward areas were always subject to continual 'stonks' by German guns and mortars. No day passed without casualties, no night without patrol activity or minor alarms. At last, the skies cleared and on 15 March, 500 heavy bombers opened the second attempt by the New Zealand Corps to capture Monte Cassino and the ruined town below.

For three and a half hours on March 15, 1100 tons of explosives were dropped in the target area with the base of Monastery Hill disappearing in a huge cloud of smoke and dust. Then, exactly at noon, 600 guns opened up with an ear-splitting barrage, behind which 6 New Zealand Brigade advanced to the attack. However, when they reached the town, the tremendous destruction wrought by the bombing made it impossible for the Allied tanks to move forward in support because vast heaps of rubble barred their way. At the same time, 5 Brigade from 4th Indian Division attempted to strike through the town alongside the New Zealanders, then up the slopes toward the abbey. In the small hours of 16 March,

the 1/9th picked a way through the rubble and collapsed buildings which were all that remained of the town of Cassino. Their task was to capture Point 435, an outcrop just below the abbey on which there was a shattered pylon which, in happier days, had carried an aerial ropeway. To the Allied soldiers, this feature was known as Hangman's Hill, one that was less than 100 yards from the south-west corner of the abbey. The 1/9th's C and D Companies were sent ahead to attack Hangman's Hill with the rest of the unit following in single file. However, C Company disappeared into the night and no one saw or heard of them until next day as dawn was breaking, when German defenders in the abbey caught sight of the Gurkhas clambering up the rugged slopes below Hangman's Hill.

Under their young commander, twenty-year-old Captain Michael Drinkall, C Company had walked up a track in the darkness on a wet night and moved in single file diagonally across the hillside to a point where they had dumped their packs. This was below Hangman's Hill. In silence, they crept up on the objective, to surprise the German outpost in a small cave, killing two of the men they found there. Those who escaped raised the alarm which was followed by heavy mortar fire on to the Gurkhas, crouching tensely behind rocks as dawn broke.

During this 'stonk', both Drinkall and his Gurkha second-in-command were wounded and undoubtedly more casualties would have resulted had not Naik Amarbahadur Khattri,* with great coolness, crawled forward and silenced the German mortar and its crew. The wounded company commander – who continued to command his men from a stretcher – had no communications with his CO as the company radio set failed to function. C Company's position was not a happy one and Captain Drinkall was on the point of ordering a withdrawal as soon as it was dark when, suddenly, the company radio began to work and communications were re-established with battalion headquarters, situated on the edge of the town. Drinkall was told to hold on at all costs and during the following night, the remainder of the battalion began moving up the mountain while noisy diversions were arranged to cover their advance. Once again it proved

* Naik – corporal in the Indian Army.

quite impossible to move any other way than in single file, and this slow and frustrating process continued until dawn on 18 March. The first sub-unit that reached C Company did so at an opportune moment because the Germans had launched a sharp attack which threatened to overrun the whole company. The Germans were beaten off and retired to the abbey, taking with them the news that a substantial force of Gurkha soldiers was now within yards of the outer walls of the building.

For nine days the ordeal of the 1/9th Gurkhas continued, a saga that made them the best-known unit in Italy and, at that time, possibly in the United Kingdom as well. The Gurkhas had moved up the hill with little beside their weapons and a light scale of ammunition because no one had expected this to be more than a temporary phase before the next move: there had been no suggestion that these lightly clad men would have to endure a long sojourn on the rocky slopes of Monte Cassino. Clinging like limpets to their rocky home under the shadow of the abbey walls, they were encircled by paratroopers from the 1st Parachute Division, the corps d'élite of the German Army who, by now, were well aware that the key to the whole operation lay in Hangman's Hill. If the abbey was to be stormed, then Hangman's Hill had to remain in the hands of the 1/9th. To this end, the Germans tried desperately to cut all communications and, in particular, sought to capture a key point, Castle Hill, through which all reinforcements and supplies had to pass. Castle Hill was held by the 1/4th Essex Regiment, to which A Company of the 2/7th was sent in order to help retain the position against determined attacks by the German paratroopers. In the end, all was to be of no avail: the German defenders in Cassino town, although shaken by the bombing, benefited from the mass of rubble that resulted. They stood firm against the New Zealand Division until, to prevent further heavy losses, the New Zealand Corps' offensive was called off. The 1/9th would have to abandon Hangman's Hill, a decision not understood by many of the Gurkhas who immediately asked which unit was to relieve them.

On 25 March, the withdrawal began after dark, with the tired force moving down the route used by messengers dispatched earlier that day. Various distractions were made by other units, with artillery concentrations being fired against known German outposts in the town, while, nearby, New Zealand tanks displayed aggression in as noisy a manner as possible. The withdrawal down the hillside was a considerable strain on men who had endured so much for so many days but it passed without any major incident. Down from Hangman's Hill Lieutenant-Colonel George Nangle led a party of 8 officers and 177 soldiers from his own battalion, together with 2 officers and 50 soldiers from the 1/4th Essex and 40 Indian soldiers from the Rajputana Rifles. Later, German patrols claimed to have counted 185 dead Gurkhas in and around the craggy feature – the price the battalion paid for the nine days spent under the shadow of the abbey. The 9th Gurkha Rifles won themselves high praise for their ordeal on Hangman's Hill: on the crest of that rugged outcrop, a giant boulder today bears the regimental badge. 'The story of how men won and held that eyrie in mid-air will be told again and again as long as memory remains' – in such a way does their regimental history end its account of this gallant action.

Despite their efforts, the 4th Indian and New Zealand Divisions had failed and it was not until 11 May that the final battle for Cassino began. This time the Germans were unable to withstand a well-planned offensive, delivered with such unexpectedly overwhelming strength.

The 1/5th, as part of 8th Indian Division, played an important part in this, the fourth battle for Cassino. The battalion's role was to follow up the other two units in 17 Brigade across the Liri River, pass through their bridgehead and then capture the village of San Angelo, at the very heart of the German Gustav Line. On 12 May the leading battalion, the 1st Royal Fusiliers, was pinned down by accurate enemy fire so when the 1/5th Gurkhas moved down to the river, they found only four of the sixteen assault boats had survived the raking fire. As a consequence, it took nearly four hours to cross the river, using a shuttle service which meant that the first company to reach the start line did so only at platoon strength and had to disengage. On the following day, and flanked by the 1/12th Frontier Force Regiment, the 1/5th waited for the next order to attack while, all the time, they had to endure heavy shelling, sniping and accurate mortar fire. The delay was caused by difficulty in getting tank support across the river but by evening some Canadian armour had reached the west bank so that the 1/5th were able to begin their second attack. Initially all went well but when the tanks bogged down in the marshy ground, further advance proved impossible, forcing them to dig in until dawn next day.

Then, in the wake of a heavy barrage, C and B Companies attacked but, once again, the supporting armour ran into difficulty in the marshy ground so that only one tank succeeded in arriving to help the Gurkhas' advance. After some fierce exchanges, the 1/5th did gain a footing inside the village, and there followed two hours of desperate fighting among the rubble. Individual acts of gallantry inspired the assailants, in particular one by Havildar Raimansing Gurung who led a bayonet charge despite heavy German fire. By his side, man after man fell until only the NCO was left; hit many times, Raimansing collapsed near the German machine-gun post but in his dying moments drew the pin from a hand grenade and threw it, whereupon the Germans were quick to surrender. For his gallantry Raimansing was awarded a posthumous IOM. Elsewhere in the village the battle continued until a second Canadian tank came forward to help and by early afternoon, San Angelo was in the hands of the 1/5th, but at a heavy price: 41 all ranks had been killed and 129 wounded. The Germans gave way and Route 6, the road to Rome, was in Allied hands at last, while the Polish flag now flew over the ruins of the abbey: the Germans were in retreat along the whole front, including the Adriatic sector where 4th Indian Division followed as the enemy withdrew to the north.

Two other formations from the Indian Army saw much service in the Italian campaign. One, 10th Indian Division, contained the 2/3rd and 2/4th, both of which had been severely mauled in their short time in the Western Desert, as well as serving in other parts of the Middle East. The other formation was 43 Gurkha Lorried Infantry Brigade which consisted of the 2/6th, 2/8th and 2/10th Gurkhas. The latter formation was to serve under six different divisional headquarters during its comparatively short but intense period of operations in Italy. For those Gurkha battalions, there had been a long and frustrating period of waiting and training before finally they joined Eighth Army, to come under command of the British 1st Armoured Division, then slowly working its way north up the Italian Adriatic coast in the face of tough German opposition.

There were some sharp encounters for the 2/3rd and 2/4th Gurkhas in Central Italy and especially up the Tiber Valley, where the Germans gradually withdrew to their next big line of defences which the Allies called

Mud – Gurkhas of the 4th Indian Division advance in Italy

the Gothic Line. Fighting expert rearguard actions, the German soldiers did not allow the advancing Indian divisions any chance to relax and each Gurkha battalion in turn had to fight spirited battles to enable the advance to continue. Names like Auditore (1/2nd), Monte della Gorgace, Il Castello (both 2/3rd), Monte Cedrone (2/4th), Rippa Ridge (1/5th), Poggio del Grillo (2/7th), these are but some of the battle honours won by the Gurkha battalions serving in the three Indian divisions before the battle of the Gothic Line began.

To achieve surprise against well-prepared defences, Field Marshal Alexander reinforced troops in the Adriatic sector until V Corps contained seven divisions. The greatest care was taken to deceive Axis agents, with complicated moves being made at night and with all insignia and formation signs removed. The staff work was brilliant and the German Commander-in-Chief, Field Marshal Kesselring, was caught off balance; nevertheless, as had happened before in Italy,

he reacted quickly so that the outcome of the offensive was only decided after weeks of intensive fighting. Up in the hills, away from the coastal sector, the three Gurkha battalions serving in 4th Indian Division all achieved victories but only after tough fighting. The 1/2nd captured the village of Auditore and a few hours later, the steep hill behind it, Poggio San Giovanni. At the same time, on 2 and 3 September and following some stiff fighting by the 1/9th north of and around Monte Calvo, the 2/7th in a spirited night attack captured the village of Tavoleto.

Thereafter, 4th Indian Division continued its advance towards the tiny Principality of San Marino, where the Germans had respected the state's neutrality, until the opening of the Gothic Line offensive. However, from the beginning of September, they demanded the use of the state's territory as well as occupying vantage points on the route to the city of San Marino. In the middle of September, the 1/9th was given the task of capturing Points 343 and 366, two

Italy – Gurkhas prepare to set out on a patrol

features on the summit that commanded the road up to San Marino. Opposition, especially around Point 366, was intense and with supporting tanks bogged down, the 1/9th was under severe pressure and forced to fall back on Point 343. It was during this engagement that Rifleman Sherbahadur Thapa won immortal glory for himself and his regiment. After his section commander had been wounded, Sherbahadur Thapa single-handedly charged his assailants, swept them before him and reached the top of the ridge from where he brought his Bren gun into play against groups of the enemy on the reverse slopes. For two hours, the young rifleman bore a charmed life and when his platoon had spent its last round of ammunition and was virtually surrounded, the intrepid Sherbahadur covered his comrades' withdrawal. He then decided to bring in two wounded men who were lying on the forward slopes but while returning for the second man, in full view of the Germans, he fell, his body riddled with bullets. Posthumously, Sherbahadur Thapa was awarded the Victoria Cross.

While the Indian divisions were battling their way north, 43 Gurkha Lorried Infantry Brigade, consisting of the 2nd Battalions of the 6th, 8th and 10th Gurkha Rifles, made its debut in the Italian campaign by leading an assault, timed for midnight on 12/13 September. Despite all their previous motorised training, in the end they fought on their feet as infantry and such was to be their role until the last few days of the war in 1945. After dark on 12 September, the rifle companies of the 2/10th moved up towards the Passano Ridge. All hell broke out when the leading groups approached the enemy positions but owing to the broken nature of the country, it was not possible to co-ordinate attacks: as a consequence, small groups of men – nothing daunted during this, their first taste of battle – closed with the Germans in fierce hand-to-hand fighting and threw them off the ridge. Then it was their turn to be buffeted by the Germans who brought down such heavy mortar and artillery fire that, for a time, it was touch and go, but the men of the 2/10th Gurkhas stood firm to win the day. The battalion suffered its heaviest casualties in Italy during this battle, a battle that was described by Winston Churchill as 'a brilliant feat of arms': truly it was a remarkable beginning by 43 Gurkha Lorried Infantry Brigade. All three battalions

were quick to establish a high reputation in battle as the Italian campaign developed in the autumn of 1944 and continued until the end of the war in Europe.

The 2/6th took over as leading battalion during the next phase which entailed seizing certain peaks on the north bank of the River Marino. Crossing the river did not prove too difficult an operation but – unfortunately for 43 Brigade – the battalions had to cross without tank or artillery support to help out the forward troops. As a consequence, during 23 and 24 September, there was a fierce battle with the Germans counter-attacking, supported by their own armour, while the Gurkhas grimly held on to their gains. The long daylight hours of 23 September proved full of anguish for the whole brigade, with confusion reigning and casualties mounting; by midday the 2/6th had to be moved forward to relieve the 2/8th which had borne the brunt of the attack. Later, as darkness fell, the 2/6th drove towards the crest of the ridge and held on to their gains after overcoming German resistance. By now a few British tanks had managed to get across the river and their presence had a marked psychological effect on friend and foe alike. By this time the whole brigade had been in continuous action for eleven days and its troops had behaved like well-tried veterans throughout.

On 6 October, 43 Brigade was transferred to be under command of 10th Indian Division, then operating in the mountains above Bologna. In such an area they were back to mule transport and on 11 October the 2/6th crossed the River Rubicon which lay between the start line and their objective, the 1,300-feet-high Monte Chicco, 'protected by precipitous ravines and approachable along a narrow hogsback'. Once again, a fierce battle ensued and the German position was only cleared after hand-to-hand fighting with kukris, grenades and bayonets. During the heavy fighting, the 2/6th lost their CO who was badly wounded; fifty-nine others were wounded and twenty were killed. As the battle for Monte Chicco raged, the other Gurkha battalions had struggled forward in turn along the ridge so that each had played its full part in the final victory achieved.

4th Indian Division with its three Gurkha battalions was fast approaching the end of its operations in Italy. Near the River Rubicon, they learnt that for them the Italian campaign was over and that others would be given the chance finally to defeat Field Marshal Kesselring's army: the division was to move to Greece forthwith.

As far as 43 Brigade was concerned, the pattern during the winter became a question of one more river to cross:

It was largely a matter of advancing from one water obstacle to the next; digging-in to withstand enemy counter-attack and patrolling forward again to reconnoitre yet another river line overlooked by high and thick banks, cleverly fortified and providing the enemy with excellent observation. (James Lunt, Jai Sixth.)

As spring 1945 approached, plans were drawn up for an offensive to attack and destroy the German Army south of the River Po. At unit level, special attention was paid to practising river crossings, including the use of assault boats and co-operation with other arms, while the tempo of fitness training was stepped up. At this stage in the war, 8th and 10th Indian Divisions were still operating in Italy in addition to 43 Brigade.

The Eighth Army plan was to attack across the Rivers Senio and Santerno with the Polish Corps taking the lead and having the responsibility for crossing the rivers before the follow-up troops struck deep into enemy-held territory. The attack began on 9 April with 43 Gurkha Lorried Infantry Brigade under command of the 2nd New Zealand Division, still led by the gallant General Freyberg, VC. On 10 April, with 8th Indian Division on their left, 43 Brigade began moving forward, with the 2/10th being the first battalion to strike with a brilliant attack across the Sillaro River in the early morning of 16 April. The crossing was secured but the unit suffered heavy casualties while capturing its objectives on the far bank, though it captured a large number of prisoners. Through them passed the pursuit group, spearheaded by A Squadron, 14th/20th Hussars and the 2/6th Gurkha Rifles. By 16 April the 2/6th was closing in on Medicina, a small town to the north-east of Bologna. The town was defended by troops from the German 4th Parachute Division but on this occasion they were bounced out of Medicina by the speed of the

Gurkhas riding on Churchill tanks in Italy

Gurkhas' advance. For the first time in Italy, the 2/6th had gone into action in Kangaroos* and by nightfall Medicina was in Allied hands, even though the German prisoners admitted that they had been ordered to hold the town and fight it out to the end, but they had been surprised by the speed of the advance. The links of comradeship between the 6th and the 14th/20th Hussars were thus forged in battle and, until 'Options for Change', the 6th wore the Hussars' hawk on the right sleeve of their uniform while their British partners in the capture of Medicina wore the crossed kukri badge on theirs. Medicina was to be one of the 6th's most prized battle honours.

That was not to be the end of the war in Italy, however, as yet another obstacle, the Gaiana River, had still to be crossed. The river was more properly an irrigation ditch with straight parallel flood banks, fifteen to twenty feet high, and a black muddy stream which could be waded by men but not crossed by tanks. It was a natural anti-tank ditch and the German paratroopers had dug themselves well into the flood banks. General Freyberg decided that he would smash the Germans first with a weighty

* Tanks with turrets removed which could carry ten men.

artillery bombardment which would precede a night attack, beginning at 9 pm. Despite the heavy barrage on to the German defenders, two companies of the 2/6th took heavy punishment when crossing and were so reduced in numbers that there was little hope of withstanding a German counter-attack. The brigade commander ordered the survivors to retire so that another stronger attack could be launched, in which the 2/8th and 2/10th both took part. This was successful. The war was virtually over for 43 Gurkha Lorried Infantry Brigade and on 2 May 1945, the news was received that the German armies in Italy had capitulated. For 43 Brigade the campaign in Italy had taken a heavy toll in Gurkha lives: as an example, the 2/8th lost 133 other ranks killed, with another 41 dying of wounds. The other two battalions had similarly gloomy statistics to report at the end of the war.

Before leaving the campaign in Europe, it is necessary to take a quick look at the situation that faced 4th Indian Division when it arrived in Greece. For the many veterans who had been on active service since the early days of the war, the peaceful liberation of Greece sounded a most attractive proposition. The initial welcome by the Greeks when units from the division landed at Salonika, Athens and Patras was genuine and warm but it did not last long. The Communist ELAS* was well organised and determined not only to eliminate collaborators and traitors whether real or imaginary in Greece but, by force, to take over the government of the whole country. Well armed, with many able leaders, ELAS soon turned their welcome of the British into direct enmity. Open warfare began in Athens where 5 Brigade, with other British troops by their side, soon found themselves deeply involved in intense street fighting, made the more unwelcome as it was so totally unexpected.

'CO 1/9 GR stated that no one in 5 Brigade had received any real briefing about the political situation, but they were warned they would probably go straight into action.' In peace and war, the Gurkha and his kukri had been inseparable but with the Communists spreading horror stories about Indian and Gurkha troops, it was decided that the 1/9th should not use their kukris in close-quarter fighting. That order caused great offence for it meant that 'full protection to the men could not be offered'. The adjutant at the time added: 'It was agreed that Nelson rather than the War Office should be our guide if difficulties arose!'

For a time the situation in Athens was touch and go but in the end the British force was successful. The casualties suffered during this phase of the fighting by the 3/10th Baluch Regiment and the 1/9th Gurkhas (both 5 Brigade) were approx-imately the same: ten killed and about sixty wounded in each battalion.

Elsewhere in Greece the atmosphere was extremely tense while both sides waited to see who would triumph in Athens itself. In the end, 7 Brigade in the Salonika area and 11 Brigade in Patras saw little fighting, although C Company, 2/7th was engaged in a spirited action near Patras, killing thirty-two rebels, wounding thirty-eight and taking several prisoners, for the loss of two Gurkha soldiers killed. At the end of December 1945 the time had come for 4th Indian Division to return to India: in the case of the 1/2nd, they served for four and a half years in ten countries before they saw their regimental home in Dehra Dun again.

* ELAS – National People's Liberation Army, Communist-dominated armed resistance movement.

7 THE FAR EAST

JAPAN made a disastrous choice in entering the war which was to lead to untold calamity and horror, but in 1941 such a decision did not appear to be eccentric or irresponsible. After her German ally had crushed Western Europe and driven deep into Russia, Japan stood aside to bide her time. Only Great Britain, alone of the European powers, still controlled her Far Eastern empire, while the United States clung to an isolationist policy. The temptation to add to her possessions was there, and the Japanese military command struck without warning on 7 December 1941. Pearl Harbor was bombed. Other disasters to the Allies were to follow in quick succession. But before the long-drawn-out war in Burma was to begin, catastrophe was to strike the nearby Federated States of Malaya. After September 1941, there were three Gurkha battalions stationed in that pleasant land, the 2/1st, 2/2nd and 2/9th. There was considerable tension and on the morning of 7 December all doubts were ended when, following the attack on Pearl Harbor, the Japanese carried out landings on beaches in Malaya, while at the same time the first air raids were made on Singapore. While no one on the Allied side expected an easy campaign, all were to be shocked by the speed and ease with which Japan conquered Malaya. As part of 11th Indian Division, the three Gurkha battalions first had a brush with the Japanese during the night of 11 December but it soon became obvious that immediate disengagement was necessary since otherwise they would be surrounded. For four days and three sleepless nights 11th Division marched south with the Japanese already using the jungle to the best advantage; their audacity and mobility spread confusion until no one knew where their leading units would appear next. A measure of defiance was shown at Gurun but it took a few days for 11th Indian Division to recover from the earlier reverses.

When the Gurkha battalions met the Japanese on even terms, they were able to repulse them but there was never to be any respite. With little or no support available from either the Royal Navy or Royal Air Force,* temporary defences were prepared and then abandoned as the retreat to the south continued. At Slim River on 7 January, 11th Indian Division initially fought with spirit but within a few hours its units were to become completely disorganised. Without any air support, the British were unable to deal with a sudden attack by some fifty enemy tanks jammed tight, head to tail, and these tanks broke through, overrunning brigade headquarters and burning British transport which lay defenceless before them: thereafter complete chaos and confusion reigned.

At this time, the 2/2nd and 2/9th found themselves cut off on the northern bank of the River Slim, behind the Japanese advance. A decision was made to split into two halves and separate routes were selected for each force to cross the river and, if possible, rejoin the retreating British formations. One party, mainly of the 2/2nd, was able to cross over a partially destroyed railway bridge, but the other two companies from the same battalion, joined by some men of the 2/9th, were not so fortunate. Many crossed the river by improvised means only to find the Japanese waiting for them. In desperation, a handful of officers decided to lead the remainder on a wide outflanking march through dense jungle and over high hills of 2,000 feet. Other small groups, each of three or four tired and ill-clad men, attempted to

---

* So great was Japanese air superiority that on 10 December their aircraft bombed and sank the British battleships *Prince of Wales* and *Repulse* off Malaya's east coast.

follow the line of a main road, moving in the undergrowth wherever possible. While a few managed to escape, many subsisted for several weeks before finally being taken prisoner. It was the end of the war as far as many men of those two battalions were concerned.

On that same day, General Sir Archibald Wavell, the Allied Supreme Commander, South-West Pacific, made the decision to abandon the Malayan mainland and to concentrate all available resources to defend the island of Singapore. At the same time, British, Indian, Gurkha and Australian units continued their long retreat back to the island until, at dawn, on 31 January, the causeway to the mainland was blown up, with the last organised bodies of British and Australian forces having safely crossed on to the island. The siege of Singapore had begun.

Unfortunately, much false propaganda had been spread around about the strong 'fortress of Singapore', but the Japanese High Command had a far more accurate picture of the true state of its defences than did the British Government back in Whitehall. Japanese agents had reported, in the main, that the fortifications built were designed to prevent a sea landing, while perhaps the most important factor of all, the huge civilian population – mainly Chinese but with strong elements of Malays and Tamils – were most indifferent to the dire predicament of their British masters, mainly because the latter had made little effort to prepare them for the war. Moreover, the water consumption of such a population in a hot climate is high and in those days the precious water had to come across the causeway from nearby Johore. When that source was captured, Singapore began living on its none too plentiful reserves.

During the night of 8/9 February the Japanese crossed in various types of craft and hurled themselves against the north-west sector, held by the Australians. On their right, 11th Division was untouched and for the rest of the day heard only rumours and the scantiest reports about the progress of the struggle. This lack of co-operation was to prove disastrous because, once the Australians were forced to withdraw, they did not – or were not able to – inform the 11th Indian Division, thus leaving an open four-mile flank which was far too much to protect

so that the depleted units had no alternative but to pull back.

Even then they found themselves being fired on from the rear as well as from the north by Japanese infiltrators who were roaming the island. Confusion reigned as groups of soldiers from both sides moved about, fought each other and moved away without knowing where their headquarters were or what the next task should be. Singapore's days were numbered and although plans were made to pull back the perimeter and defend a shortened one, the situation by now was hopeless. On 15 February 1942 at 4 pm a cease-fire was agreed.

The three Gurkha battalions had fought grimly although dead tired and dressed in a varied assortment of uniform and rags. Once they had moved back for the final stand, they had prepared positions and having benefited from a day's rest, the men were ready to sell their new position, and their lives, dearly when, to their disbelief and shocked amazement, news of the surrender reached them.

For the Gurkhas who were marched into captivity, it was to be a grim and long-drawn-out struggle for survival, a supreme test of their loyalty to their regiments and their allegiance to the British. Quickly, the Japanese separated them from their British officers while, at the beginning, treatment was lenient in an attempt to persuade them in to joining the newly raised Indian National Army (INA).* Few, very few, Gurkhas were to join and some of those who did enlist did so only to try and escape from Japanese forward positions in Burma at a later stage in the war. Inevitably, the junior ranks looked to their Gurkha officers (VCOs) for guidance and the Japanese soon realised it was necessary to break the resistance of those leaders.

The Gurkha officers were rounded up and taken to prisoner-of-war camps where they suffered every indignity, being forced to work at demeaning tasks while their guards beat them with bamboo staves or clubbed them with rifle butts. They were deprived of blankets, with no shelter at night or protection from the heat of the sun by day. The senior Gurkha officers suffered the worst hardships, one of the most noteworthy being Subedar-Major Harising Borha of the 2/2nd who, blind, demented and suffering internal haemorrhages, died after severe

* A force recruited by the Japanese from Indian Army prisoners of war.

beatings and other ill treatment. This gallant officer refused to submit to the Japanese demands and addressed a letter of protest, pointing out that his countrymen were not citizens of India and, therefore, were not interested in serving in the Indian National Army. They had taken an oath to serve the British King-Emperor and as POWs they were entitled to honourable treatment under international law. Couched though it was in the most dignified manner, this letter caused a series of brutal beatings which killed him. Nevertheless, inspired by Harising's unflinching courage, his men stood firm and it was on their testimony after the war that this great Gurkha officer was posthumously awarded the Indian Order of Merit (IOM). While these unfortunate Gurkha officers and men were prisoners of the Japanese for the next three and a half years, in Burma the long war began, first with disaster but finally, turning from defeat into victory.

On 20 January 1942 the Japanese Fifteenth Army invaded Burma from Siam (now Thailand), using 33rd and 55th Divisions to strike southward, with Rangoon as their main objective. By that stage in South-East Asia, the Allies were in complete disarray: Singapore, Malaya, Hong Kong, the Philippines, and the Dutch East Indies had all fallen or were about to fall. The reverses were sudden and complete; the list long. In Burma there was no master plan to defend the country, too few troops and, as became increasingly apparent during the final stages of the retreat, the handful of Allied planes had to operate from civil airfields which were not strategically sited. As a result, the RAF was in no position to protect the ground troops and their links to the west from constant accurate harassment.

Initially, there were four Gurkha battalions in Burma when the Japanese struck, all serving in 17th Indian Division, with 48 Brigade being all-Gurkha (1/3rd, 1/4th and 2/5th) while the 1/7th was serving under command of 16 Indian Brigade. Soon the latter brigade was to be joined by the 3/7th, one of the wartime units which, within a few weeks of completing the men's recruit training, found itself in the front line fighting a highly trained and successful enemy. During March the 1/10th arrived as part of 63 Brigade to fight in the long retreat of the first Burma campaign.

The key to Burma lay in Rangoon because the British Army depended on that port for supplies and reinforcements. Inevitably, the Japanese made for that city and, in particular, sought to seize the Sittang Bridge, a vital link to the west if their advance was not to be held up. In mid-February, the already over-stretched 17th Division learnt that a fresh force of Japanese was streaming to the west, obviously making for the bridge so that a grim race took place, with the Japanese hoping to capture the bridge intact while the retreating British planned to destroy it after their troops had crossed over to the other side. The Japanese set up a number of road blocks between the bridge guard and the British and Indian units desperately trying to escape, so that units and sub-units became separated until there was little overall control: each had to do its best against whatever opposition was encountered. Of the Gurkha battalions fighting their way towards the bridge, only the 1/4th Gurkha Rifles succeeded in crossing: the 1/3rd and 2/5th were unable to reach the bridge, as were most of 16 and 48 Brigades. The leading battalions tried desperately to fight their way through to the bridgehead guard, with a set-piece attack mounted by the 1/3rd, supported by artillery, being partially successful: one company seized a hill near the bridge but the rest were pinned down and were unable to make any progress.

An agonising decision faced Major-General John Smyth, VC, GOC 17th Division, as his big fear was that the Japanese would seize the bridge intact. At 5.30 am on 23 February, he gave the order to destroy it. For a short time after the explosion there was an unearthly silence, made worse because those still on the east bank of the Sittang did not know whether the Japanese had seized the bridge and blown it up or whether it had been destroyed by their own side. It later transpired that the commander of the bridgehead guard had reported to Smyth that the bridge could not be held any longer and although it meant sacrificing much of his division, the General had to make the painful decision to give the order for its destruction.

On the east bank of the Sittang, junior officers and their men were left to find some way to cross the river. The Sittang was about 1,200 yards wide, with a tide that flowed strongly; there were no boats but there was bamboo in the jungle and in the local villages wood was plentiful. Anything that could float was carried to the river's edge, with a few rafts being made for the wounded but most

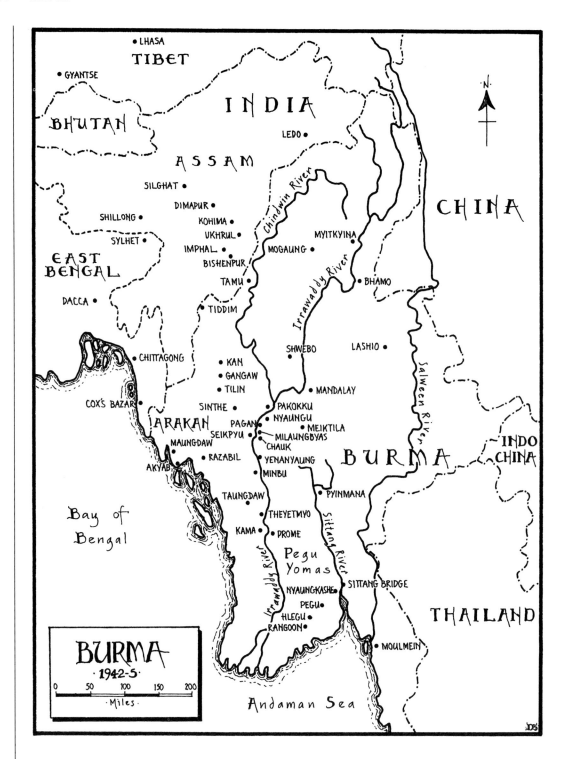

men had to wade into the river and, clinging to whatever support they could find, try and cross the wide water obstacle. Dozens drowned, others were carried out to sea by the current and even the strongest swimmers had to abandon boots and equipment before reaching the other bank. No one knows how many died and even after the war hundreds were unaccounted for and could not be traced - although later some

had undoubtedly died as prisoners in Japanese hands.

Remnants of the battalions on the west bank had to be amalgamated so that at least they could operate with some degree of effectiveness. As a result the 1/3rd and 2/5th joined forces, and became known as the 5/3rd until May of that year, when their respective units were re-formed back in India. Likewise, the two battalions of the 7th Gurkha Rifles, the 1/7th and 3/7th,

Burma, 1942 – the Sittang Bridge as seen from the Japanese side

combined to form one unit with a joint strength of about 500 all ranks, under command of a new 48 Brigade. All this meant, in terms of numbers, that 17th Indian Division had been reduced in strength to one brigade only until the arrival of 63 Brigade in Burma during March.

By now the decision had been made to evacuate Rangoon and on 7 March, Twenty-Fourth Army Headquarters and rearguards managed to move out from the city. Thereafter, it became a long agonising retreat back to India, with a series of roadblocks being set up by the Japanese which had to be cleared and that invariably meant tough fighting, even when the enemy was operating in small groups. From the beginning the Japanese displayed superior techniques in jungle fighting as well as being stronger numerically: more important still, they enjoyed generous air support 'on call'. In contrast, and as an example, the 1/10th contained 450 recruits with less than six months' training, while all units lacked efficient and serviceable radio equipment and specialists trained to operate the sets.

Occasionally the retreating forces turned on the Japanese and fought with great spirit. On 28 April at Kyaukse, 48 Brigade fought a sharp action and severely manhandled the newly arrived 18th Japanese Division in its first big battle. At that time, 48 Brigade consisted of the 1/4th and the two amalgamated units, the 5/3rd and 7th Gurkhas. The three Gurkha battalions took up positions to the east of the already gutted town and through those rearguard posts, the withdrawing Chinese Fifth Army passed on 27 April, followed by the other brigade of 17th Division, 63 Brigade. Next evening, under bright moonlight, the unsuspecting Japanese were allowed to approach to within a hundred yards of the Gurkhas' position before the latter opened up with heavy and accurate fire. The Japanese fled in confusion, only to try once more after an hour, but again heavy firing drove them back. Thereafter, attack and counter-attack continued during the next morning with the Japanese suffering severe losses until it was time for the Gurkha battalions to be ordered, one by one, to withdraw. Kyaukse was a model rearguard action as it caused the Japanese to deploy in strength, thus holding up their advance, as well as inflicting many casualties on them. One regimental historian summed up the battle: 'At Kyaukse we were masters of the situation from the start.'

However, there was no hope of holding the invading force so the retreat became a race against the weather as well as against the enemy. If the monsoon broke, the road back to India would have become an impassable quagmire. It was also a race against starvation because if the withdrawal took too long, the meagre stocks of supplies along the road would prove to be insufficient. In the end, the forces under General Alexander (then GOC Burma) made it and on 21 May, the Gurkha battalions marched out of Burma, just as the monsoon broke. They were tired and defeated but certain that it was not the end and that they would return to win the final round. With the heavy monsoon season upon them, and both sides suffering from severe logistical problems and with disease rife (in particular malaria), major operations along the Burmese border with India came to an end until early 1943.

Early next year, the Japanese showed signs of stirring, with minor incursions into the Chin Hills, where 48 Brigade from 17th Division was sent with orders to take over and protect the Tiddim area. At the time 48 Brigade consisted of three Gurkha battalions, 1/4th, the re-formed 2/5th and 1/7th. During the first few weeks of 1943 the Japanese objectives were limited in intention until the other brigade in 17th Division, 63 Brigade, took over the operational commitments.

General Wavell, by now Commander-in-Chief in India, appreciated that it would not be possible to take any major offensive action for some considerable time; as a consequence, he was attracted by the idea of British and Indian forces operating behind the Japanese forward positions, with all supplies being air dropped, whenever the tactical situation so permitted. Soon to stir the imagination of all, from Winston Churchill down to the newest recruit in India, came the exploits of Wingate and his Chindits. Appointed commander of 77 Brigade, Wingate was soon to be a famous figure in the Burma war: a man who possessed a restless temperament, eccentric in dress, speech and habit, yet who had the complete confidence of the taciturn Wavell.

Orde Wingate's part in the campaign aroused bitter controversy at the time and the debate has continued to excite historians to this very day. It was not what Wingate (soon to be promoted major-general) achieved in 1943 that mattered: indeed, the few stings his long-range penetration (LRP) columns inflicted on the Japanese were minuscule in effect and costly in lives. On the other hand, the propaganda value to the Allied cause in South-East Asia, as well as lessons learnt of immense value– even if this was grudgingly admitted by the more orthodox senior officers. Wingate held many convictions about jungle fighting which he imparted in crisp and colourful language, and these were soon to be practised by his troops in a series of tough, imaginative exercises in Central India.

Only one Gurkha battalion went on the first Chindit operation, launched on 8 February 1943 under the code name Operation 'Longcloth'. The selection of the battalion, the 3/2nd, reflected Wingate's theory that a newly raised unit could be easily moulded to his ideas: he accepted their inexperience and assumed responsibility for the training that would outweigh their immaturity. The uneven calibre of the British and Gurkha soldiers selected as guinea pigs for the first ambitious experiment made a difficult operation even more hazardous. Despite the ruthless pruning that took place during the weeks of hard training before the column set off into Burma, the results were not so fortunate. As far as the 3/2nd was concerned, all might have been well if the unit had fought under its own officers but as it was, sub-units were deliberately mixed and the junior commanders were as inexperienced as the men they led. Not surprisingly, the results achieved by the columns operating across the Chindwin River were not nearly as dramatic as reports published at the time. The cost in men was heavy, especially when the sick were added to the battle casualties. Mistakes were made; at every level a few commanders cracked, and several of the British and immature young Gurkha soldiers were found wanting. Wingate was to criticize the Gurkhas as being mentally unsuited for the role given them in the first Chindit expedition but events thereafter showed them to be ideal troops for any type of warfare in the jungle. By splitting the men up and mixing units and simply not understanding that Gurkha soldiers need a different type of leadership from the British, Wingate failed to exploit their best qualities.

Officers and men from the 3/2nd were divided up between four columns and each column was to undergo a series of harrowing experiences, including being ambushed by the Japanese. Many survived, and some without credit – while others died from drowning, sickness, and starvation, as well as by the bullet and after torture by their ruthless Japanese captors. C Company of the 3/2nd was more fortunate as it served under the command of the ex-Sapper officer, Major Mike Calvert. His column achieved much and was often in contact with the Japanese but by inspired leadership, Calvert kept them out of serious trouble until, in the end, he reluctantly decided to split his column into nine groups each of forty men, who were then sent off to attempt the return to India by various routes. Over 200 arrived back safely so that it could be claimed that Calvert and his men, despite their tribulations, had achieved worthwhile results. Back in India the 3/2nd gradually re-formed after its traumatic experiences which resulted in 446 being lost in Burma, of whom 150 subsequently returned by one means or another.

While the Allied press praised the gallant Chindits and lionised the eccentric figure of Orde Wingate, the survivors inevitably asked the question: had it been worth it? The lessons were evaluated and Wingate, with the full support of Churchill and other Allied senior commanders, then asked for troops of the highest quality for his next venture. This time the special force was to be much larger and four Gurkha battalions were selected for the rigorous training that took place before the operation began. Operation 'Thursday' was a large and complex operation involving six brigades which flew into Burma during February 1944. The initial fighting centred on 77 Brigade, under Mike Calvert (now a brigadier), who led the fly-in to 'Broadway' (the landing zone) and continued fighting there and thereafter until the final victory at Mogaung, more than four months later. Under the command of Calvert were two Gurkha battalions, the 3/6th and 3/9th, and after their fly-in, it was not long before the first big skirmish occurred when Pagoda Hill near Henu was captured: much hand-to-hand fighting occurred with bayonet and kukri before the hill was taken, with the brunt of the fighting being done by the South Staffordshire Regiment, strongly supported by 3/6th Gurkhas.

Under Mike Calvert's inspired leadership the Chindit base near Henu, code-named 'White City', was converted into a stronghold and it was not long before the Japanese made every effort to evict Calvert and his troops from that position. There was much marching and counter-marching, accompanied by bouts of bitter fighting which resulted in heavy casualties expecially among the British officers of the two Gurkha battalions. By this time, the Chindits had another commander when Brigadier Joe Lentaigne (late 4th Gurkha Rifles)* was promoted major-general to succeed General Orde Wingate, who had been killed in an aircraft crash in the jungle on 24 March. After such ordeals the officers and men in 77 Brigade were near exhaustion and fully expected to be flown out to India, but to their dismay orders were received to move over 150 miles north and capture the town of Mogaung, thus directly assisting the Chinese forces under US General Joseph Stilwell to make progress towards Myitkyina. The march was extremely harrowing, especially as the monsoon had broken in all its fury. By now the units comprising 77 Brigade were mere skeletons of their former selves, each mustering no more than 230 all ranks, while many of those who struggled to keep up were suffering from malaria, dysentery or trench foot.

The battle for Mogaung, which began one night in the first week of June, lasted for sixteen days until the Japanese withdrew: it was an action which brought great honour to the 6th Gurkha Rifles. When the battle began, Calvert's brigade was over 2,000 strong; when it ended that figure was down to 806 effectives. For three days the assaulting troops saw some hard fighting before capturing objectives outside Mogaung itself. A vital bridge on the western approaches was strongly held by the Japanese who defied, firstly, the Lancashire Fusiliers, then a company of the 3/6th which lost thirty men and were pinned down. Only after outstanding bravery by Captain Michael Almand of the 3/6th were the defenders overcome and the bridge captured. Thereafter, the Japanese fought with their normal fanatical bravery and progress was painfully slow: it was not until the night of 21 June that the centre of the town was reached. Every yard had to be fought for, every success had to be held against vicious counter-attacks.

The early hours of 3 June heralded the greatest day in the history of that wartime

* Lentaigne handed over to his Brigade Major, John Masters of the 4th Gurkhas, who had to order the evacuation of the 'Blackpool' stronghold. After the war Masters was to gain fame as a writer and novelist.

A rifleman of the 8th Gurkha Rifles with a Bren gun returns from a patrol, Burma, 1943

battalion, the 3/6th Gurkha Rifles, and in particular, B Company, which had a tough struggle against a Japanese stronghold known as 'Red House'. Only after a fierce fight was the position captured. During the attack two members of the company were to win Victoria Crosses. Captain Michael Almand – who had already distinguished himself with two acts of outstanding bravery – although suffering so badly from trench foot that he could hardly walk, struggled alone through deep mud and single-handedly charged a Japanese machine-gun post before

he fell mortally wounded. He died during the night of 23 June. Fortunately the winner of the other Victoria Cross, Rifleman Tulbahadur Pun, was to survive the attack on Red House. Accompanied by two riflemen he charged the building before going on alone when his companions fell badly wounded: firing from the hip, Tulbahadur covered some thirty yards of open ground before reaching the building, where he killed the Japanese machine-gunners and put the other defenders to flight. The outstanding courage of these two men inspired the rest of the battalion in the eventual capture of Mogaung.

Elsewhere other Chindit brigades were engaged in serious fighting, too. In June 111 Brigade was ordered to capture Point 2171, overlooking the Mogaung River, a position firmly held by the Japanese. The prolonged struggle first to capture and then hold that objective, which took place between 20 June and 5 July, was won but caused great suffering to those who participated. Taking part were the 3/4th and 3/9th and three British battalions from 14 Brigade, with every unit weakened by battle casualties and sickness. They were told that it was to be their last 'show', and that it would be over quickly: in the event, however, weeks passed until the operation became an endless nightmare. It was during an attack on a ridge from where Point 2171 was clearly visible that the 3/9th advanced despite murderous fire. Major J. Blaker, who had been an outstanding leader during the whole campaign, led the final assault until he was mowed down by bullets, but such was his example that the 3/9th moved forward in a wild charge which drove the Japanese off the peak. Major Blaker was awarded a posthumous VC.

The 4/9th Gurkhas have not been mentioned so far during Operation 'Thursday'. Originally part of 111 Brigade, they were detached in March 1944 to become the main component of 'Morris Force', whose task was to block the road from Bhamo up to Myitkyina, thus directly supporting Stilwell's advance towards that area. This they did effectively from March through to May of that year. Having carried out their mission for many weeks, they were approaching the ninety-day deadline after which they were due relief, when, in the middle of May, Morris Force was put under direct command of General Stilwell. By this time the physical and mental condition of the officers and men was deteriorating quickly, and the series of orders and counter-orders received from Stilwell's headquarters did not help their morale. An American liaison officer went to visit Morris Force and after seeing the physical state of the men, he stongly supported the view that they should be withdrawn from operations at the first available opportunity. Eventually they flew out from Myitkyina airfield on 17 July and, after a long leave, restarted their training with gusto. The 4/9th's enthusiasm was based on the experience gained during their prolonged blocking of the Bhamo-Myitkyina road. Despite their sufferings when under Stilwell's command, the officers and men had great confidence that, if employed in a recognised Chindit role, they could repeat their successes behind Japanese lines. Operation 'Thursday', however, was to be the last action in Burma by the Chindits, who shortly afterwards were disbanded, the units being sent to join other formations. It is now time to turn the clock back and look at the decisive battles of 1944, in the Arakan, at Imphal, and around Kohima.

In the spring of 1943 an abortive attempt had been carried out by the British to drive the Japanese out of the Arakan: it had been a mismanaged operation and even though it had limited objectives, the campaign was marred by mistakes and timidity on the part of the British commanders concerned. In view of this, it was, perhaps, surprising that plans for a second offensive were finalised towards the end of the same year. The country was ideal for defensive operations, with the coast cut up into islands by the muddy tidal rivers and the hills and steep valleys covered in dense jungle, with few tracks and torrential rain falling during the monsoon season. All told, it was not the sort of battlefield that a commander would choose unless he had the ability and means to launch amphibious operations, designed to unsettle or cut off tenacious defenders. Unfortunately, the necessary landing craft were not available in South-East Asia so the only other alternative, an overland offensive, was decided upon once more.

In December 1943, British, Indian, Gurkha, and West African soldiers began to advance in a mood of cautious optimism, built up during months of hard realistic training in India. The 5th and 7th Indian Divisions both contained Gurkha battalions: the 3/4th and 3/9th in 5th Division and the 4/1st, 4/5th, 3/6th and 4/8th, at one time or another, were under command of 7th Indian Division. At first all went well and only token resistance was offered by the Japanese, but after the New Year of 1944 the whole atmosphere of the operation changed completely. Around Razabil, a halt had been called to the attack as casualties had been heavy: redeployment took place and the Sappers worked hard to build vital roads that would permit necessary logistical support to be effected. The date for the renewal of the offensive was fixed for 7 February and by that time the tactical redeployment had been completed.

It was at that moment that the Japanese under Lieutenant-General Tadashi Hanaya decided to strike first, his offensive in the Arakan being launched under the code name 'Ha-Go'. Its aim was to draw off British and Indian reserves from the main central front around Imphal where the main Japanese offensive was due to begin later in the spring, code-named 'U-Go'. The Japanese had selected ideal commanders in the Arakan to lead such a bold enterprise when, confronted by at least two British-Indian divisions, their troops set out, carrying provisions for seven days only. It was intended that their soldiers should live off the spoils of war and Hanaya and his commanders had even planned to use British weapons and vehicles as soon as these had been captured. Surprise was complete and it was not long before all land links between 5th and 7th Indian Divisions had been severed by the infiltrating Japanese soldiers. The soldiers of Nippon had done well but the long-term value of such infiltrations depended on the British retiring as soon as their land links to the rear were threatened. Unlike the 1942 campaign this did not happen.

The XV Indian Corps Commander, Lieutenant-General Sir Philip Christison, had appreciated the vital importance of retaining his administrative area at Sinzweya, the name of which was to be changed by the press to 'the Admin Box'. The Japanese 'Tanahashi Force', with great daring, rounded the left flank of the 7th Indian Division and overran Divisional HQ. The GOC, Major-General Frank Messervy, managed to escape with most of his staff to reach the comparative safety of the Admin Box. Once there, Messervy resumed command of his own brigades by radio but wisely left the defence of the Admin Box in Brigadier Geoffrey Evans's hands. Evans ordered his miscellaneous force to: 'Stay put and keep the Japanese out.' Later, other units and sub-units – that had been either temporarily lost or detached in the jungle – came into the Box, including two companies of the 4/8th Gurkhas. In the Box, staff officers, clerks, administrative troops and elements of 9 Brigade of 5th Indian Division, prepared a perimeter in a dry dusty bowl of paddy fields which were surrounded and dominated by scrub-covered hills. Within this confined area, soldiers, mules, tanks, vehicles and guns were crammed together and for eighteen days they were pounded by enemy artillery, while from the encircling hills mortars and machine-guns were ranged on them.

The desperate struggle for the Admin Box continued day after day, with clouds of smoke hanging over the bowl and at fairly regular intervals explosions occurring as Japanese shells and mortars hit petrol or ammunition dumps. Supplies were dropped from Dakotas but even collecting these was difficult as every part of the area was vulnerable to enemy fire. Japanese snipers took a regular toll each day.

One of the most notorious incidents occurred when a strong raiding party of Japanese infiltrated the forward positions to enter the Box hospital. Their first act was to bayonet a number of the badly wounded while they lay helpless on stretchers: thereafter, six doctors were lined up and shot and when at dawn a counter-attack was successfully organised, the retreating Japanese withdrew behind wounded patients and medical staff, using them as human shields. As a final act of barbarity, they then murdered the hostages in cold blood. Such a horrific incident only served to heighten the defenders' resolve to stay put, to fight it out until the very end.

Elsewhere, other brigade 'boxes' were holding out and hitting back at their adversaries. Despite the fierce fighting, the British, Indian and Gurkha troops received badly needed supplies and the basic necessities by air, something that was not possible for the Japanese. They could not fight without food and ammunition; they gambled that they could live off their enemy but in spite of a long bitter siege, the rich prizes within the Admin Box were not captured. It was not possible to bring forward even a modest share of their requirements along the same jungle tracks that had been used for their strike a few days earlier. Devoid of food they were trapped and soon, for the first time in South-East Asia, a handful of Japanese soldiers began to surrender.

To describe the many spirited actions that took place would require a much longer account than this one. Magnificent fighting spirit was shown by British battalions, the squadrons of 25th Dragoons, the 4/8th Gurkhas and officers and men from the various supporting arms and services. For the defenders of the Box succour was on its way, with 26th Indian Division moving down from the north while, from the west, 5th Indian Division came across to their help and support.

At dawn on 24 February the commander of 5th Indian Division, Major-General Harold Briggs, drove into the Box to find that more than 500 wounded were awaiting evacuation: the ordeal for Brigadier Evans and his gallant men was over. Also, in the relieving force was the 1/8th, operating under the command of 26th Division. In a week of fighting near the Box, that battalion was to lose three officer casualties and twenty-three other ranks.

Elsewhere, and during the same period, the 4/1st, on a feature christened 'Abel', withstood attack after attack by the Japanese. As the tide of battle around the Box changed, so did the pressure on 'Abel' increase. For five days the Gurkhas endured constant shellfire from 150-mm guns, sited barely 3,000 yards away. Hit defences had to be re-dug and rebuilt again until, on February 22, the enemy launched a strong attack, and for two hours a fierce battle raged simultaneously at five different platoon positions. Japanese corpses piled up along the battalion's front but despite the heavy casualties the attacks were unsuccessful. Following such a costly failure of direct assaults, the Japanese tightened the ring about the defenders, with the aim of blocking all supplies into the perimenter. A measure of resupply did manage to get through by night: the defenders had to live on meagre fare – which meant half a mess tin of lentils and rice and two chapattis* a day per soldier. Water, too, was strictly rationed.

In the whole area, the Japanese were now beginning to retire but continued to attack certain defences at 'Abel' until the beginning of March, when the 4/1st was relieved and the whole of 'Abel' was cleared two days later. During the intense fighting, the 4/1st lost 6 British and 2 Gurkha officers and 225 other ranks killed or wounded.

The second campaign in the Arakan was over. It represented, as General Slim later wrote, 'one of the historic successes of British arms. It was the turning point of the Burma Campaign.' The legend of the Japanese superman, the soldier invincible in battle, had been smashed and, as a consequence, the morale of Slim's Fourteenth Army rose in a remarkable fashion. By the end of May 1944 that year, the monsoon season brought large-scale operations in the Arakan to a virtual standstill. Both sides there realised that the outcome of the next phase in the campaign, the 'U-Go' offensive aimed at Imphal, would dictate the course of their own activities after the monsoon rains had ended.

For the Japanese in Burma the tide was turning; they could see the gathering strength of the British around Imphal, fully realising that a major offensive was about to be launched which would be difficult for them to withstand. 'U-Go' was devised to counter this threat but although tactically sound in conception, its execution relied on an over-optimistic approach to administrative problems. The Japanese generals were confident that they could capture the towns of Imphal and Kohima before moving westwards to the border with Bengal – although no specific measures had been prepared for an advance that would have taken them any further into that province. The Japanese Fifteenth Army had a tough ruthless army commander in General Renya Mutaguchi, who was in a confident mood when the dramatic onslaught against the British-Indian IV Corps was launched on 7 March 1944.

On the face of it, Mutaguchi had little cause to be optimistic: his army was made up of three experienced infantry divisions, 15th, 31st, and 33rd, about 100,000 front-line troops in all. In all other respects, he was outnumbered, outgunned and, in the end, he was to be outmanoeuvred in the struggle for Imphal, his task being made doubly difficult because the Allied air forces ruled the sky. Mutaguchi staked the previous invincibility of the Japanese soldiers against the overwhelming odds which confronted them and this mistaken belief so blinded him, that he failed to appreciate the hard logistic realities which faced his men. In the past, their superior mobility in the jungle meant that they had surrounded British formations and, whenever that occurred, their opponents had withdrawn, usually in considerable disorder. But recent events in

* Chapattis – flat round pancakes of unleavened bread.

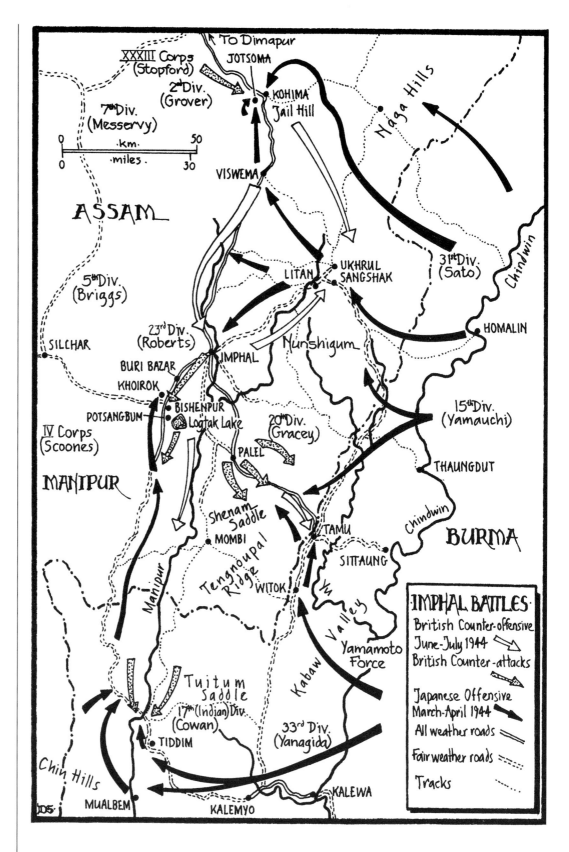

the Arakan had shown that times had changed, and with an eleborate air resupply organisation, troops who were cut off would stand fast and continue to fight.

Although General Slim was aware of the Japanese intentions, he was surprised by the speed of their initial advances towards Imphal. Thereafter he reacted with speed: reinforcements came by air, by rail and by road to defend Assam and East Bengal.

Nevertheless, east of Imphal 17th Indian Division, which included several Gurkha battalions, was to fight many battles, clear many roadblocks, and cover many miles in non-stop fighting over four months, before the overall Japanese threat was defeated.

One of the first indications that Japanese columns were moving west came from a report of a young rifleman of the 1/10th Gurkhas who became separated from the patrol he was accompanying. Soon afterwards, other reports followed and 17th Division was ordered to fall back on Tiddim. Such an order came as a shock to the Gurkha battalions, for in local clashes and by aggressive patrolling they had gained a moral superiority over the Japanese. However, by now General Slim knew that three Japanese divisions were moving west so that 17th Division would soon come under pressure, as well as being in danger of being cut off when the enemy positioned themselves across the Tiddim Road near the Tuitum Ridge.

At the Tuitum Ridge between 14 and 25 March and after three Gurkha battalions (1/3rd, 1/4th and 1/10th) had scattered the Japanese advance guards and destroyed half their number, the 1/10th was ordered to cover the first stage of the withdrawal of the division towards Imphal, the battalion acting as a rearguard as the other units retired along the road. For several days and nights the Japanese hurled themselves repeatedly against the defenders. The 1/10th took the brunt of these onslaughts, holding firm until relieved by the 1/3rd. The battle for Tuitam Ridge was probably the 1/10th's most successful action during the whole Burma campaign and as a token of his high esteem, the GOC 17th Division, Major-General 'Punch' Cowan, granted the battalion the unique privilege of flying his divisional 'Black Cat' banner, with the regimental crest superimposed upon it, outside the Quarter Guard – a custom that continued until the recent amalgamations.

Thereafter, the withdrawal continued with 17th Division having to fight on several occasions in order to clear roadblocks. As they moved westwards, other Gurkha battalions played a significant part in ensuring that the division survived to fight again elsewhere around Imphal, in particular the 2/5th, which in a series of dogfights along the Tiddim Road suffered nearly 250 casualties. During the first week in April,

17th Indian Division reached Imphal: it had taken three weeks at a cost of about 1,200 casualties but it meant that it could help blunt the next phase of the 'U-Go' offensive.

The Tiddim Road was not the only approach to the Manipur Plain as there were two other routes the Japanese divisions could move along, one leading from Tamu in the south-east over the Shenam Pass and the other from the north-east, down the track from Ukhrul. The former approach was guarded by 20th Indian Division and that sector had remained quiet, although after the first few days of March, evidence indicated that the Japanese were about to strike. The key to this route was a range of mountains, dominated by the 6,000-foot Shenam Ridge, which separated the Manipur Plain from the Kabaw Valley. It was vital that these mountains remained in British hands in order to bar any entrance to the plain along the road from Tamu. In defence of Shenam – as well as the other main routes – many battles were fought, all of which contributed to the successful defence of Imphal itself. Three battalions of the 10th Gurkhas would between them suffer over 1,000 casualties before 21 June when the last of the Japanese roadblocks was cleared on the Imphal-Kohima Road; the battle honour 'Imphal' was awarded to all three battalions, a fitting reward for the regiment's magnificent contribution to the final victory gained there in the summer of 1944.

While it is impossible to describe here, in any detail, the fighting on the Manipur Plain itself and during the siege of Kohima – when hundreds of miniature battles took place between March and June 1944 in the Naga Hills – one or two of the more important ones will be mentioned in this account. Near Imphal the battles swirled around for several weeks in an apparently random manner before the Japanese recoiled in defeat. Hundreds of encounters, ambushes, attacks and stern unremitting defence, could not be charted then and never will be now. Unlike the war in the Middle East or in Italy, important decisions often rested with junior NCOs leading hard-pressed sections, platoon commanders and sometimes company commanders, while the more senior officers commanding at headquarters level and above, could do little but hope that they had properly trained and prepared their men for this ordeal by fire. In the last resort, victory

Men of the 3/10th Gurkha Rifles consolidate after taking the feature 'Scraggy' near Imphal, 1944

depended on the morale and skill of the individual soldiers, qualities and virtues that had to be sustained for long periods under inhospitable conditions and against a foe fearless and fanatical in battle.

Three of the most significant battles during this period occurred around the village of Kohima; at the high Shenam Pass already mentioned; and at the village of Bishenpur, some sixteen miles south-east of Imphal where the Silchar Track came in from the west to join the Tiddim Road. In all these battles Gurkha battalions were heavily involved, a fact that was recognised after the war when battle honours were granted in official recognition of their gallant prowess in battle. During late May and early June the battles that were fought for the Shenam Pass features were bitter ones indeed. One of the peaks, nicknamed 'Scraggy' because of its appearance, was the foremost defended locality on the the pass and here 37 Gurkha Infantry Brigade earned itself great fame. In the brigade, the 3/3rd, 3/5th and 3/10th, all wartime battalions, played significant parts in the struggle, which did not end until 24 June when B Company, 3/10th, spearheaded a pre-dawn attack. Shouting 'Ayo Gurkha!'* the Gurkhas surged forward until eventually the Japanese had had enough, heralding the great victory won by 37 Brigade.

While the battle for Kohima raged, the Silchar track, the last link to Assam, had been closed to the defenders. From the hill village of Ningthaubang the Japanese were only twenty-one miles from their final destination, Imphal, which appeared to be within their grasp. When this struggle began, conditions worsened as the monsoon that year came early. By the middle of May life was miserable for all concerned: dry watercourses became torrents and paddy fields were swamped, while weapon pits and foxholes on the hills were soon full of muddy water. For the Japanese there was one major consolation because the thick white mist that rose from the sodden soil in the early mornings hid them from the prying eyes of the Allied pilots, who enjoyed almost complete superiority in the air. Around Bishenpur a fierce battle raged, for both sides appreciated that this was a battle of crucial importance. Deeds of valour abounded. Three Gurkha soldiers and a British sergeant from the 1st West Yorkshire Regiment each won the Victoria Cross during these battles; two of the Gurkhas were serving in the 3/5th while the third, Rifleman Ganju Lama, 1/7th, rose to extraordinary heights of courage by winning the MM and VC in two separate actions within the space of a few days. It was the bravery of such men, British, Indian and

* 'The Gurkhas are here.'

Gurkha, that restored the dangerous situation around Bishenpur.

The 32nd Brigade, which contained the 3/8th and 4/2nd, saw much fighting around this area, as did the 1/4th which had been detached from 17th Indian Division to help stem the Japanese advance. The 1/4th was involved in actions around a feature called Scrub Ridge where the battalion was to lose several British officers, including the commanding officer, in fighting at close quarters. That gloomy casualty list reveals all too clearly what easy targets British officers were at close range when serving with the Gurkhas, especially in Burma.

The epic struggle for Kohima, which is widely regarded as one of the decisive battles of the Second World War, was fought in an area measured in yards, while the numbers defending the British positions there were comparatively few. The early capture of Kohima was an integral part of Mutaguchi's 'U-Go' offensive: during the first part of the siege no Gurkha Brigade units were present but there were those of Nepalese extraction who fought with the 3rd Assam Rifles, in addition to an undertrained Nepalese State battalion, also in the garrison. Great renown was won by the garrison, especially the battalion group under command of the CO, 4th Royal West Kent Regiment. For sixteen days that small force repelled attacks launched by vastly superior numbers of Japanese troops; constant attacks which continued until the siege was lifted on 20 April.

That was first phase of the Kohima battle because there was still much bitter fighting to follow: the GOC Japanese 31st Division, Major-General Kotoku Sato, had not given up hope of winning. Soon units from 7th Indian Division were involved in attacks on Japanese positions; these included the 4/1st which, with great dash, captured Basha Hill: thereafter for two days and nights the Gurkhas were shelled and subjected to attack after attack. Defences had to be repaired and re-dug until it was time for the 4/1st to resume the offensive during which, for three days, they met fanatical resistance from the Japanese, who fought defiantly from a series of bunkers. It was a victorious 4/1st Gurkhas

Two Japanese tanks destroyed by Rifleman Ganju Lama, VC, MM, 7th Gurkha Rifles, with a PIAT anti-tank weapon in June 1944, the feat for which he was awarded his VC

Kohima – Naga village
after the battle

that was finally relieved by the 4/5th. By this time General Sato had decided that his 31st Division had had enough, and he therefore addressed a plea to his army commander, Mutaguchi, asking that his men be allowed to withdraw while there was still an opportunity to do so. Outnumbered by at least five to one, with a long tenuous supply line which the heavy rainstorms had almost closed, the soldiers of 31st Division were woefully short of ammunition, food and medical supplies. Realistic though it was, Sato's request was against all Japanese military traditions so that he was replaced after he began leading the survivors in a withdrawal towards the River Chindwin. The struggle for Kohima was over, the road to Dimapur was open and the once formidable Japanese 31st Division had been reduced to a disorganised rabble.

By now even the redoubtable Mutaguchi knew that his army could not win but being the man that he was, he continued to exhort his tired soldiers to make one final effort: 'If your hands are broken, fight with your feet... If there is no breath in your body, fight with your ghost. Lack of weapons is no excuse for defeat.' Nevertheless, at the time he made this dramatic appeal, Mutaguchi was seeking permission to withdraw and, on 2 July that was duly given him: he could now attempt to withdraw the remainder of Fifteenth Army in a search for refuge east of the Chindwin. Operation 'U-Go' was over.

About the importance of the battle for Imphal the Japanese themselves had no doubts whatever – one verdict declaring that: 'The disaster at Imphal was perhaps the worst of its kind yet chronicled in the annals of war.' Japanese official figures show that 30,000 were killed in battle, while hundreds died after the defeat

Men of the 10th Gurkha Rifles guard Japanese prisoners

became a rout, victims of sickness, malnutrition and exposure. The whole of Fifteenth Army was shaken by the defeat, with grave repercussions on the morale of the dejected soldiers. Despite all that, even in defeat the majority chose death, either in battle or from starvation, with typical stoicism and courage rather than accept ignominious surrender. The spirit of Bushido* still ruled the soldiers of Nippon.

It was now time to plan to cross the River Irrawaddy and push on to final victory. As 1944 drew to a close, General Slim's

The 17th Indian Division banner presented to the 1/10th Gurkha Rifles by the division's GOC, in recognition of the battalion's defence of the Tuitum Ridge during the siege of Imphal, and for capturing the division's first Japanese prisoners in Burma

* The feudal code of the samurai, emphasising courage, loyalty and self-discipline.

The 4/6th Gurkha Rifles cross the River Irrawaddy in January 1945

Fourteenth Army was poised to reconquer Burma. He planned a battle of movement on the North Burma Plain, the left-hand pincer aimed at Mandalay while the right struck at Meiktila, seventy miles to the south. Meiktila was the hub of the Japanese communications and was on the road and rail routes to Rangoon. In November 1944, brigades crossed the Chindwin to begin the advance to the Irrawaddy. Even reaching that river entailed hard slogging, almost entirely on foot, while such a rapid advance could only be maintained by supply by air. On reaching the Irrawaddy, the British forces were faced with a river 800 yards wide, near the east bank of which stood the ancient city of Mandalay. The Japanese withdrew the bulk of their forces across the river during the night of 14 January 1945 with the aim of counter-attacking Fourteenth Army bridgeheads as and when they were established on the east bank.

Slim ordered 19th Indian Division to go after them, and 64 Brigade, in which the 1/6th was serving, was ordered to establish a bridgehead across the river. From the moment their bridgehead was established, there were a series of Japanese counter-attacks which resulted in tough fighting. It was only on 26 February that 19th Division was able to break out of the bridgehead but

even then their advance was still contested with ferocity by the enemy. Also serving in the division was the wartime-raised 4/6th, now meeting the Japanese for the first time.

Appreciating that the battle for Mandalay could be a hard slog with heavy casualties resulting, Slim ordered 17th Indian Division to strike for Meiktila, some seventy miles south of the division's bridgehead. In addition, and again to draw off large forces of defenders from Mandalay, 20th Indian Division crossed the river opposite Myinlu: in this division were five Gurkha battalions; the 1/1st and 3/1st, 3/8th and 4/2nd, together with the 4/10th in the same brigade. The 4/10th had been given the nickname 'The Non-Stop Gurkhas' by the military Correspondent of the *The Times*, earned by their independent mission at the end of 1944 when they crossed the Wainggyo Gorge. Now, during some fourteen days and nights in the middle of February, the 4/10th was to win its finest victory. Having captured the village of Talingon, the battalion found itself attacked repeatedly by the Japanese. At times it looked as if the Gurkhas would be overwhelmed by superior numbers but they stood fast, with their CO showing great moral courage in bring down artillery 'defensive fire' close to and even on top of one of his own company positions. Between 16 and 26 February 1945, the 4/10th lost 50 killed and 127 wounded in that prolonged battle but they virtually wiped out the counter-attacking Japanese 16th Regiment by inflicting 953 casualties – which included at least 500 killed. Two armoured bulldozers had to be called on to dispose of the corpses of their enemy.

Meanwhile the battle for Mandalay could not be joined until the little village of Kyaukmyaung had been captured and then held against further Japanese attacks, which went on for nearly five weeks in an attempt to destroy the enlarged bridgehead. All three Gurkha battalions in the 19th Division, the 4/4th, 1/6th and 4/6th, were engaged in this struggle, which often entailed hand-to-hand fighting. In the end 19th Indian Division broke out on 22 February, with mixed columns of tanks, armoured cars, infantry and guns streaming across the plain towards Mandalay. On 7 March the British stood outside the gates of that city.

The Japanese had set up strongpoints among the ruined buildings and it would have been an extremely tough nut to crack, had not the British drawn off defenders by capturing Meiktila two days before Mandalay itself fell. In this important victory, the motorised and armoured troops of 17th Indian Division played a crucial part. An exhilarating sweep across the plain to Meiktila provided a complete and welcome change after countless weeks of cautious silent movement in the jungle. During the final attack on the town, 48 and 63 Brigades both had crucial roles to perform. As a consequence, all six Gurkha battalions serving in those brigades at that time played their full part in the fall of Meiktila, with General Slim subsequently writing about A Company, 1/7th's attack: 'It was one of the neatest and most workmanlike bits of infantry and armoured minor tactics I had ever seen.' It was by such tactics, in conjunction with close support from the tanks, that the Gurkha companies eventually triumphed over the Japanese defenders. By 7 March the town was in British hands but this was to be only the first phase of a tough battle. The Japanese lost no time in calling in other troops to recapture Meiktila and in a short time 17th Division, in turn, found itself besieged. A serious crisis faced the divisional commander, General 'Punch' Cowan, when his supply line fell into Japanese hands, while the British hold on the airfields nearby was contested with such violence that more than once these changed hands. Only at the end of March was Japanese resistance broken with General Hyotaro Kimura, Commander-in-Chief Japanese Burma Army Area, subsequently describing the siege and

Men of the 10th Gurkha Rifles advance through Prome, May 1945

On the road to Mandalay –
Gurkhas with a British officer
accompanied by a Grant tank

capture of Meiktila as the 'masterstroke of the whole campaign in Burma – the stroke which sealed the fate of his armies in that theatre.'

In Mandalay itself there was one feature, Mandalay Hill, which was 700 feet high, nearly a mile long, honeycombed with tunnels and passages and covered with pagodas. By 10 March, the 4/4th Gurkhas and the 2nd Royal Berkshire Regiment had secured most of the hill but still fierce fighting continued, with the Japanese rear parties refusing to give an inch. In addition, another feature, Fort Dufferin, presented a major problem for the attackers as its walls extended for 2,500 yards, being 30 feet high and 4 feet wide, backed by an earth wall and surrounded by a 40-yard-wide moat, filled with water. Moreover, the recent Allied bombing had reduced several nearby well-constructed buildings to ruins which then became ideal strongpoints during the street fighting. On 10 March, the 1/6th moved forward to take part in the battle for Fort Dufferin but using the natural advantages

they had, the Japanese defended fanatically against attempts to scale the walls, which also proved resistant to modern artillery and aerial bombing, both of which did little damage other than burn the houses within the fort. Full-scale attacks were planned for 24 March but before these could take place, the Japanese pulled out during the night of 19/20 March.

Prior to that, the task of capturing the holy Mandalay Hill had been given to the 4/4th. During their attack, outstanding acts of bravery inspired the Gurkha soldiers to fight their way up the hill and once there to reinforce those who held the crest. Individual battles within the buildings themselves were often decided by the Gurkhas drawing their kukris and closing in upon the Japanese. The gruesome killing at close quarters was too much for those Japanese who survived and they took safety in flight.

Although the war was far from over, the capture of Mandalay and the Japanese defeat at Meiktila marked a watershed in the Burma campaign of 1944-45. The race for Rangoon now began, a race not only between British and Indian divisions to get there first, but also a race against the weather, because it was essential to open the supply port before the monsoon broke and left Fourteenth Army floundering on the plains, with its vehicles and armour bogged down in a quagmire of mud. General Slim was determined that Rangoon would be occupied before the middle of May.

The first blows against Rangoon began with an airborne attack on Elephant Point, near the city, carried out by a composite Gurkha parachute battalion. The men, all volunteers, had been training for three years, waiting for such a chance. By late 1942 the 3/7th had become a parachute battalion, to be designated 154th (Gurkha) Parachute Battalion in 1943: prior to that, 153rd (Gurkha) Battalion had been raised from volunteers from the whole Gurkha Brigade, the largest number coming from the 2nd Gurkhas. Both units were redesignated as the 2nd and 3rd (Gurkha) Battalions, Indian Parachute Regiment, in November 1945.

Elephant Point was to be the only time paratroopers were used in their traditional role in the Burma campaign. On 1 May 1945 the Gurkhas dropped successfully in the area of Tawkiai on the west bank of the river, landing without any problems. Once there, however, they encountered some thirty Japanese who had either been left behind to observe or had been forgotten by their superiors. The little band fought to the death and only one wounded man survived. But the action was not one-sided in terms of casualties because the Gurkhas lost more than did the Japanese. The majority of the Gurkha casualties were caused by American aircraft which hit the paratroopers harder than the enemy did: their inaccurately aimed sticks of bombs tragically brought death and understandable bitterness at the time. As the Gurkhas battled with the Japanese, minesweepers began clearing the river: next day 36 and 71 Brigades, both from 26th Indian Division, landed on the east and west banks, ready to probe towards Rangoon as well as linking up with the paratroopers. In the end, Rangoon, which had been in Japanese hands for three years and two months, was occupied without any fighting on 6 May 1945, two days before the final surrender of Germany in Europe. The fight for Burma was nearly over

although hundreds more Japanese were to die as they tried, in vain, to batter an escape route through the cordon of British and Indian troops in Central Burma. In mid-July one major attempt to break out was made when the waiting 17th and 19th Divisions inflicted terrible punishment on the enemy. Eight days later, on 25 July, the Japanese Army in Burma capitulated.

On 14 August 1945, just after Japan had surrendered, the British landed in Malaya. Although posterity has condemned the Allied use of atomic bombs at Hiroshima on 6 August and at Nagasaki on 9 August, it

'Action stations' – a Gurkha parachutist standing in the door of an aircraft

Operation 'Dracula', the drop by a Gurkha parachute battalion on Elephant Point, Rangoon. Japanese dead outside a bunker

Operation 'Dracula' – Captain A. G. Rangaraj, the Medical Officer of the Gurkha parachute battalion, treats a Japanese prisoner, watched by Gurkha parachutists

must not be forgotten that those bombs saved perhaps hundreds of thousands of Allied and Japanese lives: if Malaya had been contested and, more important, landings on Japanese soil itself had been attempted, the loss of life, civilian and military, would have been horrific. Japan's sudden surrender, however, led to other problems in the Far East as British and Indian troops had to police areas and guard large bodies of bewildered and dejected prisoners of war: in all these operational tasks Gurkha battalions played their full part. In French Indo-China,* 20th Indian Division, which contained five Gurkha battalions, found that nationalist groups were clashing with the advanced elements of the French colonial regime who were returning to a much changed country. The division landed in Saigon to find a menacing situation, with open conflict between the French and their former subjects already resulting in bloodshed. A shortage of British troops forced the GOC of the division, Major-General Douglas Gracey,

* Now Vietnam, Laos and Cambodia.

into using Japanese prisoners of war in a variety of tasks, often as assistants and collaborators and, on one or two occasions, as comrades in arms.

For about a month the Gurkhas in Saigon were virtually at war again. The rebel forces showed they had already studied the art of guerrilla warfare and the war diarist of the 2nd Gurkhas complained: 'In such a country the Annamites always had the first shot. It was annoying they never stayed to bear the brunt of the attack but always faded into the countryside where it was almost impossible to follow them without sustaining casualties.' Years later such words would be echoed by, first, the French, and then the Americans in their respective wars in Vietnam. Only after the French were outwardly in control did 20th Indian Division leave that troubled land.

Another area where matters were even more delicate was Java, prior to the Japanese invasion, a Dutch colony. In October 1945 23rd Indian Division, which contained four Gurkha battalions, before carrying out an assault landing at Semarang, was informed that in some places the Japanese had handed over their arms and overall control to the Indonesian nationalists, who thereafter seized Dutch internees and prisoners of war as hostages.

Fortunately, the local Japanese commander in Semarang appreciated the danger and despite the fact that many of his men had been disarmed, was taking energetic steps to clear the town and protect the Dutch internment camps. That was the situation on the morning of 19th October 1945 when the leading companies of the 3/10th were put ashore from landing craft. They found a most confused situation and, inevitably, there were casualties but by evening the internment camps were occupied and the battalion was in full control. Open fighting broke out again and again: truces were negotiated but these did not last long. For nearly a year the Gurkhas in 23rd Indian Division served in various parts of Indonesia, never free from tension and always meeting insults. One regimental history described it as 'the Java Nightmare'. It did show, and not for the first time, that the Gurkha, with his happy disposition and tolerance, is in every respect as good a keeper of the peace as his British counterpart.

A Japanese officer surrenders his sword, Moulmein, Burma, 1945

The 3/8th Gurkha Rifles take the Japanese surrender at Saigon in 1945

Lieutenant-Colonel J. A. Kitson, CO of the 4/2nd Gurkha Rifles, receives a Japanese officer's sword, Saigon

Japanese officers surrender their swords

By 1946 South-East Asia had been restored to some degree of stability, even if, in some countries, this was to be short-lived. Gurkha battalions raised in wartime were disbanded back in India, a sub-continent on the verge of complete independence from the British Raj. Nepal had sent nearly a quarter of a million of her sons to fight against Germany and Japan and now major questions were being asked about the Gurkha Brigade: in particular, what was its future to be? Was it to be part of the new army of India, serving under Indian officers, or would it become an integral part of the British Army, elsewhere in the Far East? The war was over but its aftermath did not bring peace, either in India or in South-East Asia.

8 THE LAST DAYS OF THE INDIAN ARMY GURKHA BRIGADE

As the Gurkha battalions returned one by one to India, it was not long before all faced the first major problem, that of demobilisation. The problem of deciding who was to serve on and who was to return to their homes in Nepal was one that was not easy to resolve, particularly when sizeable groups of ex-prisoners of war returned from camps in Italy and in South-East Asia. Through no fault of their own, they had spent three or four years as POWs while younger and often junior Gurkha soldiers were being promoted on the field of battle and, in several cases, earning decorations for gallantry. Harsh decisions had to be made and understandably many found it difficult, if not impossible, to continue serving in a lower rank in peacetime and reluctantly left for their homes in Nepal, often without any form of pension whatever.

The celebrations of homecoming having been completed, the reality of life in India had to be faced because it was quite obvious that the days of the British Raj were drawing to an end. No one in authority appeared to know whether there was going to be any sort of future for the Gurkha Brigade after India received her independence. Rumours abounded, rumours that did little to help any of the British officers make important decisions about their own futures as well.

In the sub-continent of India the stability achieved under 'Pax Britannica' was changed almost overnight into a religious war between Hindus and Muslims. The Indian Army remained one element which gave some promise of eventual sanity – in spite of the fact that some long-established regiments had to be divided between Pakistan and India. In the middle of the turmoil of the civil war, and especially the slaughter along the Punjab border with the embryo (West) Pakistan, the Gurkha Brigade waited for decisions to be announced about its future. Irrespective of where each battalion was serving, the one question in every soldier's mind was: 'Does my *paltan* (regiment) stay with the British or remain to serve in the new independent India?'

To those who expected an elaborate conference or a degree of formality, the telegram from GHQ New Delhi which casually announced decisions on the Gurkha Brigade was indeed an anticlimax and a grave disappointment. The telegram stated that the 2nd, 6th, 7th, and 10th had been earmarked to join the British Army: the other six Gurkha regiments were to become part of the new Indian Army, including the 5th Royal Gurkha Rifles, which most people had forecast was a certainty to be retained by the British. For the British officers, it had been a most frustrating time as during the run-up to India's independence there had been so many contradictory statements about their future. In 1947, few, if any, officers at unit level, had the slightest inkling as to how these selections had been made. One theory advanced was that the British wanted two regiments from East Nepal (7th and 10th) and two from West (2nd and 6th), but such a mixture had never pertained in the original Gurkha Brigade where the ratio was eight Western units to two Eastern. It was also suggested that as all four of the regiments selected by the British had battalions in Burma, the choice had been made merely on the basis of administrative convenience: those battalions would not be required to return to India. At the time no one really knew the background. For that reason the letter sent by the Adjutant-General in India, Lieutenant-General Sir Reginald Savory, to all COs of Gurkha battalions is of interest:

I know the decision as to which regiments of Gurkhas are to go to the War Office must have been a surprise to you and that you must be wondering how on earth the decision was made. I am, therefore writing this letter that I may try to explain what may appear to you to be inexplicable.

The future of the Gurkhas has been the subject of prolonged negotiations at a very high level in which many were involved – the Foreign Office, the India Office, the War Office, the Government of India, the Government of Nepal, the High Commissioner in India for the United Kingdom, and last but not least, GHQ India. The negotiations have not only been very slow but also very delicate and were of a nature which made it quite impossible for me to give you a hint as to what was going on, because to have done so might have prejudiced the whole question whether or not any Gurkhas were to go to the War Office.

This delay has allowed us very little time between the date of the final decision and the 15th August.* The War Office, when stating which particular regiments they would like, said that they wished the units to be spread as widely as possible over the recruiting area of Nepal. They specified the 7th or 10th Gurkhas and two regiments of Magars and Gurungs. Among the last-named they particularly specified the 2nd Gurkhas owing to their close relationship with the 60th Rifles. The selection of the second regiment of Magars and Gurungs they left to us.

In making the final decision we had to be influenced by pressing problems of time and shipping.

Both the 7th and 10th Gurkhas have regular battalions in Burma. The 6th Gurkhas also have a regular battalion in Burma and we, there–fore, chose them as our free choice for Magars and Gurungs. All these battalions were serving under the War Office (SEALF) [South-East Asia Land Forces] and their transfer from Burma to their ulti- -mate home in Malaya would be a matter of arrangement by HQ SEALF.

The 2nd Gurkhas were the only Regiment which had no regular battalion overseas, but they were specially nominated by the War Office.

Prior to the decision being promulgated in all Gurkha battalions, only one week before Independence and Partition, the huge sub-continent of India had been swamped by a religious war, with Hindus and Muslims at each other's throats. No longer did Hindus wish to live side by side with Muslim neighbours, which, in many towns and villages they had done for years past. All this put a terrific strain on the armed forces and police because, in general, they found it difficult to act against their own co-religionist. The Gurkhas performed their duties impartially and with humanity in a raging sea of hate, fear and distrust, at a time when the British Army units were in the throes of demobilising and being repatriated to the United Kingdom. Hysteria swept over hundreds of millions of people in India and the new state of Pakistan, a terrible madness in which men appeared to have lost all sense of humanity. It is estimated that more people were killed in India and Pakistan in 1947 and 1948 than in all the battles fought by the British in the Second World War. Gangs of Muslims attacked Hindu villages, while mobs of Hindus slaughtered Muslim refugees. Millions left their homes, with Muslims making their way – if they could – to Pakistan, while Hindus were attempting to make their way back to India – if that proved possible.

Amidst this bloodshed and trauma, the Gurkha battalions, although Hindus, continued to be reliable and their impartiality was quite remarkable, considering the tremendous pressures imposed on them by politicians, both Nepalese and Indian, as well as the many uncertainties at the time about their own future in one or other of the armies. It is sad that during this period of civil unrest and almost complete anarchy, the future of the Gurkhas was put very much to one side: the British seemed to take the loyalty of the Gurkhas for granted so that they were kept in a lengthy suspense until eventually they were allowed to express an opinion. By that time, anti-British propaganda had been directed at them by the Indian Congress and by Gurkhas domiciled in India.

Inevitably, where accurate information was absent, rumours abounded and these were to have a considerable effect on the

---

* The date India and Pakistan obtained their independence

2nd Battalions of the 6th and 7th Gurkha Rifles, both of which were serving in cities of India where civil unrest was at its worst. One strong rumour which was to influence many of the Gurkha officers (VCOs) stated that if they opted to join the Indian Army, then there would be a strong chance that they would be granted full commissioned rank. As a result, several Gurkha officers did everything in their power to try to influence the men serving under them to follow their example. An 'Opt' was held in each of the battalions earmarked to be retained by the British Army, when every man was called before a board consisting of a British, an Indian and a Nepalese officer and asked to state his decision. The soldier could elect to stay with his battalion, transfer to a battalion that was to become part of the new Indian Army or take his discharge with a small financial compensation. All this was utterly bewildering to the young Gurkha soldiers, especially as they had been given so few details about what would happen to them if they remained with their battalions in the British Army. Where would they go, what were the basic terms of service, what were their chances of promotion, including the possibility of achieving full commissioned rank? Moreover, prior to 1947, Gurkha battalions had always served in India: now they were being asked to leap into the unknown and serve in Malaya or elsewhere in British-held or administered territories in South-East Asia. Few of their doubts could be resolved by the British officers, who knew no more than the men who were questioning them about their futures: not surprisingly this led to confusion and anger. General Tuker summed it up: 'Our own British fault. We have hopelessly mishandled the whole business.' Let that be the final comment on this unhappy period in the history of the Gurkha Brigade.

For the British officers serving in Gurkha regiments designated to go to India, it was a period of heartbreak. One colonel wrote: 'It was not our regiment going to India that hurt but our separation from it.' At the same time the Gurkha soldiers felt that they had, in some inexplicable way, been found wanting and as a consequence had been rejected by the British. Another officer was to write: 'The British officers were walking out and leaving them during conditions of near-chaos in India, leaving them moreover to be officered by the Indians in whose ability and integrity they had little faith.' It transpired that those who had fears about the calibre and integrity of the Indian officers posted in had their doubts quickly dispelled because, wisely, the Indian Army authorities selected high-grade officers for service with their Gurkha battalions during this most difficult period – and in subsequent years, too.

No one could claim that the hand-over of the six regiments, to the new Indian Army went smoothly and without any rancour. The Indian officers, some of whom had come from regiments which had wealthy unit messes, found it difficult to understand that all the silver in the Gurkha messes belonged to the British officers. It had to be emphasised to them that mess property and funds had always been the absolute property of the officers themselves. Negotiations had to take place, therefore, in one or two regiments with acrimony, while in others with remarkably little ill feeling. Much, of course, depended on the personalities involved. What can be said is that the Gurkha regiments which remained with the Indians have never lowered the standards of the old Gurkha Brigade. As the years passed, the Indian officers and those of British stock (who returned to the United Kingdom on pension) have formed a strong attachment to the regimental family tree and over the years, several ex-officers have returned, at regular intervals, to attend regimental functions in their old centres in India.

It is not part of this book to follow the six regiments after the old Gurkha Brigade divided: suffice it to say that they have played an important part in the Indian Army's operations as well as in world affairs. They have seen much active service in Kashmir, during the Ladakh border dispute with China, and in the wars with Pakistan, as well as on several United Nations operations throughout the world. After one of the battles with the Chinese, an Indian colonel of one of the Gurkha battalions wrote: 'Please assure the British ex-officers when you meet them that these new officers and their men did not consider any sacrifice too dear.' From that we can be sure that the traditions of the old Gurkha Brigade are in safe hands in the Indian Army of today. As one British officer was to write in 1970:

If you meet an officer of an Indian Gurkha Regiment nowadays, you will find that he is as proud to be serving with Gurkha soldiers as we are, and if you are lucky enough to be offered the hospitality of an Indian Gurkha Battalion, you will find that the men are as proud of their regiment and their officers as ever before.

So, with pride and with sorrow, the six regiments of the Indian Army Gurkha Brigade ceased to serve the British Crown and hence do not appear again in this book.

The four British Army Gurkha regiments had a most difficult beginning to the new era, especially in two battalions where the number of men who opted for service under the British was surprisingly low. Nevertheless, those few carried the hopes and traditions of their regiments across the seas to begin a new chapter in a long history. It was sad to see so many old friends select service with India under the 'Opt' yet, in certain respects, it was to prove easier to mould comparatively new battalions to a different life as part of the British Army in Malaya. During January 1948 the four infantry regiments, each of two battalions, left India for Malaya. For the older officers and men it had been a nostalgic and sad occasion when they said farewell to their regimental depots, now handed over to new guardians in the shape of Indian officers. Memories of the years gone by could not be lightly dismissed even when the future seemed to hold promise of an exciting life in the British Army.

9 WARS IN PEACE

FACING a most difficult time of change from Indian to British administration which, in many respects, were poles apart, the infantry battalions, one by one, left India for Malaya. Two of them, the 2/6th and 2/7th, were in a sadly truncated state: both had been subjected to every kind of propaganda while stationed in Delhi and Ahmadabad respectively. These two battalions now accepted large drafts of recruits, many of whom were ex-servicemen as well as a handful who, by one means or another, had managed to transfer from their original Indian Army Gurkha units. A sudden demand for recruits to be enlisted in a hurry, early in 1948, placed a great strain on the two recently organised recruiting depots, still to remain for a number of years on Indian soil. Many shortages had to be filled as soon as was possible; there was a dearth of senior Gurkha VCOs (retitled King's Gurkha Officers in the British Army until after the death of King George VI in 1952, when they became known as QGOs). Specialists, too, such as drivers, signallers and clerks were sadly lacking in every unit. Time was needed to rebuild battalions but that precious commodity was not given because in June 1948, with dramatic speed, the future of Malaya was threatened by a Communist insurrection.

Within days the security forces and the Malayan Government were fighting hard to prevent Chin Peng and the Communist bandits – soon to be called Communist terrorists (CTs) – from overrunning the whole country. The Gurkha infantry battalions were so hard pressed that even their recruits were sent out to guard vital points, and on one or two occasions without ever having fired their weapons on a range. Not surprisingly, they were ordered to use their kukris and bayonets in an emergency rather than risk hitting their friends while firing live rounds for the first time.

However, prior to describing the early days of the Emergency, it is necessary to take a quick look at the overall organisation of the Brigade of Gurkhas in Malaya. The 17th Gurkha Division was in the process of being formed, with a Major-General, Brigade of Gurkhas (MGBG), who would also be GOC of the division. In addition to the infantry battalions, it was decided that the Brigade would include Gurkha Engineers, Signals and Service Corps but in the event, the last-named was not formed until 1958. Initially, it had also been the intention to have all the smaller corps within 17th Division composed of Gurkhas. To that end, a Divisional Provost Company was raised in July 1949 which embodied both British and Gurkha NCOs. This Provost Company lasted just eight years before it changed its role to become 5 Gurkha Dog Company, Gurkha Military Police, only for that shortlived unit to disband later that year.

In 1950 Gurkha recruits were taken into the Royal Army Ordnance Corps, trained and posted to Brigade regiments afterwards, but no Gurkha Ordnance unit was ever formed. Likewise, in the same year, Gurkha recruits were enlisted into the Royal Electrical and Mechanical Engineers and trained but, as in the RAOC, no Gurkha EME unit came into being, with the men being eventually posted to one or other of the infantry battalions. A similar fate was to befall the Army Catering Corps which enlisted and trained 275 Gurkha recruits, but these, too, were posted to infantry regiments; no Gurkha ACC unit ever came into being.

It must be remembered that while all this was occurring, the Malayan Emergency was worsening and indeed, had reached the stage where a successful outcome was very much in the balance. One infantry regiment, too, had been subjected to extra stress through change: in May 1948, the two battalions of the 7th Gurkhas were ordered to convert to

Men of the 1/7th Gurkha
Rifles train as Gunners on a
25-pounder field gun

an artillery role, being redesignated respectively 101 and 102 Field Regiments, Royal Artillery (7th Gurkha Rifles). Commanding officers for the two battalions were posted in from the Royal Artillery and other Gunner officers followed, while basic training began at Tampin, organised by 26 Field Regiment, RA. However, as the Emergency worsened, the operational role of the 7th Gurkhas became an infantry one and in 1949, after becoming Chief of the Imperial General Staff, Field Marshal Slim (as he had become) decided that the 7th Gurkhas would change back from being Gunners to their traditional role as infantrymen. Batteries became companies and bombardiers became corporals overnight, and once more, their own Permanent Cadre officers* returned to the fold.

The Emergency started on 16 June 1948 when a fifty-year-old rubber planter, Arthur Walker, was murdered in cold blood by three Chinese Communists. A few miles away, still in the same district of Sungai Siput, two other European planters were bound to chairs before being shot by their Chinese captors. In such a way did the Malayan People's Anti-Japanese Army (MPAJA), quickly substituting 'British' for 'Japanese' in its title, declare war on the Government and the European community in Malaya. The

Malayan Government declared a State of Emergency on 17 June in the states of Perak and Johore and, the following day extended it throughout the Federated Malay States, an Emergency that was to last for twelve years. Prior to the violence breaking out in Malaya, there had been deep feelings of unrest and apprehension which stemmed from the Japanese occupation. Indeed, inspired by the British, crash training courses had been organised by liaison officers for the Communist guerrillas during the war who set up their camps deep in the jungle. By the time the Second World War had ended, the MPAJA mustered eight regiments, about 7,000 guerrillas in total. In the event, the dropping of the two atomic bombs and the Japanese surrender rendered an Allied invasion of Malaya unnecessary: thereafter inducements to the Malayan Chinese guerrillas to hand over their arms and disband were only partly successful, and thousands of weapons and large stocks of ammunition were unaccounted for, having been hidden in caches in the jungle, ready for the war of 'liberation'.

As far as the British were concerned, they had returned after the Japanese occupation, expecting to find the same beautiful and peaceful country which they had known

* British and Gurkha officers commissioned into the Brigade.

Malaya – guerrillas of the Malay People's Anti-Japanese Army (MPAJA) on parade

before the war. By 1948, tin was booming and so was rubber. Malaya's prosperity did not seem to be in doubt even if British prestige had waned in the post-war resurgence of Asia.

The decision to risk an all-out open trial of strength had been announced at a Politburo meeting of the Malayan Communist Party (MCP), held in the jungles of Pahang at the end of May 1948. Its leader, Chin Peng, had some 5,000 trained fighters under his command and these were supported by a much larger section of the community, the vast majority of whom were Chinese. These supporters, the Min Yuen (Masses Movement), grew food, delivered supplies,

A group of Gurkhas in the Malayan jungle

acted as couriers and sifted and passed on information to their comrades in the jungle. They were the life-blood of the bandits and came from all walks of life – although the majority were squatters whose huts and shacks were located ideally near the fringes of the jungle; many of them had relatives, friends or neighbours who had decided to take up arms against the British.

The cold-blooded murder of the British planters in June 1948 caught the Government unawares and for a few days the administration did not begin to appreciate that the Communists planned to seize power and form their own Republic of Malaya – after exterminating the Europeans in the Government as well as rubber planters and tin miners. Another great disadvantage as far as the Government was concerned was that the police force had a tiny Special Branch, far too small for the task which faced its members at the beginning of the Emergency. As a result, operational intelligence was sadly lacking which in turn meant that troops and police were rushed hither and thither in unsuccessful attempts to stave off attacks on isolated police posts, rubber estates or tin mines. On many occasions, the security forces arrived too late, their sudden abortive dash being the result of rumours which had been passed on to the local commander as being information of true operational value. The term 'jungle bashing' was used more and more to describe days of sweat and frustration without any reward and often without any sign that the terrorists had even been near that particular stretch of jungle. The National Servicemen in British units, and newly joined recruits serving in the Gurkha battalions, all had to learn the hard way – as opposed to their adversaries, the majority of whom were experienced in the art of living and fighting in the jungle as a result of years spent operating against the occupying Japanese between 1942 and 1945.

Initially, the security forces' first task was a holding operation, keeping the CTs on the move by constant searching, patrolling and ambushing but it was to take some time before even those operations could be organised properly. The pressure was particularly heavy on the Gurkha infantry battalions, most of whom had large contingents of untrained soldiers. Training Gurkha recruits has always been a lengthy, well-ordered business but during the dark days of the Emergency half-trained soldiers

were deployed on a number of occasions. As a consequence, the almost complete disruption of training within the Brigade of Gurkhas was to prove a handicap to the majority of the 1948 recruits for the rest of their service.

One of the first successes achieved against the Communist bandits by the Gurkhas happened during July 1948 in the Ipoh district. During the night of 12 July a rubber tapper came to the room of Major N. Neill, who was commanding B Company, 2/2nd Gurkhas. The rubber tapper, through an interpreter, told Major Neill that he had seen about fifty armed Chinese bandits in uniform, living in a large shelter in the jungle near by and he could lead the soldiers to the very spot. Early next morning, well before first light, under Major Neill's command men of his company moved in single file through a rubber estate in pitch darkness. Unfortunately the guide got flustered and lost his way and much time was spent before eventually he found the track to the jungle hut. By now it was getting light so Major Neill had to put caution aside as they moved with speed. It transpired that the CTs were hiding in a lean-to shelter, nowhere near where the informer originally had said they were.

A second or two later, ten figures in khaki uniform burst out of the shelter, moving away from where Major Neill stood. With no time available to give any orders, the officer raised his Sten gun to his shoulder, fired three bursts and brought down seven of the CTs. After searching the area, no sign of the other three terrorists were found. In such a way was one of the first successes of the Emergency achieved, for once without days of searching or weeks of patrolling – as was to become the pattern thereafter. Major Neill summed it up: 'Good fresh information coupled with good luck on our side, had given us our success.' Modesty did not allow him to add: 'and excellent shooting by Major Neill!'

The Gurkha battalions had to learn their trade as jungle fighters against an enemy who had received their initial training from British instructors and liaison officers during the war. The Chinese terrorists were masters of the jungle and they lived in its depths, coming out from time to time to commit atrocities. The onslaught of murder and arson terrified most of the local inhabitants who, without the guarantee of adequate protection, were reluctant to give

• ALOR STAR
Kedah
THAILAND
South China Sea
• SUNGEI PATANI
• KULIM
• GRIK
Penang I.
Kelantan
Trengganu
• LENGGONG
• GUA MUSANG
• SUNGEI SIPUT
KUALA KANGSAR •
IPOH •
• CAMERON HIGHLANDS
Perak
• JERANTUT
SLIM RIVER • • BIKAM
• FRASERS HILL
Pahang
Selangor
KUALA LUMPUR ■
• TITI
KAJANG • • KUALA KLAWANG
Negri // Jelebu • BAHAU
SEREMBAN Pass • TAMPIN
Sembilan • GEMAS
PORT DICKSON • • SEGAMAT
• LABIS
Malacca
Johore
• KLUANG
MUAR YONG PENG
KOTA TINGGI
JOHORE BAHRU
SINGAPORE

·MALAYA·
1948~60
0   100
·Miles·

information to the security forces. Witnesses to atrocities would plead ignorance rather than face the wrath of the Communists. To counter this dearth of operational intelligence, the security forces had to go into the jungle and search for the terrorists. Much time was wasted in 'jungle bashing'.

The sheer professionalism of the Gurkha soldiers enabled them to learn their trade as jungle fighters in a remarkably short time, and as the eight battalions serving in the Brigade of Gurkhas were to continue to operate in Malaya throughout the Emergency – with the occasional two-year break in Hong Kong – this was to spell bad news for the Communist terrorists. Not only did the Gurkhas learn to move through the dense jungle in silence but their natural

countryman's sense enabled them to meet it on even terms, instead of viewing it with suspicion as an enemy – unlike so many of the British National Servicemen, hailing as they often did from urban areas in the United Kingdom. Carrying five or more days' rations as well as weapons, ammunition and other necessities in big unwieldly packs, might have constituted a heavy load for the average European: for the highlanders from Nepal, well used to carrying even heavier loads in equally difficult terrain, such burdens did not pose any problems.

On the whole it was a campaign during which small patrols, often no more than a platoon in strength, searched for, and if possible brought to battle, a skilful and fanatical enemy who used the jungle as home ground. Operational tasks were tackled with quiet efficiency by the stocky men from Nepal and it was not long before the Brigade of Gurkhas had eliminated more than a quarter of the total number of CTs accounted for by the Security Forces – although the number of Gurkhas fighting at that time was a long way below a quarter of the total number of troops deployed throughout the Federation of Malaya. Encounters with the CTs were often over in a few minutes or even seconds. Once fire had been opened, the speed with which the terrorists disappeared verged on the miraculous – although at the beginning of the Emergency, there were several encounters in which the terrorists stood firm and on occasions even attacked, when operating in large numbers.

Year by year the Emergency continued so that each Gurkha battalion, following an operational tour, spent about two months in 'Rest and Recreation' when neglected administration had to be put in order, educational training and examinations held to qualify men for promotion, shooting practised to improve the chance of dropping terrorists in a split second, and men were smartened up to remind them that they would not always be soldiers in the jungle. During the two months, no battalion had much chance to indulge in 'rest' but it afforded all ranks with a vital break from operations. This busy tempo was aggravated by the fact that the strange, and sometimes complex, methods of British Army admin- istration had to be learned from scratch by young, inexperienced Gurkha clerks.

It is right that the operational exploits of the infantry battalions have been given pride of place – for two important reasons. Firstly; the Gurkha Brigade grew from an untried mixture of wartime veterans and recruits into eight efficient battalions, highly skilled in jungle operations. Moreover, the operational records of the battalions from 1948 until the end of the Emergency were remarkably similar. The mode of operating, the successes obtained and the routine – which became a veritable way of life – followed much the same pattern in each of the battalions. Secondly; if the Brigade of Gurkhas had not been on the ground during the dark days of 1948 and 1949, there is little doubt that Chin Peng and his MRLA* would have won the day for Communism in Malaya.

Before one or two outstanding operational successes in Malaya are described, it is worth recording the births of two specialist Gurkha corps during the early days of the Emergency. The original idea had been to raise a complete Gurkha division – but at a time when infantry manpower was at a premium, the early concept was modified until only two corps were raised in 1948. Although affiliated to their parent corps in the British Army, these units were an integral part of the Brigade and as such were designated in that way in the Army List. The reason for this was to ensure that all Gurkha soldiers, irrespective of arm or service, were administered by the same Gurkha Record Office in the Far East.

The Gurkha Engineers and Gurkha Signals were formed in 1948 or, to be more accurate, steps were taken to raise a first squadron of each towards the end of that year. The first Gurkha infantrymen attached to the Royal Engineers assembled in October 1948 at Kluang, to become 67 Field Squadron, RE. There were some who claimed that first-class infantry soldiers were about to become second-class Sappers but the initial drafts, by their enthusiasm and ability to learn, so convinced the Royal Engineers and HQ Brigade of Gurkhas of their potential that a second squadron, 68 Field Squadron, was raised two years later.

The first major task carried out by the Gurkha Engineers was the construction of a new road between Gemas and Tampin, a task which included the construction of a 342- foot timber-pile bridge, soon to be known as Gurkha Bridge. That bridge, completed by two of the squadrons during 1955, was to herald a multitude of other tasks, such as building roads, constructing airfields and helicopter landing zones, all over Malaya, culminating in a joint venture in the State of Kedah with British and Malayan engineers on a project which was to last three years. More often than not their work was designed to open up communications to enable the security forces to have quick access for mounting operations against the CTs. By the end of the Emergency, the Gurkha Engineers had earned themselves a reputation for being thoroughly efficient, with specialists who could operate all the same plant and machinery as their British counterparts. Their role in the Borneo Confrontation – as

*MRLA – Malayan Races' Liberation Army.

we shall see later – was to be of paramount importance.

Likewise, the birth of the Gurkha Signals towards the end of 1948 originated with a small cadre of Royal Signals officers and a few unit signallers from Gurkha infantry battalions, acting as a training team. During the months that followed the cadre instructors trained up the necessary tradesmen to form the first Independent Brigade Signal Squadron, and by the end of 1950, Gurkha Signals personnel were able to provide the communications for a brigade on active service in Malaya. From this modest start, and as more and more tradesmen were trained, signal Troops were deployed to the other formation headquarters; consequently, by 1954, the Signals Regiment was manning all the communications at the operational headquarters of 17th Gurkha Division. Initially, all officers and men in the regiment wore the Royal Signals cap badge but in 1954 a new badge, incorporating the Royal Signals emblem and crossed kukris, was approved: in such a way the infant regiment retained its links with both parents.

A third corps was raised in July 1958 under the title the Gurkha Army Service Corps, later in 1965 to be redesignated the Gurkha Transport Regiment. Being formed towards the end of the Emergency meant that the fledgeling corps did not see operational service in Malaya but the Confrontation in Borneo between 1963 and 1966 was to see the regiment win its spurs in a major role.

The action by Major Neill and B Company, 2/2nd, was to herald dozens of contacts with the CTs in which all the Gurkha battalions played their part: it is, of course, not possible to describe more than a tiny sample of such encounters.

Notable contacts occurred when B Company, 1/2nd, fought two major actions in the Labis area of Johore; one in January 1950 and the other over a year later, in May 1951. Initially, the January operation got off to a bad start, chiefly because Major Peter Richardson, the company commander, received his orders over an indifferent telephone line with the instructions being given in Gurkhali for security reasons. While he understood correctly that there was a large party of enemy in the area north of Labis, and that he was to move and kill as many of them as possible, what was misunderstoood was the road by which B Company should enter the area. As it turned out, if Major Richardson had understood his adjutant's orders, and acted accordingly, then his men would not have contacted the terrorists.

Two platoons went out under Richardson's command with the majority of the soldiers being young and very raw. In the early hours of 22 January 1950, the men moved into the overgrown rubber plantations and awaited the glimmerings of dawn. As soon as it was light enough to move without undue noise, they set off in the general direction of Labis but, after only five minutes, the leading soldiers of the right-hand platoon came under fire. Major Richardson ordered his other platoon, under the Company Sergeant-Major, to carry out a left-flanking movement in order to cut off the enemy, while he, at the head of No. 4 Platoon, charged straight in. As it happened, 4 Platoon was slow in advancing so that Richardson found himself, accompanied by two young riflemen only, in the middle of the terrorists, with the rest of the platoon well behind them. Fortunately – like Major Neill of his sister battalion – Major Richardson was a good man with a gun and he killed three terrorists, causing the others to scatter. They tried to cross some paddy fields but came under heavy fire from both B Company platoons. Despite the indifferent light and an early-morning mist rising off the paddy fields, the company succeeded in killing twenty-five of the enemy, for the loss of one of the young riflemen killed while accompanying his company commander in the initial charge. Undoubtedly the quick reaction and initiative of CSM Bhimbahadur Pun played a major part in the victory because, by taking the left-hand platoon behind the terrorists at speed, he drove them into a foolhardy attempt to cross the paddy fields. Both Major Richardson and CSM Bhimbahadur Pun received well-deserved and immediate awards for gallantry.

The Communist terrorists during the early stages of the Emergency did not always take refuge in flight, as Major Richardson and B Company were to discover, again north of Labis. On this occasion, 21 May 1951, B Company met a large party of terrorists but to their astonishment, their foe stood firm and, initially, pinned the Gurkhas down. Heavy automatic fire was directed at them as they crawled forward to about thirty yards from the terrorists before taking up firing positions. From here they engaged the enemy who could be seen darting back and forth among the trees. During this spirited engagement, two Gurkha soldiers were killed and it was not until 5 Platoon came in with bayonets fixed that the terrorists broke and retreated. During their retreat, short stands of defiance were made until the CTs had lost seventeen killed, with a further fifteen wounded – as later reported by a surrendered terrorist. An action like that rarely occurred in the Malayan Emergency because it was not often that the terrorists were as well armed or equipped and, apparently, with unlimited ammunition. During the long encounter, they fought with courage and remained in each defensive position until the last moment. Later, Special Branch confirmed that they were a picked body of men, acting as escort to Communist VIPs who were moving down to hold a meeting in the Labis area of Johore. By such stubborn defence, the terrorists ensured that the VIPs they were escorting were able to escape.

From the 2nd to the 2/7th, which in February 1953 carried out a most successful operation, an operation which highlights the skill of an Army pilot, the jungle craft and initiative of a young Gurkha NCO and the merciless precision of Gurkhas in attack. It all started with an Auster pilot, Captain K. Metcalf, who thought he saw a jungle clearing when on a routine flight from Seremban. He carried out various deception flights and for five mornings at dawn, flew south from Seremban, passing about one mile east of the suspected camp area. Only on the 6th day did he fly just east of the spur on which he thought the camp was located. Metcalf found that his original map fix was accurate and, while flying over the clearing, noticed that it was about the size of a tennis court with rows of cultivated vegetables clearly visible. The terrorists had tried to camouflage the jungle 'garden' with cut saplings but the leaves had turned yellow and were dead. Flying low at about 1,500 feet, Metcalf also saw what he thought to be the roof of an atap basha and, armed with this information made a definite report about the terrorists to Brigade Headquarters.

A joint plan was made with the 1st Battalion, Gordon Highlanders, which was to approach the area from the south, dropping off a company to set up ambushes to the east, and which was then to deploy two platoons to assault the camp. From the north, C Company, 2/7th, which was under command of the Gordons, was to approach the terrorists' camp and lay as many ambushes as possible on the north flank. The company commander, young Captain John Thornton, had forty-three men with him when the Gurkhas entered the jungle. After some ten months of 'no contacts' in spite of rigorous patrolling and ambushing, it appeared that C Company's luck might change, even though the original role that had been given them appeared to be a subsidiary one. Their move from Rompin was typical of the great care necessary to deceive the terrorists and their supporters, so it is mentioned in some detail. Two platoons actually climbed on to trucks but as many men as possible lay down so that any informer would think that one platoon only was going out on a routine task. A long and devious route was taken to the debussing point where the vehicles slowed down while the men jumped off and darted into a rubber estate. The night was very dark and it was raining heavily but the rain would wash their tracks away and that, in itself, helped the security of the operation.

As dawn broke, C Company moved south along the top of a ridge where movement was comparatively easy and set up a base about a mile away from the suspected camp. By now it was four o'clock in the afternoon and Captain Thornton immediately sent out seven patrols, each of about three men, who moved on compass bearings five degrees apart. One unpaid lance-corporal, Rabilal Rai, with two riflemen, moved due south and after about 300 yards heard the sound of voices. Creeping closer they saw two terrorists washing. It was obvious the camp was close by and probably on a spur to the right. With great courage, Rabilal decided to go by himself to the edge of the terrorist camp where he saw about a dozen enemy, all dressed in khaki uniform, carrying out various chores. Even then Rabilal did not think that his task was over and he moved slowly around the perimeter, trying to find out where the sentry posts were. Time was passing and it would soon be dark; he realised he could not complete the full reconnaissance and return to the temporary company base in the jungle, so Rabilal sent back one rifleman with his report, suggesting he should meet the company at an RV (rendezvous) prior to an immediate attack.

Thornton was faced with a dilemma: he could either move in at once, which possibly meant making undue noise that would scare the terrorists away, or he could delay the attack until early in the morning before carrying out an assault. Many other junior commanders in the jungle during the Emergency faced similar situations before deciding one way or the other: only with hindsight could each commander say whether he made the correct decision or not. In this case, Thornton had time to contact the CO of the Gordons who wisely decided that the Gurkhas' C Company was best placed to carry out the assault.

Early in the morning C Company moved in to 'cut-off' positions, along the route taken by Rabilal's patrol. The assault party, consisting of Thornton and nine men only, charged into the camp, running as hard as they could into the small area. At first, Thornton sensed that the terrorists had escaped but he had forgotten about his close cordon and suddenly all hell was let loose at the foot of a nearby spur. In the end, eight terrorists were killed and Thornton's lasting impression of the attack was the complete silence of it all before the firing started. There were no heroics; just quiet, determined competence shown by the Gurkha soldiers. His final words have a classical ring to them: 'One thing I was quite sure about – I'd never like to have the Gurkhas on the other side.'

And so to another patrol, this time by the 1/7th. Its target was a terrorist called Goh Sia, a man who was notorious in the Segamat district as he and his band had plundered extensively and murdered many of the local inhabitants: by now, he was gaining the reputation of being invulnerable and there was a reward of 35,000 Straits dollars on his head. In November 1955, a small party from the 1/7th consisting of Corporal Partapsing Rai and five men, was sent out to lay an ambush in the hope that Goh Sia would be accounted for, once and for all time. The site chosen was a patch of elephant grass, 20 yards by 30, growing in the middle of a rubber plantation. It was an isolated clearing near which a terrorist food dump had been discovered recently: there was no covered approach to the elephant grass which meant that once the ambush party was in position, it had to stay there.

The six Gurkhas' vigil lasted for three days with no cover from the sun by day or from the wet, damp cold of the night. Cooking was out of the question and the only water available was the limited supply that Partapsing and his men had brought with them. It required incredible self-discipline, complete silence with no movement whatever, and after it was all over, the NCO said that they had to answer the calls of nature where they lay! At about nine in the morning of the third day – when there seemed to be little hope of any success – Goh Sia suddenly appeared, full of confidence and clearly suspecting there was no danger because his carbine was slung over his shoulder. The terrorist leader approached the food dump, where he picked up a parcel before turning to leave. Partapsing had hoped to account for most of the enemy but, wisely, he realised the opportunity of destroying the ruthless Goh Sia must not be missed. At a given signal, a rifleman rose swiftly to his feet, a shot rang out and the terrorist leader dropped dead. There was profound relief among the local people when they heard that the supposedly invulnerable Goh Sia had been killed.

From 7th to 1/10th which, in June 1953, sent out a platoon under Lieutenant (QGO) Dhojbir Limbu to investigate and follow up a successful road ambush which twenty terrorists had carried out on a rubber estate. No fresh tracks were found immediately nor were any signs of the terrorists seen for at least two days. Neverthless, Dhojbir was ordered to follow the older tracks and so began a long arduous chase which was to take his platoon from one side of the Pengerang peninsula to the other, through some twenty-five miles of jungle swamp. The terrorists led them quite a chase, splitting into groups three or four times each day and then collecting together at an agreed RV. By such tactics the guerrillas delayed the Gurkhas and their follow-up until Dhojbir realised that their rations were running out: as a result the QGO ordered his men to eat but one small meal a day and to keep following the terrorists from dawn to dusk.

By 8 July, the Gurkhas had finished their rations as well as being extremely tired when, once more, the terrorist tracks were lost. Dhojbir appreciated that if they did not close with the terrorists that very day, then they would lose them for ever as his men could not continue without any food. Splitting his platoon into two groups, he led one of them himself and his boldness paid off. Suddenly and unexpectedly his group found a camp situated on an island in a swamp. The terrorist sentries and the Gurkhas saw each other at the same time and although heavily outnumbered by the enemy, Dhojbir's small party immediately attacked. A fierce firefight ensued, with the terrorists

Major Harkasing Rai, MC and Bar, IDSM, MM, 6th Gurkha Rifles

A Gurkha signaller in the jungle with his radio set

bringing three machine-guns to bear on the small group of Gurkhas as well as hurling grenades at them. Despite that, led by Dhojbir, they entered the camp and killed two terrorists before the others fled into the swamp, abandoning much food and ammunition as well as some weapons. One of the dead terrorists was found to have a price of 75,000 Straits dollars on his head, later being identified as a political commissar. Subsequently it transpired that none of the terrorists had realised they had been followed right across the peninsula and were confident that their precautions were sufficient to deceive any would-be pursuer. They had underestimated the toughness, perseverance and jungle skill of Lieutenant (QGO) Dhojbir and his platoon.

One further action will be described, that carried out by C Company of the 1/6th, under the command of Major (GCO*) Harkasing Rai. They were ordered to investigate a report that a band of CTs were taking refuge in the remote jungle near Fort Brooke, terrorising the Sakai aboriginals, forcing them to provide food as well as acting as their 'eyes and ears'. C Company, 1/6th set out on 2 January 1956 to investigate a rumour that there were fifty terrorists near by, with orders to track them down. At first temporary resting places were found, but it was obvious that these had been used four or five nights previously which meant that the CTs had a head start on them as they moved towards the west. By this stage in the Emergency, all Gurkha rifle companies had some experienced trackers among their men, as was proved on this occasion when Harkasing and his men followed the trail of a well-trained party, who obviously enforced strict discipline, both on the march and during their night stops. They covered their tracks well and on several occasions the Gurkha scouts lost the scent and had to cast around for up to about 600 yards before finding a clue which showed in which direction their adversaries had moved. It took perseverance, patience and considerable self-discipline; it also required a commander who had faith in the ability of his men to narrow the gap between the quarry and themselves. Harkasing and his company did this and by 9 January they knew they were within a day's march of the CTs.

* GCO – Gurkha Commissioned Officer (that is, commissioned from the ranks, and not by way of the RMA, Sandhurst).

Malaya – a train
derailed by terrorists

At midday, the leading Gurkha scout spotted a hut through the gloom of the dense jungle. In silence he signalled the information back but as the leading men began to get into position, they were fired on by a terrorist sentry, whereupon they charged into a small camp. An aboriginal was promptly killed but then the Gurkhas realised that fire was being directed at them from the main camp, some 200 yards ahead. Quickly re-forming, they charged into that camp and killed three terrorists. By this time the guerrillas had withdrawn across a nearby river and from there, they directed heavy automatic fire on to Harkasing and his men. When the Gurkhas tried to cross the river, a particularly brave Chinese terrorist, armed with a submachine-gun, covered his comrades' withdrawal and forced C Company to deploy before he moved back. Despite being chased, that brave man frequently turned to fire a few shots at his pursuers, before managing to escape.

That was the first episode of this epic patrol because although C Company lost contact with the CTs, by 11 March they were on the move again, following two-day-old tracks up a knife-edge ridge, 3,000 feet above a valley. A fresh trail was found, then lost, because by that time the CTs knew that they were being hunted: they slept in caves leaving only the smallest traces of their stay. They crawled like insects along the face of the cliffs, up crevices and down waterfalls, and yet, carefully though they moved, some small but just imperceptible sign of their passing was picked up by the Gurkhas, expert hunters of game in their own country. The follow-up continued: next day, a small patrol saw about fifteen terrorists in a temporary camp but by the time Harkasing had come forward in order to make a plan, only about ten minutes of daylight remained, so wisely he decided it was too late to attack. He and his men lay where they were: there was to be no sound, no smoking, and no cooking as the terrorists were only a stone's throw away.

Malaya – a wounded CT

Gurkha sappers at work

Next morning before dawn, C Company began to edge forward; inch by inch, they crawled in silence towards the camp until, just before daylight, a sentry challenged them. The whole company 'froze': time passed and the Communist sentry relaxed. By now it was light and Harkasing considered his intended cordon was about halfway around the camp when, once more, the same sentry challenged, but this time he did not wait for a reply before firing a long burst. Two Gurkha soldiers were wounded and in a flash, the CTs were up and away, scattering in terror and splitting into groups of two or three men. Harkasing appreciated that they would now make for an area where they could obtain food and help from local sympathisers – for it was clear that after such a long chase they were in a bad way. After reporting by radio to his commanding officer, other companies from the 1/6th were deployed in the north, to the south and in 'stop' positions in the jungle edge to the west. Those companies had further successful contacts with the hunted men, thus benefiting from C Company's herculean efforts. After suffering severe casualties, the gang split up for ever and thereafter ceased

to exert any real influence in the aboriginal settlements around Fort Brooke. Major Harkasing and his men had performed a remarkable feat of tracking and for his leadership in this long, arduous operation, Harkasing was awarded a Bar to his MC.*

The impression must not be given that the first ten years of the Brigade's service in the British Army, which coincided with the Emergency in Malaya, were spent solely in Malaya, and at grips with the Communist terrorists. Two, and on one occasion three, battalions were stationed in Hong Kong where, in a tour of about two years, soldiering was of a far more conventional nature. Such breaks from operations were necessary and during the first few months very welcome, as well as being beneficial during the cool winters in the Colony.

At the end of the Malayan Emergency in 1959 when the Major-General, Brigade of Gurkhas, in a special audience with the King of Nepal, presented his annual report on the Brigade, he stated:

I am happy to inform Your Majesty that consequent to the unrelenting efforts of the troops, the successes which they have achieved against the

* During his long service, Major Harkasing Rai was to win the IDSM and the MM, as well as the MC and Bar.

Terrorists of Malaya have resulted in all except one battalion (near the Thailand Border) being withdrawn from operations. The Brigade has earned a further 43 rewards for gallantry in the field and the total now gained by Your Majesty's subjects is 443.

Let those words summarise the part played by the whole Brigade in saving Malaya from the Communist threat. As a result that multi-racial country survived violence and bloodshed to enjoy a peaceful start as an independent nation. Thereafter peace in Malaya meant many things in the Brigade of Gurkhas. To the married officers and men it brought an end to a series of partings from wives and children; to those who disliked conventional soldiering, it heralded drill parades, 'spit and polish', ceremonial occasions and test exercises. But it was the first real peace since 1939 for the older British and Gurkha officers. A respite from the years of 'jungle bashing' was both welcome and essential as, without any doubt, the whole Brigade was becoming parochial in outlook.

Apart from success on operations, prodigious strides had been made in a vast range of activities. Gurkha boys were selected to go to Sandhurst as officer cadets and become the forerunners of the RMA-trained commissioned officers now found in every battalion. Children's schools were set up in the unit lines and further education made possible for the more promising children living in the family lines. Married quarters for the families, with appropriate medical and welfare facilities, changed from the primitive into something akin to the standard found in the nearby equivalent British units. By no means were these the only significant improvements: for example, Whitehall agreed to carry out a regular review of the Gurkha soldiers' pay and allowances to keep these in line with inflation. By 1960 it could be claimed that the Brigade had become an integral part of the British Army.

New ground was broken in 1962 when, for the first time ever, some 1,700 Gurkhas in all were stationed in the UK. Accompanying HQ 63 Gurkha Infantry Brigade (retitled 51 Brigade in England) went the 1/6th, 68 Gurkha Field Squadron, 247 Gurkha Signals Squadron and 30 Squadron Gurkha Army

Malaya – a photograph found on a CT killed by D Company, 1/2nd Gurkha Rifles, Gellang Patah, April 1955

Service Corps. In addition, a small proportion of the married men were accompanied by their wives and children, with the whole contingent being accommodated in Tidworth. As part of the Strategic Reserve, the Gurkha contingent trained in England and Wales and in certain European countries as well: they also survived a bitterly cold winter exercise in the then peaceful Northern Ireland. At the time the intention was to rotate each of the eight battalions with a tour in the UK, with a similar roster for the other squadrons from the Gurkha Engineers, Signals and Service Corps regiments. Events were to rule otherwise, for which President Sukarno of Indonesia was largely to blame.

For four years after 1958, the British Army was not actually engaged on operations anywhere in South-East Asia. However, the then Major-General, Brigade of Gurkhas, Major-General Walter Walker (late 6th Gurkhas), was convinced that another crisis would occur without warning so that his Gurkha battalions were trained to be ready to go anywhere at the drop of a hat. Such an opportunity was to arise in December 1962.

Seeds of the Confrontation between Britain and Indonesia were sown on 8 December 1962 when a rebellion broke out in the Sultanate of Brunei, an independent state under British protection in the Borneo territories. Borneo is one of the world's biggest islands, mountainous and covered in dense rainforest (until extensive logging began in recent years). Politically, it was divided in two, with the largest portion belonging to Indonesia, known as Kalimantan. Along the north-west coast were

Major-General W. C. Walker, CB, CBE, DSO, the GOC 17th Infantry Division and Director of Operations in Borneo, February 1964-March 1965

three territories, two of which, prior to the formation of Malaysia in 1963, were British colonies: Sabah (North Borneo) and Sarawak, with the small Sultanate of Brunei set in between them. President Sukarno had strong ambitions to establish a 'Greater Indonesia' which he hoped would include Malaya, Singapore and the Philippines as well as the Borneo colonies. During the late autumn of 1962 a large number of the citizens of Brunei were attracted by the idea of a Borneo Confederation, with many assuming that their Sultan, Sir Muda Omar Ali Saifuddin, would become the titular head of state. With such a small population in Brunei that might appear to have been presumptuous but by then, the 4 million tonnes of oil produced each year in the oilfields of Seria made little Brunei wealthy: in contrast, neighbouring North Borneo and Sarawak had little revenue and their natural resources had still to be tapped and developed.

Under pressure from the British and Malayan governments, Sultan Sir Omar agreed to the first-ever elections to a Legislative Council in September 1962, although he had considerable misgivings about the outcome. During the run-up to the election, the only organised party, the Partai

Raayatt (People's Party), exercised more and more influence, with its public aim being to establish – by force if necessary – a Confederation of Borneo States.

After the Partai Raayatt duly won all sixteen seats in the election, Sir Omar immediately nominated a further seventeen of his own supporters to keep overall control. This provocative action aroused fierce anger among many members of the population until the Partai Raayatt's military wing, the TNKU,* under the political leadership of an Arab-Malay called Azahari, launched a revolt during the night of 7/8 December 1962. Their aims were, firstly, to seize the Sultan and proclaim him titular head of the Confederation; secondly, because weapons and ammunition were urgently required, it was hoped that these would be obtained by capturing the main police stations during the first few hours of the rising; finally, as they wanted to take control of the oilfields in Seria, they planned to seize Europeans there as hostages and use the expensive equipment as a bargaining counter with the British Government and Brunei Shell Corporation. The overall plan selected by the TNKU leaders was well considered and if they had put it into effect before the British forces were able to arrive in strength from Singapore, then the story of Brunei, and the Confrontation that followed, would have been a different one indeed. However, for a variety of reasons, the TNKU did not manage to warn many of its members about the timing of the rising, so that the Revolt went off at half-cock.

In Singapore on 8 December, a Saturday, the 1/2nd was given orders to move two rifle companies that afternoon to the small state of Brunei. That the rebellion was finally quelled was, in no small measure due to the dash and resolution shown by those first two companies which landed amidst much confusion: their exploits stopped the TNKU from obtaining more arms while, with commendable speed, HQ Far East Command in Singapore completed the dispatch of the equivalent of an infantry brigade to stabilise the situation. Major-General Walter Walker, GOC 17th Gurkha Division as well as MGBG in Seremban, was appointed Commander British Forces Borneo on 19 December 1962. He was tasked to clear the TNKU from the Brunei State before the Federation of

* TNKU – Tentera Nasional Kalimantan Utara. (National Army of Kalimantan)

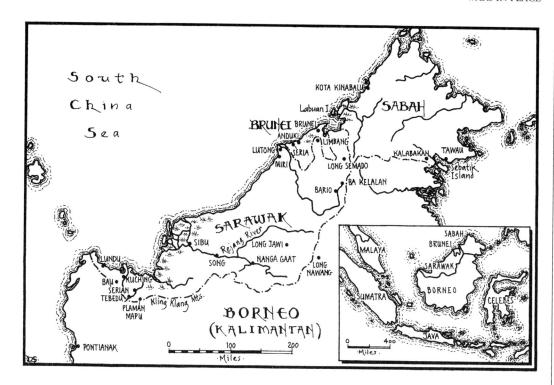

Malaysia was formally established in August 1963, a task that he had accomplished by April. No other general then serving in the British Army could match General Walker's experience of counter-insurgency operations in the jungle. During the Second World War he had commanded the 4/8th in Burma, winning the DSO and Bar. Later, in the Malayan Emergency, he first commanded the 1/6th, then a brigade on operations, before being appointed Major-General, Brigade of Gurkhas. He was an experienced commander who had strong opinions which he never hesitated to pass on to his superiors. In General Walker's eyes, the Brunei Revolt was but the prologue to an imminent and much more serious clash with Indonesia, but such a forecast was not accepted at the time by many of his superiors in Singapore and Whitehall.

Against such an ill-equipped, untrained and badly led force as the TNKU undoubtedly were, there could be no other outcome, once the Revolt had failed during the first twenty-four hours. Nevertheless, two Gurkha battalions were to lose men during the short-lived rebellion. C Company, 1/2nd, while making a dash from Brunei Town to Seria, was ambushed in the middle of a small township, Tutong. Next morning the company took its revenge when the rebel casualties totalled 7 killed, 20 wounded and 100 captured; the cost to C Company was 1 Gurkha officer and 7 other ranks wounded.

At the same time in Brunei Town, near the Government Offices, Lieutenant D. E. Stephens was hit and mortally wounded. His death brought the 1/2nd's losses to two killed and four wounded. These casualties could be considered light as the Gurkhas had been given the unenviable task of clearing a completely strange town at night and against an enemy about whose potential they knew next to nothing – and without any town maps to help them pinpoint their positions.

The Revolt in Brunei, December 1962. Prisoners being taken into custody

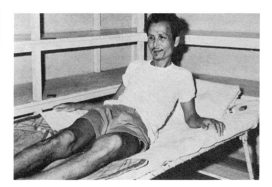

Yassin Affendi, who planned the Revolt in Brunei and who was finally hunted down and captured by the 2/7th Gurkha Rifles

Rifleman Nainabahadur Rai, who shot and killed two rebels and wounded two others, including Yassin Affendi. For his coolness and skill in action he was awarded the Military Medal

Following the New Year, the TNKU split up into small groups in an attempt to escape retribution which, by now, they knew was close at hand. Their military commander, Yassin Affendi, had a price of 15,000 Malayan dollars on his head, a reward that overestimated his ability and potential influence to a ridiculous extent. Nevertheless, in the early part of 1963, Affendi led the Gurkha searchers a merry dance and it was not until 18 May that B Company, 2/7th discovered his camp in a thick swamp and, after a painstaking approach, assaulted it. Four of the rebels went north where they ran into a tough Gurkha soldier, Rifleman Nainabahadur Rai, who was in a 'cut-off' position at the edge of the swamp, separated by about a hundred yards from the next rifleman. Nainabahadur saw four rebels at a distance of about seventy yards quickly approaching him and, with

great coolness, let them close the gap. When they were about thirty yards from him, the leader saw Nainabahadur, pointed his pistol at him and with shouts, all four TNKU charged at the rifleman. Nainabahadur fired from behind a tree when the men were less than twenty yards away: his first round killed two men, the single shot going through the leading rebel's chest before hitting the man immediately behind him. The other two rebels took cover but Nainabahadur was able to wound them both before closing in and ordering them to surrender. One of the captives was the much sought-after Yassin Affendi, the military commander of the TNKU. Nainabahadur was awarded the Military Medal and later in the year was selected as 'Man of the Year' by the British Council for the Rehabilitation of the Disabled. All this entailed a visit to the UK to attend a luncheon at the Savoy Hotel which the young rifleman much enjoyed – quite unmoved and unspoilt by the publicity, the interviews on television and by the media attention generally. Nainabahadur went on to win a Bar to his MM during a subsequent tour in Borneo.

Affendi's capture was a dramatic end to the five-month-long Revolt and no one was more pleased than General Walker, who signalled: 'I am absolutely delighted that it should be 2/7th who have pulled this off.'

Peaceful conditions returned to the jungle and waterways of Brunei but elsewhere in Borneo clouds of discord were becoming more obvious. Sukarno was as determined as ever to smother the concept of Malaysia and, to this end, training camps for irregular volunteers were set up at various points along the thousand-mile-long border between Borneo and Indonesian Kalimantan.

On 12 April 1963 a thirty-strong party of Indonesian border terrorists (IBTs) crossed into the First Division of Sarawak and attacked the police post at Tebedu. The small detachment was taken completely by surprise and a corporal was killed and two more policemen wounded. The Indonesians left behind documents intended to give the impression that the raid had been carried out by TNKU volunteers as a continuation of the Brunei Revolt, but later evidence showed that the raid had been carried out by regulars operating with the IBTs. The Tebedu raid, in itself a minor affair, was to have far-reaching consequences, for no longer could the obvious military threats be disregarded; there was a string of guerrilla bases situated on Kalimantan soil, just over the other side of the border. During the early stages of the Confrontation most of the guerrillas were volunteers, trained and often led by Sukarno's regular armed forces, with instructors coming from specialised units such as the marines, paratroopers and air force paratroopers.

In 1963 General Walker predicted that Great Britain and Malaya would be led to the brink of war and that if they did not stand firm, supported by the Commonwealth countries of Australia and New Zealand, Borneo would be conquered by force. Attempts by the Prime Minister of Malaya, Tunku Abdul Rahman, to find a peaceful solution came to naught even though at one stage a UN mission made a lightning tour of both Sabah and Sarawak to ascertain whether the people wished to join the new Federation of Malaysia. All this consultation was to be of no avail because the Indonesian-based guerrillas continued to cross the border, using every form of intimidation possible against the local people, while it was clear that more and more guerrillas were being led by regular officers and NCOs because leadership at the lower levels improved noticeably.

The Federation of Malaysia was created officially in September 1963, so what had started as a colonial war was transformed overnight into a counter-insurgency operation, waged in support of a fellow Commonwealth member. General Walker, as Director of Operations, issued the order to all his troops: 'Dominate the jungle,' and to achieve this required constant surveillance along the long and ill-defined frontier. In this task, the SAS took the leading part, acting as the eyes and ears of the security forces, but there were never enough of them so that the newly raised Gurkha Independent Parachute Company was ordered to help the SAS carry out their formidable role. Although the majority of the Gurkha paratroopers had completed their specialist training within the last three years, they were now required to operate in the jungle in small groups. Before they could take up an SAS-type assignment, all ranks had to undergo a further concentrated bout of specialised training, which included medical courses, signalling, survival techniques, river crossing and many other facets of the multi-various tasks which 22 Squadron SAS takes in its stride.

That training completed, some of the Gurkha paratroopers led extremely lonely existences after being sent to long houses astride likely incursion routes, where they were tasked to act as 'eyes and ears'. In close contact with the Dyaks and other local tribesmen, it was not an easy duty for a young lance-corporal or senior rifleman to perform because it required tact, tolerance, initiative and a high degree of self-discipline. Temptations there were, as the majority of Dyak long houses contained a friendly and hospitable people, never tardy with generous potions of their home-brewed liquor, often dispensed by comely bare-breasted maidens who were neither shy nor aloof. It would be wrong to claim that no man ever strayed because it would have been out of character if they had behaved like monks, since the

Gurkhas of the Independent Parachute Company training in 1963 average Gurkha likes his drink (*raksi*), gambling and women. That there were liaisons there could be no doubt but rarely, if ever, at the expense of their high military standards or to the detriment of their operational duties. Surveillance along the border continued to be all-important, even when Sukarno escalated the level of conflict from minor raids by 'volunteers' to incursions by the TNI (Indonesian Army).

To watch and guard the many routes into the large Third Divison of Sarawak, about the size of Wales, was a task well beyond the capabilities of a single battalion. In September 1963 the 1/2nd Gurkha Rifles had such a responsibility, so to help them in their task, local Iban tribesmen were enlisted as Border Scouts under command of the battalion. These Border Scouts carried out a short training course in the use of rifles or shotguns, but they were not enlisted to fight except in an emergency. Many of them were excellent trackers and boatmen, so their value lay in a detailed knowledge of their long houses and immediate surroundings. One of the Border Scout outposts in the 1/2nd's area was at a place called Long Jawai.

Long Jawai was about twenty miles away from the international border, with a corresponding village on the Indonesian side, Long Nawang, containing a similar large settlement of the same tribe of people. In the past, the international border, established by their colonial masters in the shape of the Dutch and British, meant nothing at all and they continued to trade with each other, oblivious to the formation of

Malaysia or the disruptive tendencies of President Sukarno in Djakarta.

The small isolated detachment which lived in Long Jawai consisted of twenty-one Border Scouts, two radio operators and five Gurkha soldiers, all from the 1/2nd, under the command of a Gurkha corporal, Tejbahadur Gurung. The detachment headquarters with its radio sets was in a hut close to the village long house and until the morning of the 27 September, life at Long Jawai had been dull and uneventful, with no information coming in at all, while the locals were generally apathetic and certainly not helpful.

At about half-past five in the morning on 28 September, the Gurkha rifleman on sentry duty heard movement near his post so that every man stood to. Shortly afterwards three or four shots were fired near by. The radio operators tried to establish communications with their company headquarters but suddenly the whole area was blasted by mortar bombs, machine-gun and heavy small-arms fire, and in the half light a party of Indonesians charged the signals hut from the north, killing the Gurkha operators as they sat at their sets, unable to hear the enemy approaching because of their earphones. All hope of communication with the outside world had gone.

One by one, the Border Scouts started slipping away; they had not been trained to fight, so they went down the side of the hill to a stream and round to the Indonesian position to surrender. However, the last one, having seen his comrades being disarmed and bound by the enemy, decided to return

Corporal Tejbahadur Gurung, MM, 2nd Gurkha Rifles, at Long Jawai, September 1963

to the Gurkhas and risk death by their side, on a small hillock, their first position.

Daylight came and the small detachment kept up an effective fire against the fighting force. The Gurkha machine-gunner was hit, his side torn open by a machine-gun bullet, while another rifleman was killed outright by a mortar bomb which exploded in a tree above him. By 8 o'clock there were only three effective men left, with two Gurkha riflemen wounded who were in great pain and the Border Scout. For two hours they fought under continuous heavy mortar and small-arms fire, until their own ammunition was down to a few rounds per man. The corporal therefore decided to withdraw his party, although one wounded rifleman, now delirious, begged to be left behind lest he should hamper their withdrawal. His request was ignored, and slowly the three Gurkhas and the Border Scout dragged the two semi-conscious men off the position. Two hours later they managed to get them down to a stream to the south, and thence into the jungle on the other side. Fortunately for them, the Indonesians had suffered casualties too which deterred them from assaulting the position during the Gurkhas' withdrawal, but at about eleven o'clock they began to attack the hillock, and kept on firing in its immediate area although by this time the small party had disappeared. Without food or medical supplies, they spent the night in pouring rain, keeping the wounded men as warm as they could. Then, having made them as comfortable as possible, the corporal and his companions left for the nearest village, many miles away. Living off roots, they had a long and hazardous journey before they reached the outpost of Belaga, weak and exhausted but with their weapons spotlessly clean, and able to give a first-hand account of the battle. Unbeknown to them, the Indonesians had tied up the other Border Scouts who had surrendered, plundered the village and returned upstream towards the border. In a camp near by they had then murdered ten of the Border Scouts.

Retribution was to follow, because in the next few days the whole of the 1/2nd Gurkhas deployed, using helicopters, and covering a wide area by boat and on foot as well as from the air. On 1 October, a Gurkha officer and his platoon from C Company ambushed two enemy boats carrying some thirty men: the ambush was admirably executed and there were few, if any, survivors when both boats capsized in the middle of a fast-flowing river. Arms and equipment recovered including weapons lost at Long Jawai, as well as the radio which the Indonesians had taken out of the signals hut near the village.

The relieving troops found that Long Jawai had been completely ransacked and 'smelt of death'. The two wounded Gurkhas had managed to survive, more dead than alive, but they recovered from their harrowing ordeal. An accurate picture of the enemy force emerged. It had consisted of about a hundred soldiers with nearly the same number of porters. The commander of the group, one Major Muljono, had been a guerrilla fighter all his life; he had fought against the Japanese, then the Dutch, had caused President Sukarno repeated trouble in the 1950s, and had even attended a British Army jungle warfare training school at Kota Tinggi in Malaya. It was not known how many of his force died before they eventually crossed the border back into Kalimantan; five graves were found during the rest of the follow-up, while another five of the enemy were killed. Of more importance was the result that the Indonesians were reluctant to make any further deep incursions into the Third Division. Corporal Tejbahadur Gurung was to win the Military Medal for his leadership and resolution. As to why Major Muljono murdered the Border Scouts, that was never known. Perhaps he wished to discourage others from joining, but this terrible act, coupled with the plunder of Long Jawai, had the opposite effect: the villagers on returning were wholly on the side of the security forces thereafter.

By this time every Gurkha battalion was serving a series of six-month tours in the Borneo Territories. The Gurkha infantrymen were quick to learn how to dominate the jungle and thus to 'own' the frontier. The ambush became the key operation both for the guerrillas and the security forces. A successful ambush required all the tricks of the Gurkhas' trade: an eye for country, expert camouflage, complete silence and strict fire control, guile and, above all, self-discipline.

In the jungle operations, the Gurkhas bore the brunt during the early stages of the Confrontation because it was to take some time for British battalions to acclimatise to the terrain and the hot humid climate. In

A patrol in an assault boat on a river in Sarawak, 1968

addition, after serving so long in Europe, the latter had forgotten how to fight, move or even live in the jungle, which meant that even after attending crash courses at the Jungle Warfare School in Malaya, the majority of British infantrymen did not reach the necessary peak of efficiency until the unit concerned came back for its second six-month tour in Borneo. Obviously there were exceptions, and some notable ones at that – the SAS and 40 Royal Marine Commando, in particular – but few British units had any

Gurkhas move off from a helipad after disembarking from a Royal Navy helicopter

veterans from the Malayan Emergency, unlike their Gurkha counterparts.

During 1964 the Director of Operations had to rely on his thinly spread surveillance screen giving early warning of incursions and, by using his air transport to its maximum, deploying troops in an attempt to stop and harass the Indonesian invaders. When incursions came singly, or on occasion overlapped, General Walker was able to cope but, as seemed increasingly likely, if three or more inroads occurred at the same time, then a situation could develop which was beyond the capacity of the forces under his command to control. In the short term, many more helicopters were required but if the campaign was to be won, more than that was needed. He had to be allowed to force the enemy's base camps away from the border, back into Kalimantan, or if political clearance for this proved impossible, then at least his forces had to be allowed to cross over the unmarked border when in 'hot pursuit'. In 1964 even this limited concession seemed unlikely to be granted by the politicians, although Walker argued most persuasively for it.

If Sukarno had continued to keep up this pressure against the Borneo Territories (now East Malaysia) alone, it is highly likely that the outcome of the Confrontation would have been as he expected, a defeat for Malaysia and its Commonwealth allies. However, he then made an error of judgement which eventually led to his own downfall as well as to defeat for Indonesia.

In the early hours of 17 August 1964, more than a hundred raiders crossed the Straits of Malacca by boat to land on the coast of south-west Johore. Three-quarters of them were Indonesian marines and parachute troops and it was evident that the intruders had been briefed to expect a rapturous welcome from the 'oppressed' citizens of Malaya and had left their boats at Pontian Kechil, anticipating little fighting. The invaders were soon to be disillusioned when they were rounded up in a remarkably quick and efficient manner.

A fortnight later came another attack against the mainland, this time when nearly 200 parachute troops emplaned in four transport aircraft at Djakarta. The original plan had been to drop near Labis, about a hundred miles north of Singapore: this area had been selected because during the Emergency it had been strongly pro-Communist as well as being situated astride the main railway line which ran northwards to Central Malaya. Nothing went right for the invaders: only two aircraft out of four eventually reached Labis in a severe electric storm, and the unfortunate parachutists were scattered over some five miles of country. Purely by chance, the 1/10th happened to be back in Malaya, resting and retraining before returning across the water to Borneo. Of equal significance, half of 845 Squadron, Fleet Air Arm, flew their helicopters from HMS *Bulwark* to enable the Gurkhas to launch a gigantic manhunt with maximum speed and efficiency. After a disillusioned TNI offficer, Lieutenant Sukitno, surrendered, a million copies of his statement were dropped over Indonesian territory from RAF Hastings and Argosy aircraft, warning his fellow countrymen that Malaysia would not greet them as liberators.

These landings, military pinpricks as it transpired, were to herald the most momentous decision taken in the whole of the Confrontation. Thoroughly alarmed at Sukarno's hostile actions, the Malaysian Government in Kuala Lumpur was now prepared to support the Director of Operations' request that cross-border operations should be approved up to a depth of 5,000 yards inside Kalimantan: faced with this request from its Commonwealth ally, the British Government gave its approval, stressing that there was to be no public announcement and that the operations were to be carried out under conditions of maximum secrecy.

Before describing a typical cross-border operation, tribute must be paid to the three Gurkha corps, each of which played an invaluable role during the Confrontation in Borneo. The Gurkha Engineer squadrons had the task of setting up operating bases for companies and platoons of infantry, usually in the most inaccessible of areas. Moreover, as far as the infantry battalions were concerned, their gratitude was centred on the efforts made by the sappers to improve living conditions in the forward bases, once these had been established. This included the construction of water points and other

An airstrip constructed by the Queen's Gurkha Engineers at Kapit, Borneo, in 1963

projects. Operationally, the sappers cut LZs (landing zones) for helicopters which meant that the security forces gained in mobility and flexibility when opposing any incursions. Another unusual duty was to take

An outboard motorman of the Queen's Gurkha Engineers in Brunei during the Revolt

Below:
A Gurkha sentry keeps watch in the jungle during the Confrontation in Indonesia

over the manning of river launches and local long boats and it was noticeable that the outboard motors of a civilian type used by the local fishermen were reliable – as opposed to types produced for the services which often fell victim to abuse by the Gurkha boatmen. Sapper history was made in January 1964 when after being lifted sixty-five miles into the jungle by a Belvedere helicopter, C Troop of 69 Gurkha Independent Field Squadron took delivery of a bulldozer and started to construct the first medium-range air transport strip built in those surroundings. Their task was made doubly difficult by heavy rain falling during the first few days but by using the local Kelabit tribesmen as labour, the assignment was duly completed on schedule. If it can be said that the Gurkha Engineers learnt to walk during the Malayan Emergency, then in Borneo they came of age. 'They left the country a better place because by their efforts they had helped to open up many parts of Borneo by improving air strips and river communications and by building permanent roads into the interior.' (E. D. Smith, *Johnny Gurkha*.)

Two out of the three squadrons of the Gurkha Signals served continuously in Borneo, providing reliable communications which enabled the security forces to maintain the initiative in some of the most difficult country in the world. That the movement of Indonesian insurgents from across the border was known almost instantaneously was due in no small measure to the communications run and maintained by the Gurkha Signals. Perhaps their most remarkable achievement was to establish VHF (very high frequency) re-broadcast facilities on some of the highest peaks, one of them being nearly 8,000 feet. Here the radio relay detachments lived in complete isolation, wholly dependent on visiting helicopters which brought in stores and rations, as well as enabling the personnel manning the remote station to be changed round. This and other re-broadcast sites ensured there were VHF communications throughout the brigade areas, a remarkable achievement, which could never have been brought about without the helicopters. These machines were used at all stages; for cutting the initial LZ, establishing the party by flying in their precious equipment and, thereafter, keeping the post resupplied to meet the operational requirements.

The Gurkha Transport Regiment (GTR) – redesignated thus in November 1965 at which time the companies were renamed squadrons – had 30 and 31 Squadrons, in turn, carrying out tours in Borneo before they moved back to Singapore in January 1967. They had detachments dispersed over a thousand miles, in places as far apart as Kuching, the island of Labuan and Tawau, away to the east. Their composite platoons gave magnificent support to the troops operating in their vicinity, while in the rear the transport platoons worked around the clock, ferrying stores from airfields and docks, as well as moving units and sub-units to and from operations. When the Confrontation ended in August 1966, the GTR reported that: 'In four months we moved back from the forward areas, the ports and airfields, every soldier and ton of stores that had taken us three years to bring forward.'

Thus the administrative efforts of the three Gurkha corps played a notable part in the final victory.

As stated before, until political clearance for cross-border operations was given, President Sukarno had every chance of winning an outright victory which would have meant the end of the fledgeling Federation of Malaysia. At the same time, the British Government was anxious to avoid an open war with Indonesia so that the rules governing these raids were very tightly drawn. The code name for the cross-border raids was 'OP Claret'.

Every operation had to be authorised by the Director of Operations Borneo himself, which meant that, in some cases, he visited the company base from where the operation was to be launched. He had to be convinced that the raid had a definite aim, which was to deter and thwart aggression by the Indonesians. No attacks were to be mounted in retribution with the sole aim of inflicting casualties on the enemy; moreover, it was vital that civilian casualties were avoided at all costs because the co-operation of the local people was crucial if the Confrontation was to be won in the end. Only tried and tested troops were to be used; in other words, no soldiers were to be sent across into Kalimantan during their first operational tour in Borneo. Initially, apart from the SAS, only Gurkha battalions were used but after British infantry units had gained the requisite

Gurkhas waiting to board a Belvedere twin-rotor helicopter

... Don't annoy the chief, don't look at the women, don't drink the water, don't forget your malaria tablets—and have a good time!'

Jak, the famous cartoonist, summed up the situation © Jak

A Vickers medium machine-gun in Borneo. This gun was reputedly used by the 2/2nd Gurkha Rifles from Neuve Chapelle in 1915 to Borneo in 1964

experience in jungle fighting, they played their full part in OP Claret raids. Nothing was to be done which could cause open warfare so that close air support could not be provided except in an extreme emergency. Finally, meticulous planning, careful rehearsals and zealous security were all mandatory ingredients of these Claret operations, each being governed by what were to be known as 'the Golden Rules'. Perhaps the most remarkable aspect was the fact that secrecy was maintained at all levels; it is doubtful that the Indonesians realised that they were at the receiving end of a new Commonwealth strategy. This was partly due to the fact that these raids took place along a lengthy border which, in certain areas, was ill-defined, and partly because the Indonesian communications and administration within Kalimantan could not cope with a series of reports or assess them quickly and accurately until it was too late.

While the Kalimantan border bases were being harassed – initially by Gurkhas and then by British and other Commonwealth troops – the world at large still thought that the Indonesians were on the offensive. One by one their bases along the border were targeted for action and although the Indonesian casualties were light, each reverse had local significance because invariably it led to a withdrawal deeper into Kalimantan territory. Three cross-border operations will be described in outline, selected as being typical of the many Claret raids that were launched.

One of the first Claret operations – though in the end not successful – was carried out on 17 May 1964 by a platoon of D Company, 1/6th, commanded by Captain (QGO) Damarbahadur Gurung. His task was to lay an

Live rations about to be loaded on to an RAF helicopter for delivery to forward units

ambush on a track used frequently by Indonesians who moved up and down the border, but when some local women spotted a Gurkha sentry, Damarbahadur had to move the ambush position to another location. Shortly afterwards disaster struck; Damarbahadur had instructed his platoon sergeant to establish a temporary base with eight men, while he took the rest of the platoon to deploy them in an ambush on another track nearby. Unfortunately, the platoon sergeant did not position his men tactically, so when the Indonesians surprised the base, two Gurkhas were killed in a short firefight, as were two of the enemy. In terms of casualties it was not a defeat but the action demonstrated that no liberties could be taken with the Indonesians, now that their regular soldiers were operating from most of the bases along the border. For Damarbahadur, there was to be retribution when under his leadership, in another Claret raid, five Indonesians were killed and four wounded in an ambush that he had laid close to the border. He was awarded a well-deserved MC.

A different type of Claret operation was the one launched from C Company, 1/2nd's base at Ba Kelalan, in the Fifth Division of Sarawak. Punitive action was called for after the Indonesians had forbidden cross-border trade, an order that caused immense hardship to the Murut tribe who lived on both sides of the border. The Muruts at Ba Kelalan duly petitioned the commanding officer of the 1/2nd to take action, but as week followed week nothing, in their eyes, appeared to happen. In reality, however, several reconnaissance patrols were being carried out and only when detailed information had been obtained about Long Medan, on the Kalimantan side of the border, did General Walker visit Ba Kelalan to satisfy himself that the raid was justified and that the military risks were worth taking. In January 1965 official permission for the cross-border raid was granted.

The C Company commander, Captain Bruce Jackman, made a simple plan but one which entailed a night approach to cover a distance of about eight miles without being detected, quite a problem for nearly 150 men when everything had to be carried, including the mortars, rocket launchers and their rockets. In addition, each Gurkha soldier carried two mortar bombs as well as his own weapon and normal load. The route taken enabled them to dump the mortar bombs near the close supporting fire positions selected prior to the next phase, an attack on the Indonesian strongpoint near Long Medan. To complicate matters even more for

A radio relay, manned by men of the Queen's Gurkha Signals, and a helipad in Borneo

Captain Jackman, General Walker's HQ had laid down that only one hour could be spent in actually carrying out the attack: such a precaution was designed to stop C Company becoming too embroiled with any other Indonesian parties which might move to cut off the patrol's return to the border. Once again, the Golden Rules were being strictly adhered to in the planning of the operation.

As C Company marched all through the night of 29 January 1965, they were extremely tired when they reached the selected 'jumping-off' position in the early hours of the 30th. Everything went as planned until the attack was sprung by an Indonesian walking towards 11 Platoon's position. That was the signal for a firefight to begin, which continued until the company commander gave the order to charge, and under close covering fire his party fought through the enemy position from bunker to bunker, using grenades and rifle fire. The Indonesian camp was soon taken but from across a river an enemy 12.7-mm anti-aircraft gun began firing, joined by a mortar and medium machine-guns in support. Casualties among the Gurkhas resulted and the situation began to look grim. The crisis was saved by a corporal who was acting as the

Mortar Fire Controller (MFC): he stood up and thus exposed himself to the Indonesian machine-gun fire while making some quick calculations. He was able to pinpoint the hostile 60-mm mortar position and blow the mortar up, as well as killing the crew. He then turned his attention to the Indonesian machine-guns and knocked them out. For this action Corporal Birbahadur Gurung was awarded the MM.

Meanwhile, 12 Platoon was doing its best to avoid being pinned down by the accurate fire of the 12.7-mm gun before the danger was removed by a corporal and two riflemen, who crawled across a paddy field taking a rocket launcher with them. The rest of the platoon kept up a noisy diversionary fire before the NCO's first rocket hit the enemy gun post. That was to be the end of the battle.

Being by now fifteen minutes over the time of one hour allowed for the attack, Jackman and his company had to withdraw – this time by a more direct route to the border, carrying with them two of their badly wounded men as well as the body of a dead Gurkha rifleman.

It had been a most successful Claret operation as, later, it was confirmed that not

A painting by Terence Cuneo of the action in which Lance-Corporal Rambahadur Limbu, 10th Gurkha Rifles, won his VC, Borneo, 21 November 1965

only had the enemy lost 50 per cent of their strength in the area, but, of more importance, they never reoccupied Long Medan: no more raids across the border in that sector were made by the Indonesians. Captain Jackman was awarded the MC for his leadership during this operation.

One of the most striking successes was achieved by the 2/10th when a fierce action was fought on a hill near Serikin, on the border between East Malaysia and Kalimantan, on 21 November 1965. The raiding force consisted of the 2/10th's C Company and platoons from Support Company, with supporting fire being given by light and medium guns of the Royal Artillery. The Indonesians occupied a strong position on top of a high sheer-sided hill which could only be approached along a knife-edged ridge. By superb fieldcraft, the leading Gurkhas reached a point barely twenty yards from the Indonesian position in complete silence. Then a machine-gun opened up on them, wounding one of the support group. Lance-Corporal Rambahadur Limbu rushed forward and killed the Indonesian machine-gunner.

That, however, caused the enemy to direct heavy fire against Rambahadur's group and

two of his men were hit, both being seriously wounded. After he had put his men in a better fire position, Rambahadur then tried to rescue the two wounded men. Under accurate fire his first attempt at crawling forward proved impossible, and he decided that speed alone might give him a measure of

Field Marshal Lord Slim with Lance-Corporal Rambahadur, VC, and his son Bhakta, aged five, at Buckingham Palace after the investiture at which Rambahadur was presented with his VC by Her Majesty the Queen, July 1966

protection. Covered by his comrades, Rambahadur reached one of the wounded men and carried him back to a position of safety. The Indonesians were ready for his next attempt but the young NCO did not hesitate for long; after one short rush he was pinned down for some minutes by intense fire but again he dashed forward to hurl himself down by the side of the second wounded rifleman. Picking him up, Rambahadur doubled back through a hail of enemy bullets and by some miracle arrived unscathed. For his gallantry Rambahadur Limbu was awarded the Victoria Cross; for the Brigade of Gurkhas and for the 10th Gurkhas in particular, that award was the climax of the Confrontation campaign.

Gradually the British and Commonwealth forces began to dominate the border area and the Indonesians had to move their camps back into Kalimantan. As a result their forays into Sarawak and Sabah became less daring and less frequent. One major incursion was to take place during the last few weeks of the Confrontation, however. In June 1966 it was learnt that a tough Indonesian soldier, Lieutenant Sumbi, was training about 100 volunteers in jungle warfare and boasting that, one day, he and his men would cross the border and march to Brunei Bay. He fulfilled the first part of his promise as, accompanied by fifty men, he moved out of his base at Bawang for 'an unknown destination'. Thereafter, a giant search operation was put into effect which involved the whole of the 1/7th, together with patrols from the Gurkha Parachute Company. On 31 July, a small patrol from that company found a label from a coffee tin in the jungle and from such a small clue did their radio report spark off frenzied activity; the chase went on, day after day, week after week and was continued without respite right into the autumn of 1966. Trails were found, followed, lost, found again, and then the whole process repeated again. False trails were examined and rejected, platoons withdrawn for rest and re-rationing, new fresh platoons inserted; days of exhilaration, nights of frustration, days without any information, then a surrender, giving further information, and on with the chase once more. The search for Sumbi's party eventually centred round Bukit Pagon, a 6,070-feet-high mountain astride the Sarawak and Brunei border. On 20 August two 1/7th platoons were winched into the remote mountainous area to the east of the

mountain, while a third platoon walked in from the west, accompanied by two captured prisoners from Sumbi's incursion group. Those prisoners showed where they had last seen their comrades and after two weeks of cliff-hanging, river crossing and painstaking tracking, twenty-four enemy were killed or captured, with a few deciding to surrender. Sumbi himself was captured on the morning of 3 September: in all forty-six of the original fifty enemy were accounted for by the 1/7th, with the remaining four being captured by the Royal Brunei Malay Regiment shortly after the 1/7th had departed for Sarawak. The aims and aspirations of Lieutenant Sumbi and his incursion group had been utterly destroyed, a victory coinciding with the end of the Confrontation with Indonesia.

As soon as the Confrontation was over, messages of praise and congratulations poured in at the same time as rumours began to appear in the British press that a large-scale reduction in the Brigade of Gurkhas was about to be announced by the Labour Government of the day. The then Major-General, Brigade of Gurkhas, Major-General A.G. (Pat) Patterson (late 6th Gurkha Rifles), faced an anxious time as he fought with wholehearted determination to negotiate reasonable terms for the men he led with respect and affection. Before the 'run-down' was publicly announced to all ranks of the Brigade during December 1966, the MGBG had briefed his commanding officers about the daunting task that was soon to face them all, that of sending over half the Brigade on redundancy prematurely, including many without any type of pension and with only a small gratuity.

Certain important principles were evolved by General Patterson, later to be accepted by the MOD in London, and without doubt these paved the way for the difficult and heart-rending business of sending home volunteer 'long-term' regular soldiers. One of those principles was a public announcement that, each year, there would be limited recruiting; in such a way, Patterson was demonstrating his faith in the future, as well as ensuring that the Brigade would have the correct rank structure if it continued as part of the British Army during and beyond the 1970s.

The official announcement was made simultaneously in December of that year by all commanding officers throughout the

Brigade. After so much speculation and so many rumours the actual announcement did not come as much of a shock. One CO was to comment: 'It was kept very low key and on the whole the men took the news very philosophically. The result they found very interesting but they did not really expect it to affect them but if it did – well that was life!' Another example of Gurkha fatalism: what will be, will be.

In the event there were remarkably few disgruntled men to be sent on redundancy, thanks to the careful preparation, meticulous briefing and deep personal interest taken in every case by the British and Gurkha officers in each unit.

In 1966 the original plan was that the four infantry regiments would be reduced to a single battalion each by the end of 1971. However, two events occurred in the United Kingdom during the middle of 1970 which changed the situation. The troubles in Northern Ireland worsened so that more British troops were required in a hurry; and the Conservative Party emerged as surprise victors in the General Election of that year. It would be unfair to put too much emphasis on the second factor since it is more than possible that the deteriorating situation in Ulster would have influenced a Labour administration into making the same decision about the Brigade as did the new Government. Be that as it may, the formal announcement about the Brigade's future stated that it would not run down below an overall strength of 6,700 Gurkha ranks, and that this total would include five infantry battalions as well as three small but viable Gurkha corps.

That decision was greeted with relief and delight as it meant that 700 more men could continue to serve in the Brigade for the foreseeable future. For the senior infantry regiment, the 2nd Gurkha Rifles, it meant that it would continue to have two battalions, unlike the other three regiments, each of which would consist of a single battalion only. Of equal importance, the three corps could plan ahead knowing that they had a definite role to play in the Brigade for some time to come.

Towards the end of the 1960s, four Gurkha battalions at a time were engaged in keeping the peace along the Sino-Hong Kong border, outstaring the Red Guards while in the city behind them, other units carried out internal security duties. In 1967 and 1968,

Operations to prevent the illegal immigration of Chinese across the border into Hong Kong. A patrol with one night's catch

A patrol arrests a Chinese illegal immigrant, Hong Kong

Internal Security training, Hong Kong

Junior Under-Officer Bejay Kumar Rawat, 7th Gurkha Rifles, winner of the Sword of Honour at the Royal Military Academy, Sandhurst, in August 1981, with Gurkhas of the Sandhurst Demonstration Company

during the height of the Hong Kong riots, the 6th, 7th and 10th all played a notable part, whether controlling unrest in the urban areas or along the border in the New Territories

Public Duties at the Tower of London. A painting by Terence Cuneo of the Ceremony of the Keys

Under the watchful eye of a Drill Instructor of the Brigade of Guards and of the adjutant, a Gurkha practises the 'challenge'

where the situation, at times, became extremely tense. Junior British officers and their Gurkha soldiers in the battalions were subjected to deliberate provocation, being forced to listen to a constant flow of propaganda, while trying to maintain an air of calm and good humour in the face of insults and planned insolence. It was a wearisome task which continued day and night, week after week, while back in Hong Kong, for the most part, life went on as normal.

By 1970 the 'heat' had been taken out of the Sino-Hong Kong border problem. As a consequence, life began to settle down into a more even pattern, especially after the momentous news that each infantry battalion, in turn, would serve a two-year tour in the UK, with the 7th Gurkha Rifles being the first to go. That announcement was greeted with relief because neither the British officers nor the Gurkha soldiers wished to serve for ever within the restricted confines of the Colony. It was not long before Gurkha soldiers, based at Church Crookham, were a familiar sight in and around Aldershot and Fleet where they became very popular locally. Each of the resident Gurkha battalions in the UK carried out Public Duties in London, and organised and ran the Bisley Rifle Meeting, as well as providing men for the Demonstration Company at the Royal Military Academy. To add to the brigade's renown, the 10th Gurkhas won the Army

Unit Rifle Championship at Bisley in 1973 and that victory was repeated, on several occasions, by one or other of the battalions.

After Hong Kong had settled down following the riots, units there had to carry out frequent ceremonial duties, including the provision of Guards of Honour in Korea, while internal security training in conjunction with the Royal Hong Kong Police remained all-important. Large-scale exercises were conducted in the hills of the New Territories and elsewhere in the Far East. These annual commitments were to be interrupted when an ever-increasing stream of illegal immigrants from China strove to enter the Colony in search of a new future in Hong Kong.

After 1975, the trickle threatened to turn into a deluge as hundreds of people were prepared to risk life and limb in a bid to escape from the Chinese brand of Communism. The climax was reached in mid-1979, when nearly 90,000 illegal immigrants were arrested trying to cross into Hong Kong; by this time, the British Army had five battalions deployed along the border. Without their vigilance, the already overcrowded Colony would have been swamped. In the early days, border duty was usually for two weeks' duration and came around every two months, duties that became 'very dull after three days'. It was during this crisis that the Gurkha Engineers had a most important role to play. Their many tasks included the important one of reinforcing and refurbishing the main border

fence, as well as building watchtowers in the Mai Po marshes and clearing new sites for company bases at various points along the border.

With the illegal immigrants also attempting to come in by sea, the Gurkha sappers also formed a Boat Troop which was trained initially by a team of Royal Marines.

Driver Deobahadur Rana, Gurkha Transport Regiment, winner of the Queen's Medal, Bisley, in 1987

An Honour Guard at United Nations HQ, Seoul, Korea. In the centre is Rifleman Begbahadur Ghale, 10th Gurkha Rifles

United Nations Honour Guard found by men of the Gurkha Transport Regiment, Korea, 1983

This Boat Troop played a vital operational role and even when the situation improved, it continued to operate well into the 1990s. With such a heavy British commitment in Hong Kong caused by the attempted influx of illegal immigrants, any further talk of reducing the Brigade of Gurkhas, and the three Gurkha corps, was forgotten until the situation gradually improved.

In 1982 a modest but most welcome expansion led to the 2/7th being re-formed in February. However, this decision was a short-term one only, brought about by the manning problems along the Sino-Hong Kong border.

Within the Gurkha Engineers, too, 69 Gurkha Independent Field Squadron was re-formed in Hong Kong, prior to moving to Chatham in the UK where it began tackling the same tasks as any Royal Engineer field squadron undertakes, including later tours in the Falklands.

The 10th Gurkha Rifles serving in Cyprus man an observation post overlooking the Turkish-Greek village of Pyla

Cyprus –
the 10th Gurkha Rifles
Reconnaissance Platoon
ready for action

When the 10th relieved the 7th as the UK-based battalion stationed in Church Crookham, the officers and men never expected that they would be sent on an operational tour when war clouds threatened Cyprus between July 1974 and February 1975. In that troubled island, an attempted Greek National Guard coup deposed President Makarios, who narrowly escaped assassination before fleeing the island. Eight days later, Turkish troops invaded, landing at Kyrenia on the north coast and, after a week of bitter fighting, linked up through the Kyrenia mountains with airborne troops north-west of Nicosia until a ceasefire was arranged between the Turks and the defending Greek National Guard.

While the battle raged, the 10th was warned to be ready for an emergency air move, a move that was carried out with great speed and efficiency by the battalion, which arrived on the island during the uneasy ceasefire that followed the initial Turkish landings. It was not long before the 10th was involved with the Turkish Army and only firm but tactful handling prevented several potentially dangerous situations from developing because, in general, the Turks were in an ugly mood. The battalion's two

Cyprus –
confiscated weapons are loaded
into a vehicle

roles were necessarily passive; firstly, to defend the territorial integrity of the Eastern Sovereign Base Area* and protect British personnel and installations; and secondly, to assist refugees, irrespective of their nationality. In carrying out these tasks the unit was extremely stretched but the Gurkhas proved adept in handling refugees, as well as having a quiet and reassuring effect on the host of foreign nationals with whom they had to deal. Once the border partitioning the island had been established

---

* Retained to this day as a British base, together with the second one at Akrotiri in the south.

Belize – a mortar fire-control section of the 2nd Gurkha Rifles on training

and agreed by the Turks and Greek Cypriots, the tension eased somewhat, although occasionally a firefight would break out. On 29 October, one which lasted almost one and a half hours threatened to break the uneasy stalemate until a local ceasefire was arranged. Another incident occurred when Klerides, the former Acting President, visited a Greek refugee camp and during his visit, Turkish soldiers seized an old Greek shepherd as well as occupying the escarpment overlooking the camp. Some 2,000 angry refugees advanced towards the Turks who adopted firing positions. In the end, a tricky situation was resolved when Major M.G. Allen with a platoon of his C Company, supported by two armoured squadrons from B Squadron, 1 Royal Tank Regiment, courageously interposed themselves between the Greek refugees and the Turks. A potentially dangerous situation was defused.

Other incidents occurred up to and including the last day of the tour when the 10th had to 'stand to' ready for action. At midday on 24 February 1975, the 10th Gurkhas left the island, knowing well that they had carried out a difficult role superbly. The GOC NEARELF,* Major-General C.W.B.

Purdon, was to write: 'I thought you would wish to know how highly I think of your splendid regiment, we will miss the 10th greatly. They have set the highest standard.'

Another overseas commitment which the UK resident battalion of the Brigade had to carry out during this period was a six-month tour in Belize. That small Central American country, formally the colony of British Honduras, had long been under the threat of hostile territorial claims by neighbouring Guatemala and therefore needed the guarantee of a British garrison, even after achieving independence on 21 September 1981. With a population of about 150,000 and a struggling economy, Belize could not raise sufficient defence forces of its own to protect lengthy land borders, stretching for some 240 miles.

The main duties of the Gurkha battalions while they carried out their six-month tours consisted of maintaining the integrity of the land border with Guatemala by manning static OPs† and by patrolling on foot through large tracts of jungle. In addition, they helped to train the small Belize Defence Force. The country was ideal for adventure training as well as granting an excellent

* Near East Land Forces.
† Observation posts.

opportunity for all ranks to deploy on jungle exercises to test their readiness and revise routines, none of which could be practised in the environment of the UK. At various times there were operational 'scares' but no conflict ever occurred during any of the tours carried out in Belize by Gurkha battalions. Now that tours there have ended, the British Army, as a whole, will certainly miss the chance of keeping alive jungle-warfare techniques and training. As ambassadors for that army, the Gurkhas got on splendidly with the local inhabitants.

The biggest challenge to any Gurkha battalion since the end of Confrontation was to come in May 1982 when the 1/7th left Church Crookham for Southampton, where they embarked on the *Queen Elizabeth II*, en route for the Falkland Islands. That Gurkhas were sent there at all had been shrouded in uncertainty from the beginning of the crisis. One officer was to write: 'Until we actually sailed I think most of us thought we would never go … there were fears that we, as a Gurkha battalion, might not be allowed to go to the Falkland Islands for political reasons.' In the event, these fears proved unfounded and the Nepalese Government responded, as it had done on so many previous occasions, by signifying its complete support for the British Government.

Before the 1/7th left its base at Church Crookham, the national press took a series of photographs of the Gurkha soldiers preparing for war, including ones that were much publicised, showing the men sharpening their kukris and waving them around with mock ferocity. Inevitably, it was not long afterwards that stories about the 'wicked Gurkhas' appeared in the Argentinian media: the fact that such a reputation was well known in advance by their adversaries played no small part in the almost bloodless victory the 1/7th achieved after landing in the Falklands.

The battalion set sail, full of trepidation about possible seasickness which, as landlocked mountain dwellers, they treat with the utmost seriousness. They were astounded, too, at the size of the *QE II*:

Such a ship had to be seen to be believed. Why, it was even larger than any building I had seen back home… Never had I slept in such beautiful surroundings or in such a big-soft bed, nor perhaps I ever will? If I was to go to war then there was no better way to go. (Rifleman Baliprasad Rai.)

Life on the *QE II* was pleasant until the Gurkhas had to transfer from the big liner on to the ferry ship, MV *Norland*, where, dressed in their full complement of Arctic gear, they swayed, shook and rolled towards East Falkland. Baliprasad was to write: 'I would have willingly sat through hours of Argentine torture than to through another minute of this ordeal!' After that long tiring journey, they landed at Port San Carlos and on 2 June moved to Goose Green, after it had been captured by the 2nd Battalion Parachute Regiment on 28/29 May. Once there the Gurkhas spent many hours climbing in and out of helicopters to scour the East Falkland hills for pockets of enemy believed to be hiding there. By now it was the weather that had become the foe with rain, mist and low clouds adding to the gloom. By good fortune the 1/7th just avoided the terrible fate that befell the Welsh Guardsmen at Fitzroy.

On 9 June, the battalion, less C Company, began to move forward on foot, a distance of about seven kilometres over extremely rough ground. The marching was hard; not one of the men was lightly laden and those with extra burdens to carry found things none too easy. To make matters worse, the Gurkhas were spotted by the Argentinians and a fierce mortar barrage followed. During this 'stonk', one QGO and three riflemen were hit and evacuated back to San Carlos, where the large sheep-shearing station at the settlement had been turned into a field hospital. It was crowded with paratroopers and included some Argentinian wounded, while teams of doctors and medical orderlies administered to friend and foe alike. Rifleman Baliprasad described the scene and added that: 'I had the dubious distinction of being the first Gurkha casualty to be taken there. I did not have to stay long because the next day I was put on the hospital ship *Uganda*.' He and the other wounded were evacuated back to England while, in the Falklands, the battalion waited for new orders, patiently remaining in reserve until 13 June when they were flown by helicopter to a point south of the Two Sisters feature: it was here that they were given orders for their role in 5 Brigade's attack on Tumbledown and Mount William, which was due to begin just after midnight on 14 June. Following a ferocious bombardment by the Royal Navy, supported

The Falklands War, 1982 –
1/7th Gurkha Rifles.
A headquarters shelters
in the lee of a stack
of ammunition boxes

The Falklands War –
an anti-aircraft sentry watches
out for Argentinian aircraft

by five batteries of 105-mm guns, the night of 13/14 June was spent moving forward slowly in fits and starts; strong winds and frequent snow showers added to their discomfort as the Gurkha rifle companies followed the 2nd Battalion Scots Guards, which had been ordered to secure Tumbledown en route. Thereafter, at the appropriate moment, the 1/7th was to pass through the Scots Guards, swing right and assault and capture Mount William.

In extremely difficult country and moving in single file, the battalion was nearing its start line when part of the column was hit by Argentinian defensive fire. Fortunately, the soft nature of the ground absorbed much of the fire and saved countless lives: it was later found that only eight men had been hit and none of them too seriously. A long and frustrating wait occurred while the Scots Guards fought for and took their objective, but just as the Gurkhas were anticipating that they would be moving into the assault, a long night of frustration, delay and fear ended in anti-climax when white flags were seen flying over Port Stanley.

Not surprisingly, the officers and men who had taken part in that night advance felt thoroughly dispirited, even cheated: having travelled so far, they had not been given the opportunity to show the world that they could fight as well as their British comrades in the Falklands. When the war was over, the Argentinians paid their own tribute to the Gurkhas and their fearsome reputation. One report claimed that when 300 of their

The Falklands War –
men of the 1/7th Gurkha
Rifles move forward on
high ground during the
advance on Port Stanley

soldiers fled from the Scots Guards, they ran into the Gurkhas' advance patrols, whereupon they immediately turned around and ran back to surrender to the Guards. Later, there were some extraordinary allegations in the Argentinian press, one or two of which claimed that the Gurkhas went into action 'drunk and high on drugs'. HQ 5 Brigade refuted all these wild stories with the words: 'None of these things ever happened. But the Gurkhas don't mind; it has added to their reputation in battle – it will help when and if there is another enemy to fight.'

Since that conflict in 1982 other units and sub-units have since followed the 1/7th to the Falklands, in particular, the Gurkha Engineers, whose 69 Squadron carried out a six-month tour there. This saw them heavily involved in the difficult and often dangerous task of trying to make the island a safer place to live in after the Argentinians had strewn mines around, often without keeping any records. While clearing away mines and other munitions, a Gurkha corporal was killed in an accident which unfortunately marred a most successful tour, one that certainly enhanced 69 Squadron's reputation.

In 1991 the sad news was received that the Brigade of Gurkhas was to be drastically reduced in strength as part of the overall reduction of the British armed forces, with details contained in the Defence White Paper 'Options for Change'. Each of the four regiments of Gurkha Rifles was to lose its regimental identity, as were other distinguished cavalry and infantry regiments in the British Army, while at the same time, the three Gurkha corps would be reduced to one squadron each under the new Order of Battle.

All this meant a heavy programme of redundancies, with a constant stream of Gurkha officers and men leaving the army for Nepal, their departure softened, to a certain extent, by pensions or gratuities. The task of selecting these officers and men has placed a grave burden on the officers, who, despite the coming and goings, have striven to maintain as high a standard of battle efficiency and discipline in the units and sub-units under their command as would be expected under normal conditions. Moreover, when units have contracted, prior to formal amalgamation, drafts and individuals have had to be cross-posted, with all the flux attendant on such postings. That there has never been a heavy cloud of doom and gloom over the Brigade has been due to sound leadership at all levels, as well as the self-discipline and resilience of the Gurkha soldiers themselves.

The truncated Brigade, soon to be based in the United Kingdom, faces an uncertain long-term future in the British Army after 180 years which have witnessed so many changes in the way Gurkha soldiers have been recruited, in the weapons they carry and fire, and the necessity nowadays to use a wide variety of sophisticated equipment. War has become so much more complicated and the modern Gurkha soldier has had to face a series of new challenges which he has met with remarkable efficiency. He has shown himself to be capable of adapting to the changes going on around him without losing his characteristics of toughness of spirit and remarkable stamina. Nevertheless, the Gurkha soldier of today is not the same simple-minded peasant boy who, in past years, came down from the hills of Nepal to enlist.

With so few vacancies to fill, the recruiters in Nepal can afford to be extremely selective, knowing that the Gurkha soldier today has to be able to speak and read English, operate computers and, in one or two cases already, even pilot helicopters – Corporal Pimbahadur Gurung (late 6th) being the first Gurkha pilot in the British Army, having received his pilot's wings on 5 March 1993. Without doubt, the young Gurkha riflemen serving today will have many more challenges to meet, challenges that will test them to the limit. What is certain is that they must retain their inherent virtues of courage, self-discipline and good humour. Those who have served in the old Indian Army Gurkha Brigade and in the post-1947 Britain's Brigade of Gurkhas, will be watching with pride, and some anxiety, the prowess of the two battalions, now known as the Royal Gurkha Rifles, as well as the three squadrons of Gurkha corps, now serving as integral parts of their respective parent corps in the British Army. Wherever the British Army Gurkhas may be serving, they will have the considerable responsibility of carrying on and upholding the high reputation won in countless battles in the past – at the Siege of Delhi, on the North-West Frontier of India, at Gallipoli, Cassino, Kohima and in all the other places for which they have won battle honours. What has not changed is the Gurkhas' attitude to soldiering and their loyalty to the British Crown. Their warcry of 'Ayo Gurkha!' has caused terror on many battlefields. Their motto, 'Kaphar hune bhanda morne ramro' (It is better to die than be a coward), is the reason why this book is called *Valour*.

APPENDICES

APPENDIX ## 1 CHANGES IN TITLES OF GURKHA REGIMENTS

SPELLINGS of regimental titles. In the early days there was little general agreement on the correct transliteration of words and place names from the local dialects and much of it was phonetic. This led to a number of variations in spelling in the titles of regiments (e.g. Nusseree/Nusseri; Huzara/Hazara), and none more so than in that of 'Gurkha'. In its earliest form it is found spelt 'Gorka', followed, at various times, by 'Goorkah', 'Goorka' or 'Goorkha'. In 1891 the form 'Gurkha' was adopted as the official spelling to be used in British service and still remains as such. The Indian Army, after Independence in 1947, adopted the official spelling 'Gorka' for the regiments in its service to conform to the spelling used in Nepal. The spelling of the titles in this Appendix are those in current use at the time shown.

1st King George V's Own Gurkha Rifles (The Malaun Regiment).

1815	1st Nusseree Battalion	1886	1st Goorkha Light Infantry
1823	6th, 1st Nusseri (Gorka) Battalion	1891	1st Gurkha (Rifle) Regiment
1824	6th, 1st Nusseri Battalion	1901	1st Gurkha Rifles
1826	4th, 1st Nusseri Battalion	1903	1st Gurkha Rifles (The Malaun Regiment)
1830	4th Nusseree Battalion	1906	1st Prince of Wales's Own Gurkha Rifles (The Malaun Regiment)
1845	4th Nusseree (Rifle) Battalion		
1850	66th or Goorka Regiment of Native Infantry	1910	1st King George's Own Gurkha Rifles (The Malaun Regiment)
1851	66th Regiment of Native Infantry (Goorkas)	1937	1st King George V's Own Gurkha Rifles (The Malaun Regiment)
1857	66th or Goorka Regiment	1947	Transferred to Indian Army
1858	66th or Goorka Light Infantry	1949	1st King George V's Own Gorkha Rifles (The Malaun Regiment)
1861	May: 11th Regiment, Native Infantry October: 1st Goorkha Regiment	1950	1st Gorkha Rifles (The Malaun Regiment)

2nd King Edward VII's Own Gurkha Rifles (The Sirmoor Rifles)

1815	Sirmoor Battalion	1852	Sirmoor Battalion
1823	8th, Sirmoor (Gorka) Battalion	1858	Sirmoor Rifle Regiment
1824	8th, Sirmoor Battalion	1861	May: 17th Regiment, Native Infantry October: 2nd Goorkha (The Sirmoor Rifle) Regiment
1826	6th, Sirmoor Rifles		
1845	6th, Sirmoor (Rifle) Battalion	1876	2nd (Prince of Wales's Own) Goorkha Regiment (The Sirmoor Rifles)
1850	Sirmoor (Rifle) Battalion		

1886	2nd (Prince of Wales's Own) Goorkha Regiment (The Sirmoor Rifles)	1906	2nd King Edward's Own Gurkha Rifles (The Sirmoor Rifles)
1891	2nd (Prince of Wales' Own) Gurkha (Rifle) Regiment (The Sirmoor Rifles)	1936	2nd King Edward VII's Own Gurkha Rifles (The Sirmoor Rifles)
1901	2nd (Prince of Wales' Own) Gurkha Rifles (The Sirmoor Rifles) 2nd Gurkha Rifles (Prince of Wales' Own) (The Sirmoor Rifles)	1948	2nd King Edward VII's Own Gurkha Rifles (The Sirmoor Rifles) The Gurkha Regiment 2nd King Edward VII's Own Gurkha Rifles (The Sirmoor Rifles)
1903	2nd Prince of Wales' Own Gurkha Rifles (The Sirmoor Rifles)	1994	1st Battalion Royal Gurkha Rifles

3rd Queen Alexandra's Own Gurkha Rifles

1815	Kemaoon Battalion	1887	3rd Goorkha Regiment
1816	Kemaoon Provincial Battalion	1891	3rd Gurkha (Rifle) Regiment
1823	9th, Kemaoon Battalion	1901	3rd Gurkha Rifles
1826	7th, Kemaoon Battalion	1907	3rd The Queen's Own Gurkha Rifles
1850	Kemaoon Battalion	1908	3rd Queen Alexandra's Own Gurkha Rifles
1861	May: 18th Regiment, Native Infantry October: 3rd Goorkha (The Kemaoon Regiment)	1947	Transferred to Indian Army
		1949	3rd Queen Alexandra's Own Gorkha Rifles
1864	3rd (Kumaon) Goorkha Regiment	1950	3rd Gorkha Rifles

4th Prince of Wales's Own Gurkha Rifles

1857	Extra Goorkha Regiment	1924	4th Prince of Wales's Own Gurkha Rifles
1861	May: 19th Regiment, Native Infantry October: 4th Goorkha Regiment	1947	Transferred to Indian Army
		1949	4th Prince of Wales's Own Gorkha Rifles
1891	4th Gurkha (Rifle) Regiment		
1901	4th Gurkha Rifles	1950	4th Gorkha Rifles

5th Royal Gurkha Rifles (Frontier Force)

1858	25th Punjab Infantry or Huzara Goorkha Battalion	1891	5th Gurkha (Rifle) Regiment
		1901	5th Gurkha Rifles
1861	7th Regiment of Infantry (or Hazara Goorkha Battalion) Punjaub Irregular Force	1903	5th Gurkha Rifles (Frontier Force)
	5th Goorkha Regiment (The Hazara Goorkha Battalion) attached to the Punjaub Irregular Force	1921	5th Royal Gurkha Rifles (Frontier Force)
		1947	Transferred to Indian Army
1886	5th Goorkha Regiment, The Hazara Goorkha Battalion	1949	5th Royal Gorkha Rifles (Frontier Force)
1887	5th Goorkha Regiment	1950	5th Gorkha Rifles (Frontier Force)

6th Queen Elizabeth's Own Gurkha Rifles

1817	The Cuttack Legion
1822	Rungpore Local Battalion
1823	March: Rungpore Light Infantry May: 10th Rungpore Light Infantry
1826	8th, Rungpore Light Infantry
1828	8th, Assam Light Infantry
1844	8th, 1st Assam Light Infantry Battalion
1850	1st Assam Light Infantry Battalion
1861	May: 46th (1st Assam) Light Infantry October: 42nd (Assam) Light Infantry
1865	42nd (Assam) Regiment of Bengal Native (Light) Infantry
1885	42nd (Assam) Regiment of Bengal (Light) Infantry
1886	42nd Regiment, Goorkha (Light) Infantry
1889	42nd (Goorkha) Regiment of Bengal (Light) Infantry
1891	42nd Gurkha (Rifle) Regiment of Bengal Infantry
1901	42nd Gurkha Rifles
1903	6th Gurkha Rifles
1948	6th Gurkha Rifles, The Gurkha Regiment
1959	6th Queen Elizabeth's Own Gurkha Rifles
1994	1st Battalion Royal Gurkha Rifles

7th Duke of Edinburgh's Own Gurkha Rifles

1902	8th Gurkha Rifles
1907	7th Gurkha Rifles
1959	7th Duke of Edinburgh's Own Gurkha Rifles
1994	2nd Battalion Royal Gurkha Rifles

8th Gurkha Rifles

1st Battalion

1824	16th or Sylhet Local Battalion
1826	11th or Sylhet Local Battalion
1827	11th or Sylhet Local Infantry
1861	48th (Sylhet) Light Infantry
1861	44th (Sylhet) Light Infantry
1864	44th (Assam) Regiment of Bengal Native (Light) Infantry
1885	44th (Sylhet) Regiment of Bengal (Light) Infantry
1886	44th Regiment Goorkha (Light) Infantry
1889	44th (Goorkha) Regiment of Bengal (Light) Infantry
1891	44th Gurkha (Rifle) Regiment of Bengal Infantry
1901	44th Gurkha Rifles
1903	8th Gurkha Rifles

2nd Battalion

1835	Assam Sebundy Corps
1839	1st Assam Sebundy Corps
1844	1st Assam Sebundy Regiment
1844	2nd Assam Light Infantry Regiment
1861	47th (2nd Assam) Light Infantry
1861	43rd (Assam) Light Infantry
1864	43rd (Assam) Regiment of Bengal Native (Light) Infantry
1885	43rd (Assam) Regiment of Bengal (Light) Infantry
1886	43rd Regiment Goorkha (Light) Infantry
1889	43rd (Goorkha) Regiment of Bengal (Light) Infantry
1891	43rd Gurkha (Rifle) Regiment of Bengal Infantry
1901	43rd Gurkha Rifles

1907	1st Battalion, 8th Gurkha Rifles	1903	7th Gurkha Rifles
		1907	2nd Battalion, 8th Gurkha Rifles
		1947	Transferred to Indian Army
		1949	8th Gorkha Rifles

9th Gurkha Rifles

1817	Fatehgarh Levy	1885	9th Regiment of Bengal Infantry
1818	Mynpoory Levy	1893	9th Gurkha (Rifle) Regiment of Bengal Infantry
1823	1st Battalion, 32nd Regiment of Bengal Native Infantry	1901	9th Gurkha Rifles
1824	63rd Regiment of Bengal Native Infantry	1947	Transferred to Indian Army
1861	9th Regiment of Bengal Native Infantry	1949	9th Gorkha Rifles

10th Princess Mary's Own Gurkha Rifles

1766	14th Battalion of Coast Sepoys	1890	10th (Burma) Regiment of Madras Infantry
1767	The Amboor Battalion	1891	10th Regiment (1st Burma Battalion) of Madras Infantry
1769	11th Carnatic Battalion	1892	10th Regiment (1st Burma Rifles), Madras Infantry
1770	10th Carnatic Battalion		
1784	10th Madras Battalion	1895	10th Regiment (1st Burma Gurkha Rifles), Madras Infantry
1796	1st Battalion, 10th Regiment Madras Native Infantry	1901	10th Gurkha Rifles
1824	10th Regiment Madras Native Infantry	1950	10th Princess Mary's Own Gurkha Rifles
1885	10th Regiment, Madras Infantry	1994	3rd Battalion Royal Gurkha Rifles

The Queen's Gurkha Engineers

1948	Royal Engineers Gurkha	1960	The Gurkha Engineers
1954	Gurkha Royal Engineers	1977	April: Queen's Gurkha Engineers June: The Queen's Gurkha Engineers

Queen's Gurkha Signals

1948	Royal Signals Gurkha	1955	Gurkha Signals
1954	Gurkha Royal Signals	1977	Queen's Gurkha Signals

Queen's Own Gurkha Transport Regiment

1958	Gurkha Army Service Corps	1992	The Queen's Own Gurkha Transport Regiment
1965	The Gurkha Transport Regiment		

Gurkha Military Police

1949	Royal Military Police (Gurkha Regiment)	October: Title Gurkha Military Police dropped; soldiers reverted to parent regiments.
1957	Gurkha Military Police	Corps disbanded.
1965	January: 5 (Gurkha) Dog Company, Gurkha Military Police	

APPENDIX 2

BATTLE HONOURS OF THE GURKHA BRIGADE

Note: Those regiments that remained as part of the Indian Army, post-August 1947, have been shown as having battle honours up to that date only, i.e. won while serving the British Crown.

1ST KING GEORGE V'S OWN GURKHA RIFLES
(THE MALAUN REGIMENT)

Bhurtpore, Aliwal, Sobraon, Afghanistan 1878–80, Tirah, Punjab Frontier, Givenchy 1914, Neuve Chapelle, Ypres 1915, St Julien, Festubert 1915, Loos, France and Flanders 1914–15, Megiddo, Sharon, Palestine 1918, Tigris 1916, Kut-al-Amara 1917, Baghdad, Mesopotamia 1916–18, North-West Frontier, India 1915–17, Afghanistan 1919, Jitra, Kampar, Malaya 1941–42, Shenam Pass, Bishenpur, Ukhrul, Myinmu Bridgehead, Kyaukse 1945, Burma 1942–45.

2ND KING EDWARD VII'S OWN GURKHA RIFLES
(THE SIRMOOR RIFLES)

Bhurtpore, Aliwal, Sobraon, Delhi 1857, Kabul 1879, Kandahar 1880, Afghanistan 1878–80, Tirah, Punjab Frontier, La Bassée 1914, Festubert 1914–15, Givenchy 1914, Neuve Chapelle, Aubers, Loos, France and Flanders 1914–15, Egypt 1915, Tigris 1916, Kut-al-Amara 1917, Baghdad, Mesopotamia 1916–18, Persia 1918, Baluchistan 1918, Afghanistan 1919, El Alamein, Mareth, Akarit, Djebel el Meida, Enfidaville, Tunis, North Africa 1942–43, Cassino I, Monastery Hill, Pian di Maggio, Gothic Line, Coriano, Poggio San Giovanni, Monte Reggiano, Italy 1944–45, Greece 1944–45, North Malaya, Jitra, Central Malaya, Kampar, Slim River, Johore, Singapore Island, Malaya 1941–42, North Arakan, The Irrawaddy, Magwe, Sittang 1945, Point 1433, Arakan Beaches, Myebon, Tamandu, Chindits 1943, Burma 1942–45.

3RD QUEEN ALEXANDRA'S OWN GURKHA RIFLES

Delhi 1857, Ahmed Khel, Afghanistan 1878-80, Burma 1885-87, Chitral, Tirah, Punjab Frontier, La Bassée 1914, Armentières 1914, Festubert 1914-15, Givenchy 1914, Neuve Chapelle, Aubers, France and Flanders 1914-15, Egypt 1915-16, Gaza, El Mughar, Nebi Samwil, Jerusalem, Tell-Asur, Megiddo, Sharon, Palestine 1917-18, Shargat, Mesopotamia 1917-18, Afghanistan 1919, Deir el Shein, North Africa 1940-43, Monte della Gorgace, II Castello, Monte Farneto, Monte Cavallo, Italy 1943-45, Sittang 1942, Kyaukse 1942, Imphal, Tuitum, Sakawng, Shenam Pass, Bishenpur, Tengnoupal, Meiktila, Defence of Meiktila, Rangoon Road, Pyawbwe, Pegu 1945, Burma 1942-45.

4TH PRINCE OF WALES'S OWN GURKHA RIFLES

Ali Masjid, Kabul 1879, Kandahar 1880, Afghanistan 1878-80, Waziristan 1895, Chitral, Tirah, Punjab Frontier, China 1900, Givenchy 1914, Neuve Chapelle, Ypres 1915, St Julien, Aubers, Festubert 1915, France and Flanders 1914-15, Gallipoli 1915, Egypt 1916, Tigris 1916, Kut-al-Amara 1917, Baghdad, Mesopotamia 1916-18, North-West Frontier, India 1917, Baluchistan 1918, Afghanistan 1919, Iraq 1941, Syria 1941, The Cauldron, North Africa 1940-43, Trestina, Monte Cedrone, Italy 1943-45, Pegu 1942, Chindits 1944, Mandalay, Burma 1942-45.

5TH ROYAL GURKHA RIFLES (FRONTIER FORCE)

Peiwar Kotal, Charasiah, Kabul 1879, Kandahar 1880, Afghanistan 1878-80, Punjab Frontier, Helles, Krithia, Suvla, Sari Bair, Gallipoli 1915, Suez Canal, Egypt 1915-16, Khan Baghdadi, Mesopotamia 1916-18, North-West Frontier, India 1917, Afghanistan 1919, North-West Frontier 1930, North-West Frontier 1936-39, The Sangro, Caldari, Cassino II, Sant'Angelo in Teodice, Rocca d'Arce, Rippa Ridge, Femmina Morte, Monte San Bartolo, Italy 1943-45, Sittang 1942, 1945, Kyaukse 1942, Yenangyaung 1942, Stockades, Buthidaung, Imphal, Sakawng, Bishenpur, Shenam Pass, The Irrawaddy, Burma 1942-45.

6TH GURKHA RIFLES

Burma 1885-87, Helles, Krithia, Suvla, Sari Bair, Gallipoli 1915, Suez Canal, Egypt 1915-16, Khan Baghdadi, Mesopotamia 1916-18, Persia 1918, North-West Frontier, India 1915, Afghanistan 1919, Coriano, Santarcangelo, Monte Chicco, Lamone Crossing, Senio Floodbank, Medicina, Gaiana Crossing, Italy 1944-45, Shwebo, Kyaukmyaung Bridgehead, Mandalay, Fort Dufferin, Maymyo, Rangoon Road, Toungoo, Sittang 1945, Chindits 1944, Burma 1942-45.

7TH GURKHA RIFLES

Suez Canal, Egypt 1915, Megiddo, Sharon, Palestine 1918, Shaiba, Kut-al-Amara 1915, 1917, Ctesiphon, Baghdad, Sharqat, Mesopotamia 1915-18, Afghanistan 1919, Tobruk 1942, North Africa 1942, Cassino I, Campriano, Poggio del Grillo, Tavoleto, Montebello-Scorticata Ridge, Italy 1944, Pegu 1942, Kyaukse 1942, Shwegyin, Imphal, Bishenpur, Meiktila, Capture of Meiktila, Defence of Meiktila, Rangoon Road, Pyawbwe, Burma 1942-45, Falkland Islands 1982.

8TH GURKHA RIFLES

Burma 1885-87, La Bassée 1914, Festubert 1914, 1915, Givenchy 1914, Neuve Chapelle, Aubers, France and Flanders 1914-15, Egypt 1915-16, Megiddo, Sharon, Palestine 1918, Tigris 1916, Kut-al-Amara 1917, Baghdad, Mesopotamia 1916-17, Afghanistan 1919, Iraq 1941, North Africa 1940-43, Gothic Line, Coriano, Santarcangelo, Gaiana Crossing, Point 551, Imphal, Tamu Road, Bishenpur, Kanglatongbi, Mandalay, Myinmu Bridgehead, Singhu, Shandatgyi, Sittang 1945, Burma 1942-45.

9TH GURKHA RIFLES

Bhurtpore, Sobraon, Afghanistan 1879–80, Punjab Frontier, La Bassée 1914, Armentières 1914, Festubert 1914, 1915, Givenchy 1914, Neuve Chapelle, Aubers, Loos, France and Flanders 1914-15, Tigris 1916, Kut-al-Amara 1917, Baghdad, Mesopotamia 1916-18, Afghanistan 1919, Djebel el Meida, Djebel Garci, Ragoubet Souissi, North Africa 1940–43, Cassino I, Hangman's Hill, Tavoleto, San Marino, Italy 1943–45, Greece 1944–45, Malaya 1941–42, Chindits 1944, Burma 1942-45.

10TH GURKHA RIFLES

Helles, Krithia, Suvla, Sari Bair, Gallipoli 1915, Suez Canal, Egypt 1915, Sharqat, Mesopotamia 1916-18, Afghanistan 1919, Iraq 1941, Deir ez Zor, Syria 1941, Coriano, Santarcangelo, Senio Floodbank, Bologna, Sillaro Crossing, Gaiana Crossing, Italy 1944-45, Monywa 1942, Imphal, Tuitum, Tamu Road, Shenam Pass, Litan, Bishenpur, Tengnoupal, Mandalay, Myinmu Bridgehead, Kyaukse 1945, Meiktila, Capture of Meiktila, Defence of Meiktila, The Irrawaddy, Rangoon Road, Pegu 1945, Sittang 1945, Burma 1942-45.

11TH GURKHA RIFLES

Afghanistan 1919

ROYAL GURKHA RIFLES

QUEEN'S GURKHA ENGINEERS

QUEEN'S GURKHA SIGNALS

QUEEN'S OWN GURKHA TRANSPORT

THE GURKHA WELFARE TRUST

THE GURKHA WELFARE TRUST, established in 1969 for the relief of poverty-stricken Gurkha ex-servicemen of the British Crown and their dependants, was the brain-child of Major-General A. G. Patterson, CB, DSO, OBE, MC, the then Major-General, Brigade of Gurkhas.

The impetus for the Trust's formation was the realisation that many of the large numbers of Gurkhas who were discharged from the British Indian Army after the Second World War with less than fifteen years' service, and therefore without an army pension, and the additional numbers who left the British Army on redundancy without a pension in the late 1960s, would be likely to fall on hard times as they grew older and became increasingly unable to support themselves and their dependants. The key difference between those Gurkhas and their British contemporaries, many of whom also received no military pension, was that the British lived in a welfare state which provided old-age pensions and a national health service whilst Nepal, one of the poorest countries in the world, was not able to provide such support for its citizens. Those who set up the Trust believed that a debt of honour was owed to any Gurkha who had served the British Crown.

The Trust is registered with the UK Charity Commission and today (1997) has a small office in London employing four full-time staff. Its fourteen trustees, some with first-hand and up-to-date knowledge of Gurkhas and the current situation in Nepal, and others with specialist investment, accounting and legal expertise, decide the Trust's policy.

The Trust derives its income from a variety of sources, primarily in the UK. All Gurkhas and their British officers currently serving in the British Army donate one day's pay each year. The Ministry of Defence makes an annual grant to the Trust to pay the administrative costs of its field arm in Nepal – the Gurkha Welfare Scheme. Other sources include income from investments carefully husbanded over the years, a faithful band of regular supporters, among them both those who have served with, or have family connections with, Gurkha regiments, and also many who have no other Gurkha connections. The Trust has a framework of regional supporters' branches across the UK. Periodic fundraising appeals are organised and various other UK-based grant-making charities and trusts, among them the Army Benevolent Fund, the Queen Mary's Roehampton Trust and the Jerwood Foundation, also generously support the Trust.

The Trust also receives generous support from the Gurkha Welfare Trust Foundation (USA), the Gurkha Welfare Appeal (Canada) and the Hong Kong-based Kadoorie Agricultural Aid Association. These three autonomous organisations combine with the Trust to form the Gurkha Welfare Fund which enjoys the patronage of HRH The Prince of Wales. In addition the British Overseas Development Administration (ODA) funds water projects in Nepal under the Gurkha Welfare Trust's auspices. As a result of support from all these various sources the Gurkha Welfare Scheme was able to disburse a total of £2.7 million in Nepal during 1995/96.

The headquarters of the Trust's field arm, the Gurkha Welfare Scheme, is based at Pokhara in western Nepal. It operates through a network of twenty-four area welfare centres spread across the Brigade of Gurkhas' traditional recruiting areas in Nepal and also one in Darjeeling, in India. It provides financial, medical and community aid to alleviate hardship and distress among Gurkha ex-servicemen and their dependants (the latter being wives and children up to the age of eighteen). The Scheme has a director who is the senior British Army officer in Nepal (a colonel) and also employs the full-time services of two other British Army officers and some 240 Nepalese. The vast majority of the latter are retired British Army Gurkhas.

The area welfare officers, with their staffs of assistants, medics and runners based at the welfare centres, bear the brunt of the Scheme's field work. They must know their areas and local populations intimately (which involves frequent and lengthy travel, often on foot over rugged terrain), investigate cases of hardship and destitution, and decide on appropriate assistance. They must be men of integrity and are indeed renowned in the hills for being firm but fair. Their welfare centres are a focus of aid for the local population and no one in genuine need is ever turned away.

Welfare pensions are by far the largest single category of aid currently being disbursed by the Gurkha Welfare Scheme – 10,700 pensions worth approximately £10 each per month. The vast majority of current welfare pensioners are Second World War veterans and widows. Recipients of welfare pensions are restricted to those who do not already receive a service pension. It is estimated that the number of welfare pensioners will continue to increase until it peaks some time between 1998 and 2000. Thereafter it should start to decline as the Second World War 'bulge' starts to thin out. During 1995/96 the Scheme also made hardship grants averaging about £25 per case to 4,224 ex-servicemen suffering as a result of catastrophes caused by fire, landslides, floods and hailstorms damaging or destroying their dwellings, fields and crops.

Medical aid was also provided for 58,489 treatments at an average cost of £2 per treatment. The vast majority of these treatments were made at area welfare centres. The Scheme has a medical orderly based at each centre who treats the simple cases. More serious ones are treated by local Nepalese civilian doctors retained by the Scheme who call at each area welfare centre for a few hours per week.

In 1995/96 the Gurkha Welfare Scheme also paid for the education of 628 children of needy ex-servicemen, and built 9 new school buildings in the hill areas of Nepal. During the same period the Overseas Development Administration constructed twenty water projects bringing fresh water to various hill communities in Nepal and nine latrines for hill schools. The Kadoorie Agricultural Aid Association also constructed twenty-nine water projects and fifteen latrines as well as fourteen footbridges on various mountain paths.

Although the Brigade of Gurkhas is today much smaller than it was ten years ago, and infinitely smaller than its Second World War strength, there will be work aplenty for the Gurkha Welfare Trust in looking after the welfare of Britain's Gurkha ex-servicemen and their dependants as best it can for many years to come.

BIBLIOGRAPHY

Regimental histories

BELLERS, BRIGADIER E. V. R., *The History of the 1st King George V's Own Gurkha Rifles (The Malaun Regiment)*, Volume I, Aldershot, Gale & Polden, 1956

SHAKESPEAR, COLONEL L. W., *The History of the 2nd King Edward VII's Own Goorkha Rifles (The Sirmoor Rifles)*, Volume I, Aldershot, Gale & Polden, 1912

STEVENS, LIEUTENANT-COLONEL G. R., OBE, *The History of the 2nd King Edward VII's Own Gurkha Rifles (The Sirmoor Rifles)*, Volume II, Aldershot, Gale & Polden, 1912

BARCLAY, BRIGADIER C. N., CBE, DSO (ed.), *The Regimental History of the 3rd Queen Alexandra's Own Gurkha Rifles*, London, William Clowes, 1953

MACDONNELL, RANALD, CBE, and Macaulay, Marcus, *History, 4th Prince of Wales's Own Gurkha Rifles*, Volumes I and II, Edinburgh, William Blackwood, 1940

MACKAY, COLONEL J. N., DSO, *History, 4th Prince of Wales's Own Gurkha Rifles*, Volume III, Edinburgh, William Blackwood, 1952

History of the 5th Royal Gurkha Rifles(Frontier Force), Volumes I and II, Aldershot, Gale & Polden, n.d. and 1952

RYAN, MAJOR D. G., DSO, STRAHAN, MAJOR G. C., OBE, AND JONES, CAPTAIN J. K., *The Historical Record of the 6th Gurkha Rifles (Queen Elizabeth's Own Gurkha Rifles)*, Volume I, Aldershot, Gale & Polden, 1925

GIBBS, LIEUTENANT-COLONEL H. R. V., *The Historical Record of the 6th Gurkha Rifles (Queen Elizabeth's Own Gurkha Rifles)*, Volume II, Aldershot, Gale & Polden, 1955

MESSENGER, CHARLES, *The Steadfast Gurkha*, London, Leo Cooper, 1985

LUNT, JAMES, *Jai Sixth*, London, Leo Cooper, 1994

MACKAY, COLONEL J. N., DSO, *History of the 7th Duke of Edinburgh's Own Gurkha Rifles*, Edinburgh, William Blackwood, 1962

SMITH, E. D., *East of Katmandu*, Volume II, London, Leo Cooper, 1976

HUXFORD, LIEUTENANT-COLONEL M. J., OBE, *History of the 8th Gurkha Rifles*, Aldershot, Gale & Polden, 1952

POYNDER, LIEUTENANT-COLONEL F. S., MVO, OBE, MC, *The 9th Gurkha Rifles*, Volume I, London, Royal United Services Institute, 1937

STEVENS, LIEUTENANT-COLONEL G. R., OBE, *The 9th Gurkha Rifles*, Volume II, London, Royal United Services Institute, 1937

MULLALY, COLONEL B. R., *Bugle and Kukri: The Story of the 10th Princess Mary's Own Gurkha Rifles*, Edinburgh, William Blackwood, 1957

Other works

In addition to the ten regimental histories listed above, the following books afforded me great assistance:

ALLEN, CHARLES, *The Savage Wars of Peace*, London, Michael Joseph, 1990

ALLEN, LOUIS, *Burma: The Longest War*, London, Dent, 1984

BIDWELL, SHELFORD, *The Chindit War*, London, Hodder & Stoughton, 1979

BULLOCK, CHRISTOPHER, *Journeys Hazardous*, Worcester, Square One, 1994

CALVERT, MICHAEL, *Prisoners of Hope*, London, Jonathan Cape, 1952

CHAPPLE, JOHN, *The Lineages and Composition of Gurkha Regiments in British Service*, Winchester, Gurkha Museum, rev. edn, 1984

FARWELL, BYRON, *The Gurkhas*, London, Allen Lane, 1984

GAYLOR, JOHN, *Sons of John Company*, Staplehurst, Spellmount, 1992

HICKEY, MICHAEL, *The Unforgettable Army*, Staplehurst, Spellmount 1992

JAMES, HAROLD, *Across the Threshold of Battle*, London, The Book Guild, 1993

--, AND SHEIL-SMALL, DENIS, *The Gurkhas*, London, Macdonald, 1965

--, AND SHEIL-SMALL, DENIS, *A Pride of Gurkhas*, London, Leo Cooper, 1976

LEWIN, RONALD, *Slim: The Standard-Bearer*, London, Leo Cooper, 1976

MASTERS, JOHN, *Bugles and a Tiger*, London, Michael Joseph, 1956

MOOREHEAD, ALAN, *Gallipoli*, London, Hamish Hamilton, 1956

PEMBLE, JOHN, *The Invasion of Nepal*, Oxford, Clarendon Press, 1971

POCOCK, TOM, *A Fighting General*, London, Collins, 1973

PRAVAL, K. C., *The Red Eagles*, New Delhi, Vision Books, 1982

RAMBAHADUR LIMBU, VC, *My Life Story*, London, Gurkha Welfare Trust, n.d.

REID, CHARLES, *Delhi Centenary: The Diary of Charles Reid*, 2 GR Publications, n.d.

ROBSON, BRIAN W., *The Road to Kabul*, London, Arms & Armour, 1986

SMITH, E. D., *Britain's Brigade of Gurkhas*, London, Leo Cooper, 1973

--, *Battles for Cassino*, Shepperton, Ian Allan, 1975

--, *Battle for Burma*, London, Batsford, 1979

--, *Malaya and Borneo - Counter-Insurgency Operations*, Shepperton, Ian Allan, 1985

--, *Johnny Gurkha*, London, Leo Cooper, 1986

--, *Victory of a Sort: The British in Greece 1941-6*, London, Robert Hale, 1988

TUKER, LIEUTENANT-GENERAL SIR FRANCIS, *Gorkha: The Story of the Gurkhas of Nepal*, London, Constable, 1957

In addition, I have consulted copies of *The Kukri*, issued since 1950 by HQ, Brigade of Gurkhas

INDEX